The Psychoses

FOUNDATIONS OF MODERN PSYCHOLOGY SERIES

Richard S. Lazarus, *Series Editor*

The Psychological Development of the Child	*Paul H. Mussen*
Tests and Measurements	*Leona E. Tyler*
Motivation and Emotion	*Edward J. Murray*
Personality and Adjustment	*Richard S. Lazarus*
Clinical Psychology	*Julian B. Rotter*
Sensory Psychology	*Conrad G. Mueller*
Perception	*Julian E. Hochberg*
Learning	*Sarnoff A. Mednick*
Language and Thought	*John B. Carroll*
Social Psychology	*William W. Lambert and Wallace E. Lambert*
Physiological Psychology	*Philip Teitelbaum*
Educational Psychology	*Donald Ross Green*
The Nature of Psychological Inquiry	*Ray Hyman*
Organizational Psychology	*Edgar H. Schein*

The Psychoses

ELTON B. McNEIL

Prentice-Hall, Inc., Englewood Cliffs, New Jersey

C—13–736421–0

P—13–736413–6

Library of Congress Catalog Card Number 77–94423
Printed in the United States of America

Current Printing (last digit):
10 9 8 7 6 5 4 3 2 1

PRENTICE-HALL INTERNATIONAL, INC., London
PRENTICE-HALL OF AUSTRALIA, PTY. LTD., Sydney
PRENTICE-HALL OF CANADA, LTD., Toronto
PRENTICE-HALL OF INDIA PRIVATE LIMITED, New Delhi
PRENTICE-HALL OF JAPAN, INC., Tokyo

Preface

Most of you will catch only the briefest glimpse of psychotic human beings during your lifetime. You may, in perplexity or fear, be tempted to shun them because they pose a threat to a rational and predictable way of life. Even the word "psychopathology" has an alien connotation. This book seeks in part to render the psychoses less alien, less perplexing, and, I hope, less frightening.

As difficult to understand as the disordered human psyche may be, it ought to make at least some sense in contrast to the "normal" state. The human mind has many regions that are not yet charted, and those maps we have are often little better than guesses and speculations about an obscure internal landscape. We need not apologize for the state of the art of psychopathology. We have advanced a remarkable distance from ancient days, and the future of the scientific study of man is rich and full of promise. Properly viewed, the many uncharted areas we will traverse together constitute a challenging heritage of unsolved problems that each generation always passes, reluctantly, to the next.

Man at his most disordered is the topic of our inquiry. The study of the psychoses, which anchor one end of the continuum of human behavior, may furnish clues to a better understanding of so-called normal man and better equip us to deal with those who deviate from our expectations.

Contents

The Psychoses

MAN AND MADNESS I

Aspects of
Psychosis

1

How does one make sense of the highly complicated and diverse history of psychotic disorder in mankind? One sweeping way of ordering history is to divide it into "prescientific" and "scientific" eras, using present-day scientific methods as a convenient dividing line (Kiev, 1966). The advantage of such a system is that it allows us to understand the substantial gaps in theory and treatment that exist between Westernized, industrialized, "modern" societies and rural, less educated, "primitive" societies the world over.

PRIMITIVE AND ANCIENT MAN

"Primitive" and "ancient" are not identical terms. Primitive man lives isolated in the midst of a modern world; ancient man lived in a totally ancient world. In a sense, time has stood still in some parts of our planet. Existing tribal notions of why disorder occurs and what to do about it resemble those of ancient times. The supernatural, witchcraft, possession by demons and evil spirits, and punishment by long-dead ancestors still influence native healers unaware of the existence of modern psychiatry. Our modern primitives believe mental disorder is caused by violation of important social taboos (Gillin, 1948).

Treatment of severe emotional disorder among primitives reflects directly their view of its cause and nature. If the mentally ill are thought to carry evil spirits within them, pain and punishment are administered; if their madness is thought to be a sign of divinity and special psychic

3

powers, they are likely to be elevated to a position of social prominence and holiness. As Kiev (1966) noted, "to propitiate, exorcise, or coerce unwanted spirits possessing the sick, various cultures have used prayer, sacrifice, fumigation, starvation, heat, frightening, bloodletting, catharsis, and scapegoats. To recover lost souls, confession, expiation, and purification of the sinner, as well as counter-sorcery and threats against the sorcerer, have been used " (p. 170). There are sects and cults of persons within our own modern culture that rely on "speaking in tongues," visions, and highly charged emotional atmospheres to treat the mentally ill.

Treatment in every age must offer the patient freedom from the anxiety, fear, and doubt that accompany the disorder. The healer, whoever he may be and whatever his method, must convey the same ancient psychological message—hope—to the patient. He must say, with authority, "I know why you are disturbed and I can heal you." In primitive and "modern" approaches, the *why* of the disturbance and the *how* of healing match the spirit of the time and conform to existing social and cultural beliefs about the nature of human existence.

Armed with the idea that the way in which emotional disturbance is appraised and treated reflects the shape and stage of evolution of man's view of the universe, we are in a somewhat better position to make sense of the history of psychosis. Our consideration of man's reaction to madness over the centuries should also help us to accept the observation of two prominent psychiatrists, Frederick Redlich and Daniel Freedman (1966): "It is never surprising but always sobering to discover that much of what we cherish as contemporary achievement existed before, and much of what we deride as obsolete and shameful still plagues us" (p. 28).

Ancient man could understand little of what hurt or disturbed him and could do even less about it. He "cured his minor troubles through various intuitive, crude, empirical techniques: he cooled his injuries with saliva, alleviated his fevers by lying in cold water, extricated foreign matter from his skin as best he could with his fingers, rubbed his wounds with mud, sucked snake bites to rid himself of venom" (Alexander and Selesnick, 1966, p. 7). The cause of a wound is obvious, and picking at it is a natural response still unchanged among the young of our species. But what of emotions, feelings, urges, thoughts, and dreams? What of the hurts whose causes are not obvious? What of the itches one cannot scratch and the pains that will not be assuaged? In those early days of cave man and primitive gatherer and hunter there was little distinction between medical and psychological treatment, for the fine line between physical and mental disorders must have been almost invisible. Early man was unaware of more than one aspect of self.

We know little of the early healers, who buried their failures. But magic must have come first—and magic had much to recommend it. The healer of antiquity must have had great insight about how to influence feelings and effect a change in behavior. Having the aura of the supernatural made him more authoritative and effective. Imagine that, in this day and age, all the patients in a mental hospital believed you to have command of the magic and secrets of the ancients. You could "heal" as did the ancients if the patients truly believed in the absolute power and invincibility of your magic.

Today we live in an age of superstition and magic despite our pretensions to pure science. Harmless, sugarcoated, physiologically neutral pills—placebos—still produce dramatic improvements in the patient's sense of well-being. This is magic as modern as today and as ancient as time itself. There is a timeless quality to our view of the nature of our seriously disturbed fellow humans; there may be less than a comfortable distance between drilling a hole (trephining) in the skull of a caveman to release evil spirits (Selling, 1943) and the "death of mercy" practiced by the Nazis.

Some of the great names in psychopathology we will encounter as we follow the history of abnormality will be listed later.

THE GRECO-ROMAN ERA

Aesculapius (*fl.* 100 B.C.), Aretaeus (*ca.* A.D. 150), Galen (*ca.* A.D. 131–201), Hippocrates (*ca.* 460–*ca.* 377 B.C.), and many other theorists and practitioners of the Greco-Roman era adopted a rational view of human disorder that seems remarkable to modern theorists.

The Greeks and Romans had only dim notions of the interconnection of mind and body, and their great philosophers propounded many theories on the various possible seats of mentality in the body. The Greeks in particular anticipated, in crude form, many of our modern conceptions of the nature of man and his disorders. There was a time, for example, when the influence of Aesculapius was so strong that the Greek and Roman countrysides abounded with temples that put into practice, in somewhat altered form, the basic teachings of humane treatment of mentally disordered persons. Erected in peaceful settings, the temples were places where patients could go for rest, sleep, and quiet counsel, and to benefit from the magic rendered by temple priests.

Ancient theories of disorder distinguished between acute and chronic disorders, excited and apathetic states, and differentiated among illusions, hallucinations, and delusions. The priests of these temples even practiced a primitive form of dream interpretation (Mora, 1967).

The conclusions about emotional disorder reached early in the history of man are startlingly numerous. It is surprising to realize they were arrived at as long ago as the six-hundred-year span ranging roughly between 400 B.C. and A.D. 200. These insights include observations of the nature of depression, psychotic disorders following childbirth, epilepsy, phobia, hysteria, and the function of dreaming.

These six hundred years were indeed a Golden Age of rationality compared to the primitive, ancient era from which it evolved. The Romans conquered and enslaved the Greeks and, incidentally, shared this age with them by becoming a host for Greek psychiatric thought. The Romans, concerned as they were with the more practical matters of warfare, architecture, road building, and law, simply borrowed the Greek themes and insights with regard to madness. When the Roman Empire was overrun with plague and devastated by conquering barbarian hordes, the historical stage was set for the Middle Ages in which this seeming progress in thought was to be discarded in favor of a new religious demonology. The motive force of civilization shifted, and mankind retreated to a less rational theoretical view of humanity.

THE MIDDLE AGES

God or the Devil became a suspected invader of the body of man. After all, didn't the Bible, a document well filled with recorded instances of possession by evil, describe Cain who slew Abel, Abraham who tested God, and Saul who disobeyed Him? With gesturing, incantation, prayer, ritual, and purgatives, man sought to relieve himself of his disturbances caused by God.

The Middle Ages became a time of flagellantism (self-injury), lycanthropy (the delusion one is an animal), tarantism (dancing mania), and mass madness. Attitudes reflected a psychology influenced by the belief that "whom the Gods will destroy, they first make mad." Madness, as an expression of the will of God, became epidemic. Its cure became a religious ritual designed to use the psychotic as a target for religious persecution and as a means of reaffirming the worth of the blessed, innocent, and pure. Blessed were those who exposed persons who had sold their souls to the devil. The classic "hunt of the witches" was a side product of the search for salvation.

During the thirteenth and fourteenth centuries the body was entrusted to the physician, but the mind and the soul remained the property of the Church. According to Alexander and Selesnick (1966), this became an age needing, but lacking, a scapegoat to explain away the diseases, the spreading religious disaffection, and the rapidly crumbling social order. Internal difficulties in the Church needed solutions, and the times were ripe for the invention of a clearly visible Devil to be exorcised. Sexual lust was one dangerous form of the Devil's handwork, and it was most likely to appear in the form of an inviting, sexually insatiable, female witch. The "witch-hunt" seemed to fit the spirit and fill the need of the times, and the Dark Ages closed about man (Robbins, 1959).

Mental disturbance suggested two possibilities: seizure by the Devil of an unwilling victim abandoned by God or the deliberate signing of a blood pact with Satan for personal gain. Witch detection was legitimized as the proper work of Christian man by a treatise—*The Witches' Hammer* (*Malleus Maleficarum*)—proving the existence of witches, detailing the signs by which they could be identified, and describing the means and methods of condemning and trying them (Summers, 1928). These signs that identified witches paralleled many of the symptoms of mental disorder, and the seriously emotionally disturbed were at once suspect (Zilboorg, 1935). Lea (1957) reports that some epileptics were caught up in the nets designed to gather witches and that their excited seizures furnished "incontrovertible evidence" of possession by the Devil. They were burned for their symptoms of muscular and nervous system disorder.

Exorcism was a favorite method for casting out a suspected devil. The theory was that if the Devil could be insulted by a string of curses he would abandon his victim's body. From ancient accounts of exorcism, any devil might well have been driven to despair. When words failed, "scourging" was tried. Unfortunately, to reach the Devil one had to mistreat the body of the disturbed victim who contained him. The professional "scourger" still slept the sleep of the innocent since, in his distasteful labors, he was an instrument of God's work.

The important issue is the horrendous equation medieval citizens made between possession by demons or by the Devil and behavior we now describe as psychotic. As a result of the witch-hunts, those suffering from psychoses were tortured, maimed, and killed. While such actions may have served religious and social purposes very well, they mark the high water mark of inhumane victimization of severely emotionally disturbed human beings.

A NEW RENAISSANCE

Although the twenty-ninth edition of *Malleus Maleficarum* was published as late as 1669, the beginnings of a New Renaissance and a New Humanism in the view of man can be traced to the thirteenth century. It did not reach full expression until the latter years of the sixteenth century, when the social madness of demonology began to wane and was replaced by a different perception of the disturbed.

The early asylums were places of containment, where those suffering severe psychological disturbance were treated more like animals than people. Adequate hospitals for the mentally ill were not established until near the end of the nineteenth century, but men such as Pinel (1745–1826) and his pupil Esquirol (1772–1840) heralded the movement by instituting humanitarian reforms in the face of the resistance of an uninformed public that could hardly comprehend the importance of treating emotionally disturbed persons as if they were "normal" human beings.

Pinel's work in the late 1700's and early 1800's was matched by that of William Tuke, whose York Retreat in England was characterized by an accepting, warm atmosphere in its treatment of patients. Tuke was a wealthy Quaker and his gentle religious philosophy was an integral part of his theory of how one human being should respond to another, even in the face of severe emotional disorder. In 1796, in a heroic and significant departure from common practice, he converted his private estate into a model institution for the treatment of the disordered.

The beginning of the nineteenth century witnessed the appearance of the psychological theory that could buttress practice and make rational those methods that had been developed emotionally out of sympathy for one's fellow human beings.

Dorothea Dix (1802–1887), for example, devoted four vigorous decades of her life to the reform of hospitalization practices for the emotionally disordered. She worked unceasingly for the establishment of humane, professionally-run mental hospitals. Her reforms were not without flaw, however. She unwittingly encouraged a type of isloated mental hospital in which, in the early days, psychotics, criminals, and mental defectives were all confined together in a hopeless jumble. Dorothea Dix forced the society of her time to do an about-face with regard to their view of the emotionally disturbed and to institute new forms of treatment for them. In so doing, she established a pattern that is uncomfortable for the modern era. She solved one social problem while unintentionally creating another for the generations yet to come (Foucault, 1965).

THE PSYCHOLOGICAL ERA

It is incredible that the inhumane medieval views of psychopathology prevailed for nearly one thousand years. The burning of "witches" marked the lowest point in man's treatment of psychotic patients. The last "witch" died as late as 1782 (in Switzerland), but the "renaissance" had already begun. In the next century the organic period of psychopathology made its appearance, followed by the psychological era. These periods overlap in the nineteenth and twentieth centuries.

The belief that psychic disorders were founded in organic disorder was championed, in the early years, by William Griesinger (1817–1868), Emil Kraepelin (1856–1926), and Eugene Bleuler (1857–1939), among others. Broadly, the organic viewpoint stressed the importance of brain malfunctions in emotional disorder. Since each disease was considered a separate entity, it was thought there ought to be a predictable course and a specifiable cure for each illness. The body, nervous system, and brain became targets for those honestly searching for toxins and cellular pathology as a source of disordered thought, emotion, and behavior. Scientific breakthroughs, such as the discovery of a biological basis (syphilis) for the disorder of general paresis, gave encouragement to the organicists searching for medical bases for mental disorders. The organic movement (which continues vigorously today) furnished the means of making a clear break with demonology, established a new system of classifying mental disorders, and provided the impetus for the scientific research that is now bearing fruit in the treatment of mental illness.

The organic movement, however, produced too little in the way of concrete advances and explained too little of human behavior to be accepted unquestioningly by theoreticians educated more in the humanities than in science. As the search for damaged brain tissue failed to produce results and as disturbed human behavior sometimes reversed itself (as it could not if biological damage were its cause), it became evident that additional explanations were needed.

Beginning in the late 1800's, what is now labeled the "psychological revolution" took place (Dain, 1964). Sigmund Freud (1856–1939) observed the work of Franz Mesmer (1734–1815), Jean Charcot (1825–1893), Ambrose-August Liebeault (1823–1904), Hippolyte-Marie Bernheim (1840–1919), and Pierre Janet (1859–1947), and from these observations came his formulation of the theory and practice of psychoanalysis. It was this juncture in history that has dictated so much of the direction of the modern era. Freud unmistakably established the importance of purely psychic events in the behavior of man; he reaffirmed the vital impact of early experience on later behavior; and he elevated the concept of the human mind to a properly complex status. Freud, too, developed methods for the exploration of the human psyche and for its treatment at the same moment that he elaborated a dynamic philosophy of the basic nature of man and of the interplay of biological, social, and psychological factors in his development (Kraepelin, 1962).

Freud and his successors ushered in the modern era of scientific method, eclectic theory, chemotherapy, community mental health centers, and federal responsibility for mental illness. Freud's work gave sanction to many psychological and scientific endeavors that would have seemed inappropriate to the century that preceded him.

Impetus for the psychological era in its earliest days was also furnished by Clifford Beers's personal account of emotional disorder in his book *A Mind That Found Itself* (1908). He helped mental hygiene to become the concern of an increasing number of influential American citizens (Bockoven, 1963). The study and treatment of emotional disturbance continue to be a responsibility of state and local agencies, but recently the federal government has begun to provide massive financial and technical assistance. Mental illness has acquired the status of a national liability and its amelioration—if not its eradication—has become the responsibility of all the citizens of the nation.

The psychological era has established a firm and promising foothold in part because of the medical and biochemical advances that have converted bedlam into order and reason, and this addition of medical and psychological science to the diagnosis and treatment of mental disorders has had its greatest impact on the seriously disturbed. Therapists have come almost full circle now and are discussing again the advantages of open hospitals and home care for those with psychotic disorders. This psychological era is one of optimism based on the hope that the scientific method will finally solve man's most burdensome problem (Freedman and Kaplan, 1967).

What we choose to call the modern era is a blend of many ideas and approaches to severe emotional disorder. We have begun to abandon an exclusive belief in physical illness as a proper model for emotional disorder; yet we have retained an emphasis on the unity of mind and body in any form of disturbance. Since the turn of the century, a dynamic view of the learned nature of psychological disorder, of its complex social and individual facets, and of the advances in understanding that can be the outcome of controlled experimentation, have all been realized. During our lifetime, we hope to learn how to detect the early signs of impending disordered behavior and how to deal with it before continued neglect allows it to blossom into a full-grown distorted shape.

Coleman's (1964) analysis of the modern state of theoretical agreement underlying contemporary viewpoints states that there seems now to be widespread acceptance of a dynamic view of both normal and abnormal human behavior and an emphasis on a team approach to social and individual pathology. Among the most spectacular modern developments are, of course, the advances in chemotherapy that have "unchained" so many of our mental patients. An additional and equally spectacular direction of modern thought is demonstrated in the proliferation of community mental health centers across the nation. These new centers are not only dedicated to reaching the unreached in our land but are committed to devising new and unique methods of dealing with our age-old problems.

One issue has become critical in the modern era—mental health manpower. As long as we define mental health service along traditional lines—as long as psychiatrists, psychologists, and social workers take years to be trained, recruit so few new members to their ranks, and continue to use individual, one-to-one therapeutic and diagnostic methods—our society's mental health needs will remain well beyond the reach of our capacity to service them. We have provoked new problems of supply and demand and this may occupy our energy and scientific effort for some years to come (Felix, 1967).

TABLE 1.1   GREAT NAMES IN PSYCHOPATHOLOGY

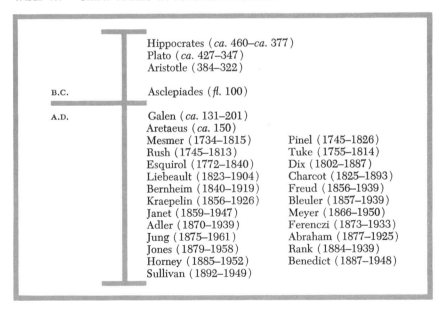

Hippocrates (*ca.* 460–*ca.* 377)	
Plato (*ca.* 427–347)	
Aristotle (384–322)	
B.C. Asclepiades (*fl.* 100)	
A.D. Galen (*ca.* 131–201)	
Aretaeus (*ca.* 150)	
Mesmer (1734–1815)	Pinel (1745–1826)
Rush (1745–1813)	Tuke (1755–1814)
Esquirol (1772–1840)	Dix (1802–1887)
Liebeault (1823–1904)	Charcot (1825–1893)
Bernheim (1840–1919)	Freud (1856–1939)
Kraepelin (1856–1926)	Bleuler (1857–1939)
Janet (1859–1947)	Meyer (1866–1950)
Adler (1870–1939)	Ferenczi (1873–1933)
Jung (1875–1961)	Abraham (1877–1925)
Jones (1879–1958)	Rank (1884–1939)
Horney (1885–1952)	Benedict (1887–1948)
Sullivan (1892–1949)	

CLASSIFICATION OF PSYCHOTIC DISORDERS

In the field of psychopathology, theorists and practitioners meet regularly on the well-worn, common ground of discontent over the way in which we classify emotional disorders. The most rabid among us rave and rant about the inconsistency, unworkability, and senselessness of the nosological system. Those of us less directly concerned with the issue accept the fact that classification of emotional disorders is, at best, a crude approximation to the reality of disturbance. It is a truism among practitioners that the better you know a patient (or, for that matter, a normal person), the more difficult it becomes to find a single label that adequately describes him.

After discussing some differences between the psychoses and the neuroses, we can proceed to a more detailed examination of the current system for describing the psychoses and look critically at the problems posed by this attempt to fit human beings into pigeonholes.

*Neurosis and Psychosis—Similarities
and Differences*

If psychosis can be described as a massive disintegration of the human personality in which the victim is no longer capable of dealing effectively with himself or his surroundings, we might be tempted to bypass the difficulties of definition by suggesting that neurosis is nothing but a "little" psychosis—a matter more of quantity than quality. Norman Cameron (1963) maintains that neurotic and psychotic processes are much more different than alike and, despite the fact that many aspects of each can be distinguished by how severely they disorder daily life, being neurotic is different in kind from being psychotic.

TABLE 1.2   PSYCHOSIS AND NEUROSIS: A COMPARISON

	PSYCHOSIS	NEUROSIS
Emotional Distortion	Severe	Mild
Cognitive Distortion	Severe	Mild
Hallucination	Present	Absent
Delusion	Present	Absent
Reality Contact	Distorted	Not Distorted
Decompensation	Severe	Mild
Disturbed Social Relations	Severe	Mild

Most neurotic persons are handicapped, perhaps severely, in day-to-day interpersonal relations, but they are so much like the rest of us that they are hard to detect. The irrational parts of the neurotic are reasonably limited—he is not grossly confused and disoriented—and he still participates actively (if somewhat angrily or demandingly) in the game of life everyone plays. Over time it may become inescapably evident that someone's behavior is neurotically based and flawed in its rationality, i.e., that he or she is excessively anxious, unusually obsessive, or determinedly and persistently afraid or depressed about everyday life. It may also become apparent that few of the events of real life have an exactly predictable impact on the personality of the neurotic because the needs he must fulfill are rooted deeply in unresolved childhood emotional problems.

Still, the neurotic does not lead a life as totally dominated by the irrational, fearful, unrealistic, or fantastic segments of the self as does the psychotic. The psychotic withdraws from life to fill his waking hours with the preoccupations of fantasy and distorted perceptions of the real world, and in so doing he effectively burns behind him those bridges to assistance by others. His world differs so much from our own that, according to Cameron (1963), "the process of socialization by which he came to be an integral part of society is at least partly undone" (pp. 462–63). No one can function effectively in an adult, social world if plagued by active infantile impulses, fantasies, conflicts, fears, and attitudes. "It is this revival of infantile dynamics that forms the core of every psychosis" (Cameron, 1963, p. 463). The nightmare terrors of the normal and the neurotic become the constant waking experience of the psychotic, and the desperate moves he must make to protect himself dominate his daily life and appear strange and incomprehensible to his fellowman.

It is in the process of symptom formation that we can get a glimpse of the ways in which neurosis and psychosis differ. As Cameron (1963) notes, psychotic and neurotic reactions have a common base in tension, anxiety, and the threat of ego disintegration. The neurotic may meet these threats with defensive and regressive moves that work because the person's basic "ego resources," i.e., the fundamental soundness and strength of his psychic apparatus, are adequate to the task. The psychotic may lack these resources or may experience such a great sense of threat that he fails to manage the assault with the first defenses he turns to. As a consequence, the psychotic may be driven to a deeper, more regressive, and primitive way of meeting threat, and these extreme self-protective devices will mark him as a strange, "abnormal" person. Severely regressed or fixated at an infantile level of conflict and problem solving, the psychotic may be forced into a world of hallucination and delusion that distorts reality into a more comfortable or manageable shape. Like those who have ingested LSD or some other psychotomimetic drug, he experiences a sense of revelation and escape that makes a mockery of the urgent messages calling him back to the troubled real world. In psychosis, infantile fantasy is untrammeled and unfettered, drives and urges are naked and unadorned, and conscience and social regulation are less pressing. This world differs clearly from that of the troubled neurotic.

Those who develop psychosis may be unusually vulnerable when faced with the loss of some primary and major source of gratification, e.g., a parent or a loved one, and this vulnerability may be coupled with a diminished ability to defend against the onslaught of hostile, erotic, or guilt-laden impulses. As their defenses crumble before the threat, they become very much like infants who happen, accidentally, to occupy adult bodies.

Whether the precipitating differences between neurosis and psychosis are constitutional, environmental, or both, has yet to be resolved scientifically. Psychotic parents, for example, are likely to disadvantage a child in the process of socialization, but we cannot be certain that the child was not constitutionally vulnerable to such injurious influences. No single factor seems in itself to be sufficient to produce the severe interpersonal distortion we call psychosis, but we do know that many of the children who display neurotic symptoms in childhood (particularly male children) are hospitalized later in life bearing a diagnosis of schizophrenia (Gardner, 1967).

The Classification System

Let us look now to the classificatory system in the official diagnostic manual of the American Psychiatric Association (1952) to see how this problem of classification has been handled. In the category of functional disturbances (disorders of psychogenic origin and disorders without clearly defined physical cause or structural change in the brain), diagnosis is based primarily on symptoms the patient displays and only occasionally on definitively established causation.

Psychotic Disorders

DISORDERS DUE TO DISTURBANCE OF METABOLISM, GROWTH, NUTRITION, OR ENDOCRINE FUNCTION

INVOLUTIONAL PSYCHOTIC REACTION. Severe depression and agitation or paranoid thinking occurring in middle and late-middle age with no previous history of psychosis.

DISORDERS OF PSYCHOGENIC ORIGIN OR WITHOUT CLEARLY DEFINED TANGIBLE CAUSE OR STRUCTURAL CHANGE

AFFECTIVE REACTIONS. Exaggerated moods accompanied by disturbances of thinking and motor behavior appropriate to the mood.

1. MANIC DEPRESSIVE REACTION, manic type. Recurrent episodes of elation, flight of ideas, and excitement.
2. MANIC DEPRESSIVE REACTION, depressive type. Recurrent episodes of depression accompanied by inactivity and behavioral retardation.
3. PSYCHOTIC DEPRESSIVE REACTION. Severe depression perhaps with depressive delusions and no previous history of psychosis.

SCHIZOPHRENIC REACTIONS. Psychotic reactions with disturbance of perception, thought, verbal and motor behavior, affect, intellectual functions, or marked distortion of reality.

1. SIMPLE TYPE. Seldom apparent hallucinations, delusions, or intellectual loss or impairment. Marked by general apathy or social withdrawal.
2. HEBEPHRENIC TYPE. Hallucinations, delusions, inappropriate affect, regressive, wild, or "silly" behavior.
3. CATATONIC TYPE. Stupor or excessive agitation and excitement with easily visible motor disturbance.
4. PARANOID TYPE. Delusions that are fragmentary, unorganized, and usually accompanied by auditory hallucinations.
5. ACUTE UNDIFFERENTIATED TYPE. Schizophrenic symptoms having a sudden onset that may be a temporary phase preceding the appearance of another clearer type of schizophrenia.
6. CHRONIC UNDIFFERENTIATED TYPE. Mixed but prolonged symptoms of schizophrenia with no dominant type.
7. SCHIZO-AFFECTIVE TYPE. A mixture of affective and schizophrenic reactions.
8. CHILDHOOD TYPE. Reactions resembling adult schizophrenia but occurring before puberty.
9. RESIDUAL TYPE. Schizophrenic symptoms remaining as a residual of more severe episodes. Symptoms usually mild.

PARANOID REACTIONS. Delusions predominate with little intellectual impairment and usually without hallucinations. Behavior organized and appropriate to the content of delusional systems.

This skeletal outline of the most popular classificatory system employs a number of terms that have, over the years, come to have a sometimes special and technical meaning to the diagnosticians intent on ordering and organizing emotional disturbance (Menninger, Mayman, and Pruyser, 1963).

The schizophrenic reactions, according to Bellak (1958), may be a series of disorders "of many different etiologies but with a shared final common path of ego disturbance" (p. 52). This assumption would make more difficult the task of diagnosis, since long- and short-term variations of ego functioning occur among healthy, "normal" persons. Diagnosticians have attempted to deal with this eventuality by describing a series of "not-quite" schizophrenics using terms such as "potential," "borderline," "incipient," or "latent."

Latent schizophrenia, for example, might describe a person whose processes of thinking and emotion are distorted but who manages still to present an appearance that is within the normal range. By clinical definition the patient is experiencing a schizophrenic reaction, but this may become apparent only if some sudden environmental change or alteration of life circumstance makes it manifest. It is possible for an individual to display a great many characteristics of the schizophrenic reaction—perceptual distortion, loss of control over emotions, or loss of ability to cope with anxiety—and yet achieve a stability that, given favorable life circumstances, can be maintained as a precarious balance for life. In the ranks of such persons are those we label as latent schizophrenics, schizoid characters, incipient or borderline schizophrenics, or potential schizophrenics. These makeshift terms are probably born of desperation as human beings shift back and forth along the continuum of disorder and refuse to stand still while being labeled.

In many respects we face the same diagnostic situation with acute and chronic undifferentiated types of schizophrenic reaction. The acute undifferentiated form was once described as a ten-day schizophrenia because its overt symptomatology usually diminished after a brief but severe appearance. The agitated state of the acute schizophrenic may include hallucinatory and delusional experiences with a mixture of symptoms characteristic of classic forms of the syndrome. If the symptoms persist without evolving clearly into an identifiable form, the label "chronic" is attached to it.

The "residual" category of schizophrenic reactions is an interesting one, for it introduces a new collection of commonly and uncommonly used terms. If a patient recovers enough to participate even at a reduced level in daily life but retains some modest or mild symptoms, he may be called a residual type. But this label conveys very little useful information. Coleman's (1964) collection of terms used to describe this state includes "ambulatory schizophrenia, pseudo-neurotic schizophrenia, and pseudo-psychopathic schizophrenia" (p. 284). Each of the terms is almost self-defining, since each describes a kind of mixed bag of symptoms that do not quite fit common diagnostic categories.

Faced with this collection of slippery labels and tags, Brill (1967) has recalled the often repeated suggestion that all forms of psychiatric classification be abolished on the ground that all cases are different and must, therefore, be described individually rather than grouped artificially into ill-fitting categories.

The Problem of Classification [1]

There is one immediately apparent advantage of a diagnostic and classificatory system to describe the psychoses—human peace of mind. Thinking man is made uncomfortable by confrontation with a shifting, amorphous, indistinguishable mass of events that have no name, no label, and, consequently, no easily available meaning. The human mind finds its comfort in categories even if reality will not fit neatly into pigeonholes. We need now to explore the principal shortcomings of the current system to place our consideration of the psychoses in a proper perspective.

1. Agreement and Disagreement

Diagnosticians disagree with one another and "miss" too frequently for anyone's comfort. Nearly half a century ago Elkind and Doering (1928) compared the diagnoses given a group of patients at the Boston Psychopathic Hospital with diagnoses previously given to the same patients at various other state hospitals and found 42 per cent disagreement among the diagnoses. The degree of agreement was highest when specific organic syndromes were being considered. Had the researchers used the modern system of broad groupings of diagnostic categories, their batting average would have been improved.

In a later study, Norris (1959) reported that degree of agreement varied regularly by diagnosis and averaged out at about 60 per cent. Diagnoses are particularly subject to variation when they are made independently and when they are separated by long spans of time. Lewis and Piotrowski (1954) found that the time lapse between diagnoses produced a general and startling movement in the direction of finally labeling the patient a schizophrenic. Roughly one-half the patients diagnosed manic-depressive or psychoneurotic were relabeled schizophrenic when viewed at a later date.

Things may not be as bad as they seem, however. Schmidt and Fonda (1956) detected much less disagreement when diagnoses were separated in time by as little as two weeks. When independent diagnoses are made close together in time there is about 80 per cent agreement, with the highest rate reported for the schizophrenias in general (91 per cent), and

---

[1] The issues of diagnosis and classification have been examined and criticized by a great many theorists and practitioners. Extensive references for further study are available, and the interested student might begin by consulting the works of Ash (1949), Boisen (1938), Foulds (1955), Hoch and Zubin (1953), Hunt, Wittson, and Hunt (1953), Jellinek (1939), London (1968), Mehlman (1952), or Schmidt and Fonda (1956).

the lower rates of agreement for specific subtypes of schizophrenia (51 per cent).

2. Words—Elastic Abstractions

Agreement in diagnosis is made difficult by the fact that all words do not mean the same thing to all persons. Almost every term we use to describe human beings and their behavior is highly relativistic; i.e., we don't know how much is a little and how much is a lot. If "how much" cannot be measured by any scientifically valid yardstick, we are forced to rely on the personal judgment of those we entrust with the diagnostic process. If a group of us decides to build a house, each using a yardstick of a different length, we will have more than a little difficulty erecting anything but a fairly slipshod final edifice, and this is the basic difficulty with diagnostic and classificatory systems. When five diagnosticians try to determine how aggressive an individual is and complete their task using five different terms—"quite," "very," "frequently," "seriously," and "regularly"—we do not yet know *how* aggressive he is.

Shifting terminology is a problem, but correspondence between the word and the reality is even more vexing. As Redlich and Freedman (1966) put it so succinctly, "the logical rules for diagnosing are quite clear; one pigeonhole for every disorder and no overlap between them" (p. 429). Our difficulty is in adhering to this admonition; practice falls woefully short of theory. We are not certain that such a tight and consistent way of compartmentalizing disorder is consistent with reality. If people actually occupy every intermediate position between diagnostic categories, always have symptoms that overlap a number of labels, and come only in a variety of shades of gray, then any attempt to force them into pigeonholes is bound to fail.

The problem of diagnosis and classification is complicated in yet another way. Classification assumes that cases have similarities more vital than their differences. Since words are elastic abstractions of these similarities and differences, i.e., we cannot list and detail every behavioral and emotional event in anyone's life, we stand in constant danger of reducing the nature of disorder to a dehydrated and unrecognizable abbreviation of the facts (Chapman and Chapman, 1967). Few diagnostic accounts bother to list all the ways in which the patient *fails* to fit the category into which he is being placed.

3. The Effects of Culture

We are certain that the nature of a culture alters the shape of schizophrenia and changes the details of its pattern and the frequency of its appearance. We are fully aware that these influences vary from time to time during the natural history of every society. A system of classification of human behavior should either be absolute and reflect unchanging truths about mankind, or it must necessarily change continuously to fit the changing times.

The myth of the Hutterites of the northwestern United States and southwestern Canada is a case in point (Eaton and Weil, 1955). The first investigations of these subcultures embedded within a dominant culture reported their members essentially free of mental disease. Closer checks of incidence and prevalence made these observations suspect. An accurate statement would declare that we have not yet determined, to the satisfaction of all scientists, that schizophrenia is a constant that rears its ugly head in every and all cultures. Among patients of differing cultural backgrounds in the United States, for example, the form of schizophrenia may vary—there is schizophrenia Irish style and Italian style.

Opler (1954) studied hospitalized patients of Italian and Irish background in a search for cultural differences in schizophrenia. The two patient groups were matched to one another in age, sex, marital status, intelligence, educational level, and length of hospitalization—they differed primarily in terms of ethnic extraction and, presumably, the kind of family cultural setting in which they had been reared. On seven dimensions (homosexuality, preoccupation with sin and guilt, behavior disorder, attitude toward authority, fixed delusional system, hypochondriacal complaints, and chronic alcoholism) the Irish could clearly be differentiated from the Italians. Statistically, the schizophrenics of Irish extraction were latent rather than overt homosexuals who were preoccupied with the problems of sin and guilt, were less likely to act out their impulses, were compliant rather than rejecting of authority, displayed a greater fixity in their delusional systems, were less hypochondriacal, and were more likely to suffer from chronic alcoholism than their counterparts from Italian homes.

The theoretical explanation of these differences in form and pattern of schizophrenia in two ethnic groups in the United States is a complicated matter. For Opler, a number of variables may be crucial in such development. Thus, the nature of the family authority structure (an oppressively powerful or ineffective father or a subtly rejecting mother), how the child learns to channel emotional expression (open violence or repressed emotion), and the form of sexual identification or misidentification in early life become the foundation for later severe psychological distortion. The form of the Italian family differs drastically from that of the Irish, and these types of family organization are reflected in the symptom patterns of serious disorder. Families sharing a common culture learn from that culture a style of family interaction that can determine the kind and quality of emotional and interpersonal experience to which the growing child will be exposed. Each kind of family poses a different problem for its children to solve. Failure to resolve these social and emotional difficulties produces a characteristic pattern that appears as one component of extreme psychopathology.

IS MENTAL ILLNESS
REALLY ILLNESS?

Perhaps we have become obsessed with classification and have become entangled in an unnecessary web of our own weaving. We name, we classify, and we tend to believe that all objects or persons put in a pigeonhole must share the same characteristics. But the original Kraepelinian system was based on a disease model, and only much later was an attempt made to attach to it a coherent psychological theory of man.

For some theorists (Adams, 1964; Szasz, 1960; Zigler and Phillips, 1961), the issue is not how to improve or alter our system of classification; the issue is how to abandon it completely and view mental disorder as a form of interpersonal behavior rather than a disease.

Zigler and Phillips (1961) concluded that there was little substantial evidence to show that knowing a patient's diagnostic category would be very helpful in predicting that patient's behavior. In their massive and carefully executed study of the relationship between symptoms and diagnostic categories, the degree of relationship was found to be so slight that it would call into question the validity and usefulness of any such system of describing complex human behavior.

Adams (1964), on the other hand, states flatly that there is no such thing as mental illness in the medical sense of the term "illness." In his words, ". . . organic physical illnesses and the functional types of mental illnesses are defined by *different kinds of criteria,* and they are modified or ameliorated ('treated' or 'cured') by *fundamentally different procedures"* (p. 191). He maintains that most attempts to describe mental disorder have treated human behavior as though it were "just like" other natural events such as medical events (illness, health, prevention, cure), physical events (psychic energy, tension, stress, drive), or biological events (homeostasis, development, growth).

For Adams, "mental illness" is a phrase applied to patterns of inappropriate social conduct based on faulty or inadequate social learning experiences. Some victims of "mental illness" become that way as a consequence of inadequate opportunity to learn the required social skills, and others lack the requisite resources and skills when faced with a particularly difficult set of social stresses. Psychotherapy for serious mental disorders must, then, be characterized by the acquisition of social skills that will allow a more appropriate and successful means of solving problems.

In the forefront of modern objectors to current conceptions of mental illness is the psychiatrist, Thomas Szasz (1960). He sees mental illnesses as quite complicated expressions of problems in human living. Mental *illness*, for Szasz, is a myth. He agrees it was a natural evolutionary step to describe mental disorder as illness as theorists emerged from the historical period of an organic view of all man's behavior but notes that the flaws of such a prescription have become increasingly evident. Szasz feels we have waited too long for an adequate physiochemical explanation of human behavior, that it may never arrive to solve our problems, and that we need now to look to redefinition of emotional disorder in more productive terms.

Mental illness should be considered an unsolved "problem in living" —a deformity of the personality. Mental illness is not so much an organic concept as it is a psychosocial, legal, or ethical one—a deviation from "some prescribed norm of behavior" (Ellis, 1967; Sarbin, 1967). Legally, "mentally ill" patients in our society are judged to occupy that category not because they have a demonstrable lesion in the brain or central nervous system, but because they do not behave according to the rules of our society.

Szasz insists the concept of "mental illness" has outlived its usefulness in modern society and is no more than a convenient myth closely akin to the myths of witchcraft. As he indicates, "It is the making of good choices in life that others regard, retrospectively, as good mental health!" (p. 118).

SUMMARY

An appropriate summary of the material in this chapter is provided by an adaptation of Rosen and Gregory's (1965) principles for the interpretation of abnormality through the ages.

1. Since time began, societies have devised some means for responding to and dealing with mental disorder in their citizenry.
2. The past is riddled with error and superstition, but it also contains the forerunners of modern scientific theory and practice.
3. Understanding of different aspects of psychopathology has developed at different rates, i.e., the psychoses were recognized and described before the neuroses.

4. Progress and regress in our view of abnormality is related to the social, political, and cultural progress or regress of the age, i.e., the mentally disturbed are a vulnerable minority in times of social conflict or upheaval.

5. There is no guarantee that the future will not witness a regression in our view of abnormality if we experience new social crises.

6. Theoretical insights based on advances in the immediate past have, in history, been discarded in favor of those of the remote past; i.e., modern trends may bypass Freud and return to an organic view of causation of the psychoses.

7. The modern era is more sensitive to the mild and moderate disorders ignored by the ancients.

8. Systems of classification of disorder are proving increasingly unsatisfactory.

9. Psychopathology, today, is confronted with a choice: Should it follow a medical or a psychological model; i.e., is it mental illness or a disorder of living?

10. Experimental evidence may one day substitute for clinical evidence, in describing disorders, and bring the scientific method to bear on psychopathology.

The Dimensions of Disorder

THE INCIDENCE OF DISORDER

In 1880 it was estimated that our hospitals contained nearly 41,000 mental patients, with yet another 51,000 cared for at home. By 1904 a census of mental hospitals recorded almost twice the patient rate of 1890. This confinement rate continued to rise as hospital facilities became available, and by 1910 we were hospitalizing 204 out of every 100,000 persons. The hospitalization rate changed to 245 per 100,000 by 1923 and became 381 per 100,000 by 1950. The trend since then has been ever upward and has given rise to the statistically oversimplified conclusion that man's sanity has been the price he must pay for civilization.

How Frequent, How Much?

Our population has increased slightly more than fourfold since 1880, and during that time the number of patients confined to mental hospitals has expanded more than 18 times. By 1964 our hospitals contained 750,000 mental patients, and there is little reason to believe that the decade to come will differ from those preceding it. No one can accurately estimate how many disturbed persons are free of hospital confinement, but a conservative estimate of the incidence of abnormal behavior in the United States, by Coleman (1964), calculates functional psychotic disorders to number 700,000 coupled with over one million acute and chronic brain disorders and perhaps 30 million psychophy-

23

siologic and psychoneurotic disorders. It is hardly a pretty picture viewed from any angle.

Statistics vary—the figures are dependent upon the type of agency that supplies them and the locale and time in which the compilation was made. Public mental hospitals routinely record rates of admission, residence, and discharge of seriously emotionally disturbed patients. These figures reflect only a small and "official" portion of those seriously distressed in our society, but they do form a basis for some projections and speculations. Tables 2.1 and 2.2, and Figure 2.1 give a representative account of the mental condition of one portion of our society in the recent past.

TABLE 2.1   A COMPARISON OF FREQUENCY OF FIRST ADMISSIONS AND PATIENTS
WHO BECAME RESIDENTS IN MENTAL HOSPITALS IN 1959 *

	ADMITTED FOR THE FIRST TIME	REMAINED IN HOSPITAL
Acute Brain Disorder	3.6%	0.8%
Chronic Brain Disorder	31.4%	26.3%
Schizophrenia	23.0%	49.8%
Other Psychoses	8.6%	10.0%
Psychoneurotic and Personality Disorders	22.9%	11.9%

* *Patients in Mental Hospitals.* Part II. U. S. Dept. of Health, Education and Welfare (Washington, D.C., 1959).

Table 2.1 indicates clearly why our hospital beds are occupied primarily by schizophrenics and secondarily by those with chronic brain disorder; both kinds of patient remain hospitalized in higher proportion than those with other mental disorders.

Figure 2.1 shows that in state and county mental hospitals rate of admission is rising steadily but is matched by a doubled rate of release to produce a generally reduced patient population in our hospitals. It is difficult to determine whether this is a trend that will continue and grow in the years ahead or whether this reflects merely a transitional phase of adjustment to the new psychoactive drugs and the new theoretical investment in community mental health concepts.

Numbers and Their Meaning

This statistical portrait of the mental health of modern America is not as grim as it might first appear. It is not that our society is suffering such

FIGURE 2.1   TRENDS IN STATE AND COUNTY MENTAL HOSPITALS—1955–1966 *

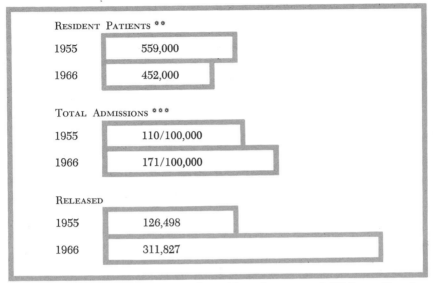

* Based on U. S. Department of Health, Education and Welfare. *Mental Health Statistics: Current Facility Reports.* Series MHB-H-11 (Washington, D.C., 1967).

** The resident patient population has dropped 19% in the 11-year period 1955–1966. In 1966 a rate of 4.4% was the largest ever recorded and was double the reduction in patient population between 1960 and 1961.

*** The rate of admission to the hospital continues to rise, but the rate of release has nearly doubled in 11 years.

a staggeringly higher rate of psychic decay year by year, it is, rather, that the incidence of hospitalization of mental patients rises in direct proportion to:

a. the increase in available hospital facilities
b. the growth in sophistication with regard to early detection and successful treatment of emotional disorder
c. the shift from home to hospital care of patients
d. reduction of the age-old equation of emotional disturbance and social stigma.

In 1880 most children were born in the home; this year almost all children in our society will greet life in the maternity ward of a hospital. We cannot draw any conclusions from the fact that the locus of birth has shifted to hospitals; it has nothing to do with the increased birthrate; similarly, the rise in hospitalization of mental patients tells us nothing about the frequency of the incidence of emotional problems in our midst.

It is in the refinement of the gross emotional distress figures and in the examination of their subdivisions that we can gain insight about the size and form of the problem our society faces. Let us take as an example the vital statistics of schizophrenia interpreted by Lemkau and Crocetti (1958). Plagued by the continuing difficulties of shifting definitions of the behavior called schizophrenia, they question whether schizophrenia is a disease entity, a type of behavioral reaction, a malfunction of the person, or a process of psychic maldevelopment.

They note that in any counting process it is important to distinguish between incidence (the occurrence of new cases during a fixed period of time) and prevalence (the total number of active cases in the population at any one time). For example, prevalence figures might be the same over a two-year span; yet in one year there might have been many new cases coupled with a high rate of cure, and in the second year there were fewer cures but also fewer new cases added to the total count. Although the vital statistics of schizophrenia or schizophrenic-like reactions have been collected, tallied, adjusted, interpreted, and reanalyzed again and again, complete accuracy has not been achieved.

The conclusions of Lemkau and Crocetti seem most sensible, since they are cast in the form of estimates of reasonable limits and probable incidence. They state that in western European societies the lower limit of incidence could be set at 50 cases per 100,000, the upper limit at about 250 per 100,000, with a median figure of 150 per 100,000 in any one year. A best guess at prevalence would list 290 cases per 100,000 in the population with approximately 150 of these hospitalized. Lemkau and Crocetti put it another way: "It is probable that for each 1,000 children born, between 14 and 20 will be hospitalized . . . within their lifetime" (p. 80).

Several studies note an unequal distribution of occurrence of the psychoses across the various socioeconomic levels in our culture, and this complicates the process of counting and interpreting the meaning of numbers. Hollingshead and Redlich (1958) found that differences in frequency of appearance of the psychoses were significantly correlated with social class membership with the psychoses most prevalent among those occupying the lowest end of the social scale. Studies by Rennie, et al. (1957), reflecting an intensive coverage of a residential area of New York, reported a 3 to 1 ratio of psychotic disorders, with the greatest frequencies among those occupying the least affluent rungs of the social ladder (13 per cent psychosis in the lower classes versus 3.6 per cent in the upper stratum). This is not to say that members of the lower socioeconomic classes are more disturbed than others. It underscores, rather, the observations that:

    a. the form of mental illness is associated with the style of life peculiar
       to the social status of the individual and

b. the availability of psychological help in the early stage of disorder clearly favors the affluent members of the middle social classes.

The form and frequency of mental derangement has a host of correlations with other life circumstances and we cannot attribute causation exclusively to any one of these.

Rates of disorder vary with marital status, for example. The married suffer less than do those single, widowed, divorced, or separated (Jaco, 1960). In addition, being male or female makes a difference in first admission to hospitals (see Table 2.2); approximately four males are admitted for every three females. This ratio does not hold true for all forms of disorder but is a roughly accurate overall figure. Age, urban or rural residence, intelligence, education, occupation, religion, and a number of other variables are found related to incidence, prevalence, and form of disorder.

We cannot produce a coherent portrait by adding one piece to another, since each piece is really a part of every other. Being white or nonwhite is correlated with the incidence of psychosis in our culture. But, as we know, race is also significantly correlated with education, socioeconomic status, occupation, religion, and a host of other indicators of the external and internal condition of man's life.

In this welter of discrete items related to psychosis must be hidden a single, overriding factor that can connect all the disparate parts into a meaningful whole. Being white, having a stable marriage, being gainfully employed, being educated, and being intelligent may all summate to a condition called security and freedom from anxiety. Having all these "advantages" may be the critical factor in determining how easily and successfully one copes with the tasks of living. The absence of any one of these conditions may diminish the human capacity to adjust. The absence of a great number of them may spell psychosis.

We must not lose sight of the fact that statistics represent people and that mere numbers are poor clues to the nature of the disordered state we seek to understand. We must look, now, at the unique, personal experience of the individual for whom life has become disordered.

THE COMPONENTS OF DISORDER

The components of psychosis are many and varied, but they can be assembled in terms of the alteration of the five basic aspects of human functioning: motivation, perception and sensation, emotion, behavior, and thinking. Distortions of these basic components of human life, in combination, produce the symptoms of psychotic disorder.

1. Motivation

Disorder in the motivational system may take a number of forms. An individual's urge to act (in thought or deed) can be paralyzed by conflict to the point where he ceases to make volitional movements or decisions about life. Or, he can retain the ability to make shaky decisions and subsequently be haunted with doubt about their correctness. The victim may reverse himself so often that variability and changeability become characteristic of his behavior. The motivation to act may be marred by excess—too weak or too strong; overdoing or underdoing.

LAURIE M.

What has finally driven her family to despair is Laurie M.'s total inability to make up her mind and to stick to a decision once it is reached. Laurie dreads living in a world that overwhelms her with options, alternatives, and a thousand possibilities. She fears that with each choice she is inching that much closer to some unknown personal horror. Choosing correctly means life; making wrong choices means death. So, Laurie moves only when told to and passively accepts whatever others decide for her. She has become increasingly unresponsive to the outside world and is almost totally absorbed with nagging worry about the wisdom of past decisions and apprehension about those that have yet to be made.

Motivation has as its aim satisfaction of biological and psychological needs. Needs may go unsatisfied if the means to their attainment are ineffectual or inappropriate, since our society limits the form of expression of many motives and restricts the choice of time, place, and object deemed proper for motivational fulfillment. This suggests that socially appropriate motivation and behavior are often judged by assessing what Murray (1938) labeled the TPMO (time, place, mode, and object) of putting motivation into action. When social customs of TPMO are violated, the individual may be judged emotionally disordered or criminal, depending on the current rules and stage of enlightenment of the society.

2. Perception and Sensation

When perception and sensation get distorted, the individual can no longer understand his world. Man's senses can be disordered via abnormally increased or decreased sensitivity or by the partial or total absence of necessary sensations. Imagine the impact on your psychic well-being of a sudden increase, decrease, distortion, or diminution of any or all of your sensory capacities or of a combination of them. Suppose you lost your sense of touch (with no detectable organic basis for the loss). How could you maintain composure and lead a "normal" life? Suppose that you frequently saw that the objects and people closest to you were changing their shape, form, and outline without rhyme or reason. That these "physiological" disorders can be triggered by emotional "causes" is vital to our understanding of the psychoses.

Perception is a psychic response to sensation. From the interpretation of sensation and from its integration, synthesis, and conversion into a reasonable response, we fashion normal behavior. Hallucinations represent an extreme form of distortion in which any of the senses may be perceived as feeding false information into the psychic system. Nothing is probably more disconcerting than to experience sensations for which there are no appropriate physical stimuli and the sense of which others cannot accept as reasonable.

The most common hallucinations are auditory and involve the hearing of nonexistent voices. These voices are strange ones or those of friends or neighbors. Sometimes the voices speak to the individual directly, threatening him or accusing him of unthinkable crimes or of his failings as a person. What the hallucinator is hearing, of course, is the sound of his own thoughts.

GENE P.

Gene P. is a 45-year-old male whose home has been the state hospital for the past nine years. He is a paranoid schizophrenic who complains continuously to all within earshot that men with high-pitched voices are talking about him. The experience, according to his description, is very much like being in a crowded, noisy room and suddenly hearing fragments of a conversation in which people are talking about him. Gene isolates himself from his fellow patients, sits in a corner of the ward, and strains to filter out the noise in order to hear more of what is being said. Invariably, "they" seem to be talking about homosexuality and laughing as they use such terms as "fairy" and "queer" in referring to him. During one particularly distressing episode Gene became severely agitated. The voices suddenly became louder and clearer and unmistakably accused him of having homosexual relations with his younger brother. When spoken to in the ward, Gene reacts with arrogance and sometimes cups his hands over his ears to shut out this unwelcome interference with the voices that so repel and fascinate him.

Visual hallucinations are the next most frequent, and these false visions may be as real to the patient as a three-dimensional movie in color. These, and hallucinations of touch, taste, and smell, may command the patient's full attention during his waking hours.

3. Emotion

Just as sensation, so emotion can become disordered; there can be too much or too little emotion, or it can be inappropriate to the occasion. It can become distorted or confused. A simple increase of intensity in emotional response, for example, may be deemed inappropriate by others, even if there is a high tolerance for a wide range of emotional expression in the culture. When emotion exceeds social limits, when one is too happy or too sad, or when emotion takes a form that does not fit the social definition of the situation, the behavior is labeled abnormal, and steps are taken to deny the individual free access to the community.

The ways in which disordered emotion can find expression in behavior are extensive. The patient can develop disturbing ways of expressing emotion, he can become negativistic (reacting with emotions opposite from those expected), or he can experience emotions for which there seems to be no visible, environmental cause. Schizophrenics may experience emotions of a kind, quality, and degree unlike those felt by any "normal" person, and their terrifying apprehensions, religious ecstasies, and disconnected mixing of emotions may be beyond our comprehension.

WARREN N.

The psychologists called it "flat affect," but Warren's friends and acquaintances simply shrugged their shoulders and muttered "no sense, no feeling." In fact, his fellow workers observed that "he never felt one way or another about anything." Interestingly, those closest to him were divided about whether this emotional unresponsiveness was the mark of a calm, wise man or an indication that he "didn't show up when they were passing out feelings." Warren was, for example, the only member of his work crew whose facial expression remained totally impassive when fellow workers suffered painful, disfiguring, and bloody accidents on the job. Warren had acquired the reputation of being a cold fish; some of his fellow employees were afraid of him, some avoided him, and some teased him unmercifully. But nothing perturbed Warren as he steadily and dependably repeated the same simple punch-and-polish mechanical task he had done for years. Warren did his job, stared blank-eyed into the distance, and didn't feel anything one way or another.

Since anxiety is the common denominator of many disorders, it belongs in any discussion of emotion. In our time—as in every era—we have defined a relationship between stimulus and response and have determined what parts of this relationship are to be called normal and abnormal. To be considered normal, one must not be too anxious in situations where others are calm and not be too fear-free when everyone else is nervous and upset. The boundaries of normal anxiety shift, culture by culture and from era to era, because each society defines its own limits. The degree of anxiety experienced, then, becomes diagnostic of one's overall adjustment to life.

4. Behavior

When we speak or act we are engaging in verbal or motor behavior, and speech can become distorted or disordered in as many ways as any other aspect of the self. Again, there can be too much or too little; there can be distortion and interference—all can add up to mean "inappropriate," and it is on this basis that we judge the seriousness of the individual's deviation.

A disturbance of verbal behavior severs communication with the rest of society and becomes a means of retreat from social participation. Verbal distortion may take the form of simple incoherence via the production of empty, obscure, or seemingly meaningless mouthings. Or, communication based solely on his internal psychic experience may become so personalized that he may invent new words (neologisms) to express what he is feeling. He may become mute and inhibit verbal communication; he may indulge in the senseless repetition of the same phrases or or words (verbigeration); he may use only a stilted, rigid, formal, or complex and grotesque way of conversing; or he may choose to repeat and echo the words of others (echolalia), if he responds at all. In short, language can be as revealing an expression of disorder as can any other aspect of behavior.

DORWIN C.

He was 12 years old and he had not spoken one intelligible word for the last three years. He could communicate but he would not speak. He would do what he was told (if it was repeated firmly in a no-nonsense tone of voice) and, surprisingly, he still attended school regularly. His peers proved to be no problem since they at once assumed he was organically handicapped in some strange way. They serviced and protected him much as they would a baby. Peers and adults alike quickly learned to understand the needs reflected in the look in his eyes and the posture of his body and would respond with appropriate actions designed to satisfy his needs and wishes. Dorwin didn't really need to speak. He did very well being mute. His parents were mystified about his refusal to speak but they seemed, oddly, to accept it stoically and to treat it as a startling but not distressing turn of events. They knew, however, that the day of judgment was not far distant. Adolescence and manhood lay ahead, and something had to be done about the silent Dorwin. His private world was about to be invaded by mental health specialists who would be intolerant of his verbal disconnection from the world.

Bodily movement can be a symbolic form of communication with the outside world, and it, too, can be distorted in a number of ways. In addition to exhibiting the extremes of stuporlike inertia and strong agitation, the body many imitate the movements of others (echopraxia); it may respond automatically in a robotlike way; it may regularly use grimaces or other mannerisms to punctuate its movement; or it may simply move in stereotyped, repetitive patterns reflecting an individual's symbolic or magic thoughts.

Motor behavior that departs from accustomed patterns becomes a prime indicator of psychic disturbance. When perceptions, sensations, thoughts, and feelings are translated into overt behavior that does not conform to socially proper actions, and can therefore not be tolerated, we decide the individual is too disturbed to roam in our culture. If one cannot control his overt behavior, he becomes a threat to other members of society and must be treated accordingly.

5. Thinking

We make every effort to teach the child the "reality" of the physical world—the concepts of size (tall and short) or direction (up and down). We invest a similar but less obvious amount of energy in defining proper and improper modes of thought, because thinking that follows its own unique and highly personalized rules in defiance of social norms is declared deviant. The thinker of "forbidden" thoughts is treated as though his thoughts posed a threat to cultural survival.

The threat to society posed by disorders of thought and intelligence is confined primarily to the communication loss that takes place. An interlocked, interdependent, civilized society requires common acceptance of a code governing thought processes, the application of intelligence, and the factors which constitute logic and believability. Delusional thinking, for example, puts the schizophrenic in conflict with all others not so persuaded. The frequency of delusions is reflected in Figure 2.2, and the forms delusional thinking takes are examined in Table 2.2.

Certain disorders of intelligence and thought could have found a comfortable niche in other times and other places, but the inexorable complications of technology demand that rules of thought and communication be more rigid, more restrictive, and less tolerant of individual idiosyncrasies of direction and form. In every culture a contest is waged between those who think (and express) avant-garde thoughts and those who are comfortable with conventional thinking. If thoughts alien to the culture are too extreme, or come too suddenly for the impact to be absorbed easily, then the purveyor of the thought is declared beyond the pale of social acceptance. It is not always easy to distinguish between

FIGURE 2.2   FREQUENCY OF KINDS OF DELUSIONS AMONG SCHIZOPHRENICS *

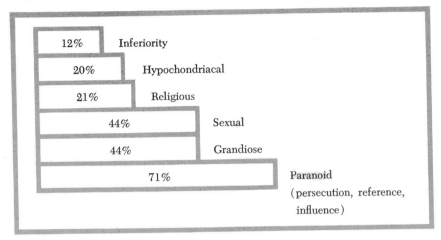

* Based on C. J. Lucas, P. Sansburg, and Joyce G. Collings, "A social and clinical study of delusions in schizophrenia," *J. Mental Sci.*, 108 (1962), 747–58.

** Patient may have more than one type of delusion. The percentages, thus, will add to more than 100%.

TABLE 2.2   THE FORM AND CONTENT OF DELUSIONS

SELF-DESTRUCTIVE

Guilt	*Nihilism*	*Hypochondria*
Unforgivable sins that have brought tragedy to others.	The world does not exist. Nothing is real.	The body is diseased, rotten, dying, or invaded by poison.

SELF UNDER ATTACK

Persecution	*Influence*	*Reference*
People are after him. Plotting, planning, threatening, attacking.	Enemies are controlling or influencing the victim's life.	People are making reference (derogatory) to him in various media (TV, radio, newspapers, etc.).

SELF-ENHANCING

Grandeur

The victim sees himself as a famous, notable, talented, brilliant person, envied (and thus persecuted) by others.

the constructive, creative, and gainful departure from the norm and distortions of the norm that lead nowhere.

CLYDE C.

At first Clyde was considered brilliant by his parents, but it became inescapably evident that his thinking was better described as bizarre. Clyde's intellectual constructions clearly plowed new and unfurrowed ground, but when the crop was harvested it consisted of strange fruit indeed. The cuteness of his unusual ideas in early childhood gave way to an obsessively pursued, elaborate, and weird master-system of power, energy, and influence that was beyond comprehension by anyone. He became secretive about his "system of mysterious life" and devoted all of his time to making journal entries and drawing strange figures behind the locked door of his room. Clyde graduated from high school (an undeserved "gift" from the educational establishment) and entered a small and not too selective college. He lasted exactly three months. Away from the supportive influence of his parents, he had decorated his dormitory room as a psychedelic "holy place," appointed himself the "Hip Pope," and demanded obeisance from his fellow students. They went along with the joke for a while. But, three "special delivery" papal bulls addressed to the president of the college failed to strike a responsive chord, and his papal reign was ended following a visit to the "holy place" by the vice-president for student affairs.

The disorders of thinking and knowledge are difficult to comprehend for those of us who have learned to think according to the usual rules. Suppose, for example, you treated two objects as identical only because they had certain similar features—features that were important to you personally but irrelevant to the rest of us? Schizophrenics are reported to assemble their world using unique segments and parts rather than common conceptions of the "whole" of things and events. It is this departure from common rules of logic and the substitution of personal, internal rules that render psychotic thinking incomprehensible to the rest of us.

It has been suggested that schizophrenics rely on primitive-symbolic-magical forms of thinking that include an unusual proportion of content drawn directly from unconscious regions (primary process thinking), and this makes for further difficulties in deciphering the complicated messages that are presented to us. Primary process thinking is, in many respects, like trying to communicate to others by describing the dream process or the internal experience of taking LSD. It comes out garbled and incomprehensible as though language is not an adequate container to hold it all.

Finally, thought disorder may appear because the schizophrenic cannot focus on one topic at a time; he cannot limit the things he thinks about, screen the flood of stimuli, and select rigorously from the variety of thoughts that fill his mind. Or because he becomes "overinclusive" in his thoughts, he cannot discard those parts of the topic that are not relevant to appropriate communication with others.

On Being Psychotic—Paul S.

Let us now try to assemble a composite symptomatic picture of what it is like to be psychotic. "Composite" because it is the combination of these components that forms the symptom patterns we diagnostically label as various forms of psychosis.

The case of Paul S. is a fictional account of the experience of being psychotic and suffering severe disturbance in every component of disorder. It is illustrative even as it mocks reality.

Paul S. was never "quite right," according to his near relatives, and they were not too surprised when he was admitted to the state mental hospital. "Not surprised" is probably a charitable way of describing their feelings about Paul S., since, in their accounts of interaction with him during his childhood, it was evident that any hope for his entry into civilized society had been abandoned long before his behavior made confinement necessary. Rejection, isolation, and tongue-clucking sympathy by Paul's friends and relatives came early in his life, but a much more destructive set of experiences occurred even before he was born.

Paul was a product of alcohol and uncontrolled passionate impulse. He was conceived in a drunken, crude sexual union of parents who were making one last futile denial of their unspoken mutual intention to separate. His mother, filled with disgust for the male of the species, found herself pregnant with an unwanted child, a constant reminder of the failure of her marriage and of the husband who deserted her. Paul never saw his father.

Paul was not only rejected by a resentful mother who had no other target for her bitterness and rage; he was also viewed as a burdensome brat by his older brothers and sisters. Hate is probably too strong a word for the feelings Paul sensed in his siblings. He only knew they ignored him most of the time and hurt him the rest of the time. He began early to scuttle away from them, whining like an animal, whenever they came near.

At mealtimes he began to take his plate of food underneath the table where he could eat with his hands while unobserved. He was soon banished to a corner of the kitchen where he ate alone most of the years of his life.

In school, Paul's teachers thought of him as an unusually shy, quiet, and not too bright child. But, since he rarely caused trouble, he was left to his own devices. He dropped behind one year in elementary school and was held back an additional year in junior high school. Following this second failure, he was referred to a school counselor who talked to Paul briefly and noted on the school records "undermotivated, but is probably a late bloomer who will grow out of it."

Paul never grew out of it. He was fifteen now, and his behavior had become even more erratic and "strange." His mother thought it was the "stubbornness and meanness he got from his father" and reported with some pride: "I did my best to whip it out of him." In high school he was a "rotten mess," according to his classmates; they called him "Putrid Paul" because he would not bathe, brush his teeth, or comb his hair. They teased him unmercifully and made him the butt of an unending series of pranks and jokes. Paul missed more school than he attended, but the school's effort to make him return was, by any measure, less than vigorous and enthusiastic.

The breaking point came when Paul's mother discovered him sitting cross-legged and transfixed staring at a crucifix. He had covered his naked body with a think layer of cold cream and antennalike wires were attached to bands around his ankles, wrists, and forehead. When he did not respond to his mother's shrill command to "stop all this foolishness," he was taken to the police station "to be put in the reform school." After psychiatric examination and psychological testing, Paul was committed to a nearby state mental hospital.

In the alien setting of the hospital, Paul reacted badly to the mass of strangers who kept talking to him, sticking him with needles, and ordering him to go places and do things when he did not feel like it. Paul became stubborn, and the nurses had difficulty in dealing with him. However, he continued to communicate to the ward psychiatric resident.

It became clear that Paul had been actively hallucinating for nearly a year before his hospitalization. He reported regular visitations by a half-man, half-woman named Tal-Rec from the planet Uranus. At first, Tal-Rec had appeared only at twilight just before Paul fell asleep, but he could hear Tal-Rec's voice very faintly all during his waking hours. Tal-Rec was a kindly, shimmering-gold, giant being who told Paul he had been chosen to lead humanity out of its troubles. Tal-Rec's message was boringly trite (man is too uncivilized to have the bomb; he will be destroyed if he does not learn the ways of peace) in its recital but like a mystic revelation to Paul. Paul became, in fantasy and without effort, mankind's savior.

There were the forces of evil, of course. There were the Uranians who had fallen from a state of grace and had come to Earth to foil Tal-Rec's plans. As Paul said,

They look like earthlings but you can always spot them. If they are disguised like women, they always give it away because they act more like men than women. Men who act a little like girls are the same.

Paul was convinced his mother was one of "them" and that "they" had also taken over the bodies of his brothers and sisters. He had identified most of the "agents" in the ward and was planning to strike back at them when the time was right.

Paul's delusional and hallucinatory experiences were not nearly so well organized and systematized as they at first appeared. New characters floated in and out of the scenario he had constructed; the voices sometimes became clamorously strident, confused, or incoherent; and, his "enemies" of one day became his friends of the following day. Once, when Paul could no longer tell friend from foe, he tried to shed his bodily form to join the "good" Uranians by hanging himself with a sheet tied over his closet door.

Paul remains hospitalized despite an extended series of electroconvulsive shock treatments and administration of psychoactive drugs. He is now totally preoccupied with his almost continuous hallucinations and has ceased to communicate with anyone. Hopes for his recovery are about zero, and he has been shifted to the "back" wards of the hospital where he is receiving only custodial care.

Paul's psychotic disturbance was a defensive attempt to deal with an intolerable set of life circumstances that brought him nothing but pain and anxiety. As he retreated to the less difficult world of fantasy, he constructed a fictional life populated by accepting and near-perfect people who epitomized everything he longed to be and could never become. To achieve this state he withdrew from contact with others, disconnected himself from a rejecting world, abandoned socially acceptable patterns of motivation, thinking, behavior, and emotion, and responded only to the distorted perceptions and sensations that flooded his consciousness.

Paul's case illustrates a diffuse and massive disruption of normal psychic functioning. His is a composite case, but it does provide some feeling for the nature of the psychotic experience.

THE PSYCHOTIC PROCESS

Decompensation

An important aspect of what occurs in psychotic disorder can be described by the term "decompensation." In the normal course of living—

attempting to solve problems and defending one's self against the experi-ence of severe anxiety—the individual makes a number of adjustments in his patterns of thinking, feeling, and behaving. He compensates for the pressures he is experiencing, and, if the stress intensifies or the defen-sive maneuvers he undertakes prove to be insufficient to the task, there is a sudden decompensation in which wild and deviant forms of behavior appear as the integration of his psychic structure deteriorates and re-pressed impulses and urges come to consciousness. Ego disintegration under stress in called decompensation.

An example might make this process more explicit. At the first sound-ing of a fire alarm you may respond rationally, hurriedly gathering valued objects as you head for an exit. Thinking, feeling, and behaving are integrated, purposeful, and calculated to solve the problem of escape. Anxiety naturally mounts and disintegration begins if you become aware that the fire is spreading more rapidly than you at first gauged it would. Worried now, you drop some of the cumbersome articles that have sud-denly become a valueless burden, make some hasty, emotional decisions, and begin to run pell-mell and close to panic for the nearest door. If you discover the revolving door is jammed by the crush of others trying to escape, you may begin to scream incoherently and fall to your knees sobbing and cursing the unjust fate that signals your end. At this moment of total panic you may be incapable of saving your own life by smashing the large plate glass windows that stand conspicuously unnoticed on each side of the blocked revolving door.

Replace fire with some other personal, inexorable anxiety, and the force behind the process of decompensation becomes comprehensible even though it remains invisible. Your alteration of psychic and biological energy to meet an emergency situation is marked first by heightened tension, agitation, and alertness in an attempt at self-control and mastery of the circumstances confronting you. You mobilize resources to meet threat, and new or altered forms of defensive behavior appear. These patterns may deviate considerably from past behavior and may provoke concern among those who know you but are unaware of the threat you perceive. If these attempts fail to reduce stress, even more violent and disconnected responses may occur and assume a recognizably neurotic or psychotic form. Severe hallucinations, delusions, or serious distortions of reality can mark the outcome of your response to an internal emer-gency.

As the ego integration dissolves it will be paralleled by biological decompensation. The alarm sensed psychically is echoed in the muscular, glandular, and hormonal systems of bodily functioning. When the organ systems operate at full throttle for long periods of time, the limited and fallible human vehicle will break down. As physical decompensation occurs, additional stress is added to the unbearable burden the victim is already carrying. In concert, psychological and biological decompensation produce the characteristic symptoms and patterns of behavior we have come to recognize as serious disorder.

When the individual undergoing decompensation and psychotic transfiguration begins to sense that he differs from others and is drifting away from close emotional contact with them, he may experience a disturbing sense of depersonalization. Depersonalization can be the outcome of a flowing together or distortion of each of the basic components of motivation, perception and sensation, emotion, behavior, and thinking.

Depersonalization

The peculiar phenomenon of depersonalization has been explored and interpreted by a number of theorists (Bergler, 1950; Bird, 1957; Blank, 1954; Jacobson, 1959; Sarlin, 1962). Some patients complain of feeling that things have become unreal and that their ability to respond with appropriate emotion is severely diminished. The body and the external world become alien, and the person feels detached from it as though he moves through familiar paces—robotlike—while observing himself from outside his body (see Table 2.3).

TABLE 2.3   FORMS OF DISTURBANCE OF THE BODY IMAGE

ANGYAL (1936) *	FISHER (1962) †
1. Body unity impaired (disconnection of parts; falling apart)	1. Body enlarged
2. Body continuity impaired (body an empty shell; not human)	2. Body reduced
3. Body dimensions changed (shrinking, flat, withering)	3. Body changing
4. Body parts displaced (legs pulling into abdomen, eyes sinking into skull)	4. Body openings blocked
5. Body parts dead (hair falling out, skin dead, limbs wooden)	5. Body not part of the self
	6. Body contaminated
	7. Body boundaries shifting or lost
	8. Body skin sensations are unusual

* A. Angyal, "The experience of the body-self in schizophrenia," *Arch. Neurol. Psychiat.*, 35 (1936), 1029–53.

† S. Fisher, "Body image and psychopathology," *Arch. Gen. Psychiat.*, 10 (1964), 514–29.

Patients plagued with fears of going insane are usually distressed by this experience. These patients are not delusional; they are reporting a sense of detachment from life and a loss of the emotional capacity to respond to it.

The sensation of depersonalization is not restricted to psychotic patients; it can exist in varying degrees in otherwise normal persons and, in a mild form, is probably a part of the experience of most of us at one time or another. Any drastic change in one's environment may be sufficient to trigger this response as can special precipitating circumstances such as extreme isolation, sleep deprivation, violent physiological changes, or drugged states (Cattell, 1966). Thus, depersonalization can be an occasional part of normal existence or it can be steadily characteristic of severe neurosis or psychosis. Depersonalization may occur but go unrecognized in the early stages of any emotional disorder, but it may forecast the appearance of a massive delusional or hallucinatory experience.

There is little accurate clinical evidence about the frequency or duration of episodes of depersonalization. One plausible explanation is that depersonalization removes the person from close contact with painful reality and is an ego action that protects by withdrawal. This splitting-off of part of one's emotional and cognitive experience may signal the failure of the ego's resources—a sign that more sophisticated forms of coping with conflict and anxiety are needed. Or, something like a "habit" of withdrawal may be learned and practiced in early childhood and become a frequent defensive maneuver in one's adult years.

It is interesting to speculate about possible relationships between the phenomenon of depersonalization and the members of our society who "turn on, tune in, and drop out." This terse rallying cry may reflect a way out for those alienated from the standards and goals of our society. Detachment and drug-induced hypnagogic states may be their only means of coping with emotions. In unity there is strength, and the "hippie" movement may offer via LSD a biochemical solution for a lack of ego resources for problem solving. Banding together in common cause to search for escape from contact with fellow human beings is an ancient phenomenon. Any careful reading of religious or philosophical history will unearth similar instances of individual or group-organized withdrawal as a solution to life's problems—problems that exist in every age.

The Criteria of Deviation

One approach to the nature of deviation is to be found in Lazarus's (1963) list of criteria of maladjustment. Although such lists are informative, they do not constitute an answer to the problem of defining mental health or disturbance.

Lazarus suggests that one obvious indicator of maladjustment is the experience of a high degree of psychological discomfort. The chronically depressed, frightened, or anxious person knows of his maladjustment simply by comparing his subjective experience of life with that of others. Each of us has a rough idea of where we fit on the scale of comfort-discomfort in daily life. The absence of any sense of discomfort is, of course, an untrustworthy indicator of the presence or absence of disorder, since many hospitalized patients report that they are perfectly content with their conflict-laden pattern of life.

Most frequently, cognitive distortion or intellectual inefficiency is used as an index of maladjustment. The social world is designed along narrow dimensions in a technological society; the definition of reality must be clear, concise, and nearly absolute. A machine culture offers fewer alternatives than does a rural, primitive society. Up, down, right, left, real, and unreal have fine tolerance limits, and intellectual and cognitive inadequacy or inefficiency are handicaps that reduce one's social status. Whether cognitive disorganization is sudden in its development or whether it is part of a pattern of lifelong increasing ineptitude, a social and economic penalty is exacted. If cognitive inefficiency is coupled with a lack of awareness that one's thinking does not match that of others, the level of social rejection increases accordingly.

One additional criterion of deviation is distorted or unusual behavior. Each of us has a personal tolerance for the miscreant behavior of others, and each of us is forgiving, within limits, of temporary deviation. Since what is deviant is primarily defined by the current social mores of our particular cultural group, this definition is bound to be highly elastic.

During a period of social change, it becomes particularly difficult to fasten adjusted-maladjusted labels on people. Who is "crazy" and who is not, who is potentially harmful and who is not, is hard to determine in a time of social transition. Some individuals breach new entries into the future; others cling to the stable criteria of an earlier and perhaps more peaceful age; the rest stand confused and undecided. Which way is normal? What is the best path to the goal?

Perhaps a reasonable way of viewing mental disorder is to consider it one aspect of the unitary process called living. As Karl Menninger (1960) suggested, each of us might simply possess differing degrees of mental health—ranging from abject misery and disorganization at one end to happiness and success at the other—at different times and periods in our life.

This cursory exploration of the psychotic process needs a final note to return it to its starting point. According to existing reports, strange or unusual combinations of symptoms occurred at various times and in different cultures—symptoms that do not fit the present mold very snugly. We will consider briefly below some of these rare and exotic syndromes.

EXOTIC AND RARE DISORDERS

Silvano Arieti and Johannes Meth (1959) underscore the difficulties inherent in getting symptom patterns to fit into a classification system when they discuss psychotic syndromes that simply refuse to fit prescribed patterns. Although these syndromes are difficult to classify and are sparsely reported in the literature, and even though they are not always reliably recounted, the reader should nevertheless be aware of their existence.

Some of these special patterns of serious disorder are indigenous to a specific locale and show the influence of the culture in which they were observed. As Arieti and Meth point out, "among the islanders of Dobu (Melanesia), no sane woman leaves her cooking pots unguarded for fear of being poisoned." To us this behavior would indicate paranoia. Among some Eskimo tribes, the mother accepts the killer of her son in her son's stead. Among the Papuans it is traditional for an uncle and nephew (mother's brother and son) to practice homosexuality (p. 560). Although there are differences in frequency and form of symptoms, there is general consensus that psychotic disorders known currently to the Western world were present in primitive peoples.

Among the functional syndromes reported in other cultures are *latah, amok,* and the more controversial *thanatomania* (voodoo death). *Latah,* in Malaysia, most often afflicts middle-aged and elderly women who, often after a sudden fright, become seclusive and unusually fearful. *Latah* may be coupled with a verbal and ideational disorder which is manifested by the imitation of the words and actions of others even though it may bring abuse and punishment on the victim's head. This syndrome is considered a primitive form of relief from unbearable anxiety.

Running *amok,* a Malaysian behavior pattern found in other parts of the world, applies to a member of any culture who goes berserk and assaults or kills anyone in his path.

The public has always been fascinated by the exotic quality of the behavior disorder called Voodoo Death. Death by magic is not uncommon in primitive cultures, but full and reliable documentation is difficult to secure. Reports simply state that when an individual violates an important taboo or transgresses a vital social standard, he is "frightened to death." Since there is no clearly evident cause for death, there has been a great deal of speculation about the possible linkage of emotion and human physiology, but this hypothesis remains yet to be explored. The persistence of tales of death by voodoo suggests that something beyond old wives' tales is involved, but we may be past the point in history in which we have sufficient data to find a definitive answer to this phenomenon.

To dwell on the various speculative explanations of each of these strange syndromes would lead us too far afield. Perhaps it is sufficient to indicate that the often subtle and frequently invisible pressures of prescriptions and proscriptions imposed by society are capable of molding the form of severe disorders and giving them a form to the society and to the age in which they exist.

Psychotic behavior has been described as a helpless and mute cry for help. An individual driven beyond reasonable limits of toleration may "choose" the most dramatic form possible of communicating to others the desperate state in which he finds himself. *Latah, amok,* or *thanatomania* are such dramatic attempts at communication. In other times and in other places where anguished voices are more easily heard by other members of the society such extreme measures would not be necessary.

Arieti and Meth's examination of the literature reports collective psychoses of almost epidemic form recorded in the past. The flagellants who scourged themselves publicly to atone for their sins, the victims of St. Vitus's dance with its violent activity culminating in unconsciousness, lycanthropy (the belief that one had been transformed into an animal), and tarantism (the belief that one becomes sick after being bitten by the tarantula), all may be examples of the impact of ignorance and superstition. It is evident that these outbreaks reflect some mixture of hysteria and schizophrenic delusions and hallucinations, coupled, perhaps, with some degree of mental retardation.

We pride ourselves, in this half of the twentieth century, with being too sophisticated ever to succumb to such exotic or collective psychoses. Yet one never knows whether there will not be an unforeseen social situation of high anxiety that will trigger masses of human beings to react with new and strange patterns of symptoms.

SUMMARY

The dimensions of psychotic disorder include some conception of the frequency of psychosis in our culture. Figures on frequency are useless, of course, until they have meaning attached to them in terms of incidence (new cases in a fixed period of time) and prevalence (the total number of active cases that exist at one point in time). It is also necessary to interpret the relationship between available facilities and the rate of those hospitalized in our society.

The fundamental components of disorder are made up of distortions of our systems of motivation, perception and sensation, emotion, behavior, and thinking. These disordered aspects of relating to the world and the people in it combine to produce a psychotic experience of the kind undergone by Paul S. As stress and anxiety erode the ego resources, which normally would be adequate to cope with threat, a process of psychological decompensation occurs and response is focused on an internal emergency at the expense of dealing successfully with the outside world.

The decompensatory experience can bring with it a sense of depersonalization and alienation from others that contributes significantly to deviant behavior by causing intense psychological discomfort. When cognitive and intellectual deviations occur the victim cannot easily be accepted as a functioning member of a technologically sophisticated culture that relies heavily on predictable, cooperative interactions among its members.

Since patterns of psychotic behavior are influenced by the time, place, and culture in which they occur, history has recorded a series of exotic or rare forms of total human breakdown seldom seen in our society. The importance of these deviations in the "usual" pattern of psychosis is contained in the lesson they teach with regard to the degree of man's normal and abnormal response to the social pressures of civilized living. Civilization indeed has its discontents, and psychosis may be a part of the price we pay for group living.

THEORIES OF PSYCHOSIS II

The Causes of Psychosis

3

In considering current theories of causation, we have arbitrarily divided into two classes—psychogenic and biological—the vast array of complicated, overlapping, differently focused views of how psychosis originates. Yet, a simple declaration that such a division is arbitrary and artificial is not enough to prevent the reader from compartmentalizing theories into exactly these oversimplified niches.

To provide a proper context for the theories that we labeled "psychogenic" or "biological" we will detail one theoretical effort to combine these perspectives into a single class. This "combined" theory of Leopold Bellak (1952, 1958) is representative of one set of modern views, even though we may not agree with all of his conclusions about schizophrenia. Bellak has been one of the most dedicated explorers of schizophrenia, and his observations reflect the increasing need to assemble the many views of schizophrenia into a single, meaningful portrait.

A MULTIPLE-FACTOR THEORY OF SCHIZOPHRENIA

Bellak reviewed the literature of schizophrenia for the last thirty years and concluded "the evidence seems overwhelming that schizophrenia is not a single disease, that therefore, there is no single cause and thus no single cure. So far, none of the dramatic claims for one or another somatic factor, supposedly characteristic for schizophrenia, has been satisfactorily substantiated" (Bellak, 1958, p. 16).

47

Working from this conclusion, Bellak attempted to assemble a comprehensive theory of schizophrenia that would account for as many of the available data as possible that were relevant to the symptoms, diagnosis, therapy, and prognosis of this disorder. Schizophrenia is, for Bellak, a syndrome (a collection of symptoms, not a single disease) with variable features brought about by several conditions that combine to produce severe disturbance of the ego. In his multiple-factor theory there is room not only for infections, arteriosclerosis, constitutional and genetic factors, but for traumatic and toxic events and learned psychogenic ego defects.

For Bellak, schizophrenia can be the consequence of various biological and psychogenic forces. A number of etiologic factors contribute in producing an individual's specific pattern of emotion, thought, and behavior. Bellak's theory might be described, succinctly, as one in which no two schizophrenias need be exactly alike; each may be based on its particular combination of personal events and forces that culminate in patterns of human behavior that, for convenience, we lump together and call schizophrenia. Bellak argues that the various forms of schizophrenia may be more different from than similar to one another; he suggests that most theorists have been laboring under the misconception that schizophrenia is a disease as well as a unitary phenomenon. Bellak insists that although organic factors may be relevant to schizophrenia, their contribution may be only a "fractional" or "secondary" spurring on of the psychological pressures that produce the massive group of human beings we diagnose as schizophrenic.

For Bellak, schizophrenia (on a psychogenic level) is as often a failure of development as it is a regression to previously learned patterns of response. Psychoactive chemicals used freely in modern therapy may alleviate or disguise the nature of these conditions, but it will always be necessary to spend considerable time to teach schizophrenic persons to "habilitate to" or "adapt to" life in a socially more acceptable way. Learnings absent or distorted in early parent-child relationships may be a prime contributor to adult disorders that reflect developmental or regressive failures. Bellak has observed that child-rearing is one of the few occupations in civilized society for which absolutely no training is required. This may be a fatal oversight for some members of our society.

Bellak feels that most of our theoretical notions about schizophrenia have been of limited usefulness, since they are addressed only to a part of the total process of the disorder. And in view of his belief that schizophrenia is a combination of psychogenic and organic conditions, he espouses a multiple-factor, psychosomatic theory. Histological, chemical, metabolic, or genetic events may also combine with psychogenic factors to produce schizophrenia.

But, Bellak places his heaviest theoretical emphasis on ego functions and their disturbance. One's relation to reality, the regulation and control of drives, the capacity to form adequate relationships to others, and the management of thought processes and attempts to ward off anxiety are essential to his understanding of schizophrenia. Included in these ego disturbances are the so-called autonomous functions (perception, intelligence, cognition, thinking, and language). It is not possible to consider each of Bellak's views of these components of schizophrenia in detail at this point, but his comments on autonomous and synthetic functions of the ego deserve mention.

When autonomous functions are disturbed, some parts of the ego, or self, may still be capable of adequate performance despite severe disturbance in this area. In paranoid schizophrenics, to be specific, massive areas of intellectual functioning (such as the ability to use numbers correctly) may remain intact despite the obvious deterioration of other parts of their cognitive and emotional functioning; e.g., the patient may still do his job productively, although he believes that others are jealous of him and are plotting against him. Some psychological capacities seem autonomous, i.e., capable of unimpaired operation and performance despite the decay or distortion of related aspects of the self.

The synthetic functions are particularly vulnerable to disorder in the schizophrenic. Facts, feelings, events, and impressions flood in and must be organized, evaluated, matched, interpreted, and formed into meaningful wholes. Without the ability to synthesize, or integrate, the world becomes a dangerous jumble of chaotic happenings that can never be comprehended adequately or reacted to appropriately.

It will seem that synthetic functions resemble what we usually call intelligence: It is one's intelligence that may well determine at what *level* and in what *form* facts, feelings, events, and impressions get organized into meaningful patterns, and intelligence coupled with education may refine the sophistication of the conclusions reached. But each human being organizes his world into a sensible shape for himself at his own level of intellectual functioning. The ability to synthesize one's experience adequately to guide behavior in the culture in which one must live is the crucial test. In all honesty, behavioral scientists have yet to explore in depth the relationship between intelligence and the autonomous and synthetic functions in the human psychic structure. Conclusions of the kind reached in this area, then, are only speculative—mere guesses based on theoretical and clinical experience and not much more than that.

When an individual's ego is incapacitated, it can no longer direct coherent action designed to solve problems that confront him. And civilized living demands order and regularity. A person who cannot fit into this "civilized" schema suffers what Murphy (1957) has called an "inability to cope" with the stimuli of life, and he is given the shortest of shrift by his fellowman. Bellak does not rule out the role of physical, constitutional, or organic factors in the formation of the schizophrenic response for *some* of those so labeled, but it is evident his theoretical bent is toward a psychogenic view of life.

If we accept Bellak's views in a literal fashion, it would probably be necessary to attach to each schizophrenic an individual designation that reflects the unique combination of psychological circumstances and biological events that have fashioned him. Such a system is, at this moment, too cumbersome to envision as practical, but the idea has theoretical merit.

Let us turn now to the categorization we proposed originally. We shall look first at biological views of causation and then examine psychogenic concepts of psychosis.

BIOLOGICAL VIEWS OF DISORDER

The physiological, biological, and genetic facets of man provide a major area of consideration in the search for the cause of schizophenia. The discovery of a discrete organic basis for severe emotional disorder has long been man's dream—a dream born in the prepsychoanalytic era and fostered by theorists who balked at dealing with the intangibles of feeling and emotion. Almost every conceivable part of man has been probed by researchers. Man's physique, his nerve arrangement, the enzymes that flood his brain, the electrical impulses that vibrate through his body, his blood chemistry, the metabolic processing of his life-giving substances, and the philosophic intersect of his mind and body have all been examined (Rainer, 1967).

Genetics and Psychosis

Genetic theory suggests that psychoses result from an inherited disposition formed by genetic defect or metabolic error, a theory that would make our concern with parent-child relationships and the character of the growing child's environment an incredible waste of time. Some geneticists, however, think that both an inherited defect and a negative environment are needed to produce the full-blown, overt symptoms of psychosis.

Theoretically, an individual may inherit any of a number of biochemical, constitutional, or nervous system defects that "prime" him for psychotic disorganization. The disease called *Huntington's Chorea,* for example, is one in which atrophy in parts of the brain produces a progressive intellectual and emotional deterioration. Victims of Huntington's Chorea have at least one parent who has also suffered this disease.

Twin studies occupy a prominent position in the genetic approach. Identical twins (monozygotic or one-celled twins) are assumed to have identical heredity, and fraternal twins (dizygotic or two-celled twins) are assumed to be similar but not identical in heredity. Comparison of one kind of twin with the other and of both kinds with ordinary siblings has been a prime device for the researchers of heredity. When the rate of psychosis is measured for the two kinds of twins and then compared with the incidence of psychosis in the general population, a base for statistical and theoretical speculation is formed. Among theorists who pursue such twin-studies are Kallmann (1953, 1959, 1962), Planansky (1955), Fuller and Thompson (1960), and Shields and Slater (1961).

The rate of psychosis among near blood relatives of schizophrenics ought to be higher than the rate in distant relatives if there is an inherited, genetic basis to this disorder. Buss (1966) summarizes several studies of this rate, noting, "It is between 3 per cent and 4 per cent for distant relatives, between 4 per cent and 14 per cent for close relatives, and between 3 per cent and 17 per cent for dizygotic fraternal twins" (p. 319). The rate for monozygotic identical twins ranges between 67 and 86 per cent. Since 1 per cent is the expected incidence of psychosis in the general population, it is evident that degree of blood relationship is congruent with the presence of psychosis in those whose genetic inheritance is similar to that of schizophrenics.

Kallmann's rates for incidence of psychosis (Figure 3.1) fit, roughly, the estimates others have made. The interpretation of these facts produces the central theoretical issue: Do these facts tell us about genetics and inheritance, or can they as easily be explained by an environmental focus and learning theory?

For the affective disorders (manic-depressive psychosis) a base rate of one half of 1 per cent is assumed by most theorists for general population—about half the expected rates for psychoses. Kallmann's (1953) rates of concordance for twins and siblings are as follows: identical twins, 95.7 per cent; fraternal twins, 26.3 per cent; siblings, 22.7 per cent. Kallmann views these percentages as evidence for the inheritance of manic-depressive disorder even though the number of manic-depressive cases available for study is much smaller than the samples of schizophrenics and subject, thus, to a greater degree of unreliability.

One criticism leveled against such statistical studies is that blood lines tend to be traced with little regard for the fact that an individual who becomes psychotic may have been raised by psychotic parents who pro-

FIGURE 3.1   DEGREE OF BLOOD RELATIONSHIP AND INCIDENCE OF DISORDER IN
RELATIVES OF SCHIZOPHRENICS *

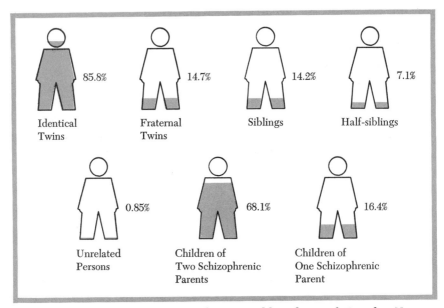

* Based on F. J. Kallmann, *Heredity in Health and Mental Disorder*. New
York: Norton, 1953.

vided a unique environment and influence. Another criticism is that since
psychosis in identical twins is a rare phenomenon, a very few cases could
inflate statistical conclusions out of proportion to their meaning (Jackson,
1960).

Twins occur only once in every 85 births, and only one third of these
twins are identical. Almost all identical twins are reared together, and
the chance of finding a testable sample of psychotic identical twins
reared apart is slim indeed. And, "reared-apart" must mean reared in
separate households almost from birth. Jackson has criticized some of
the genetic studies by indicating that "being reared separately" has been
defined as meaning that identical twins lived apart only after reaching
an average age of 15 years. This separation (only after growing up
together) is clearly an unacceptable basis for developing a genetic theory
to the theorist who believes that child-rearing experiences produce or
contribute to the psychotic process. That normal or abnormal identical
twins reared together resemble one another psychologically should hardly
surprise us. Whether this similarity is in response to genetic or environmental forces, we are not now in a position to state.

HERB AND KEITH S.

Herb and Keith had only dim recollections of each other despite the fact that they were identical twins. If you met one and then saw the other you would be startled by the physical resemblance and have the feeling you were "seeing double." They were each long-limbed, thin, bony, and awkward, and neither of them wore clothes that were suited to their physical frames. Their moderate baldness was identical, with a "widow's peak" predominant, and jet black, ungrayed hair a striking feature.

They both were hospitalized and diagnosed chronic hebephrenic schizophrenics—the most disorganizing form of serious disorder. They were young—only 18—but both had abandoned the human race with a disturbing completeness and finality. They had, together, suffered much in the first six years of their lives—three foster homes, an accidental succession of cruel, rejecting foster parents, and incalculable pain and loneliness. Finally, separately adopted, each had gone his own way, but each bore the identical scars of early childhood, and each responded to his new home with terror, self-protection, and withdrawal.

The outcome was hardly surprising. Both Herb and Keith failed to master the challenges appropriate to their age and both responded poorly to the increased pressure generated by the new parents. Faced with certain failure, anticipating only pain, and bewildered by incomprehensible demands, both chose the only way out—disconnection from an alien and threatening world. Their identical heredity and experience produced breakdown at the same juncture in life.

Many of the studies of genetic inheritance of the psychoses have been primitive, unsophisticated, and, perhaps, biased and less than scientific (Weiner, 1967). Despite the bitter argument over the pursuit of a genetic base for psychosis, we can reasonably accept the position of Rosenthal (1962) that even though the early studies may have suffered from inflated statistical artifacts they still suggest a fruitful field for further and more sophisticated research. We are without evidence that heredity alone can account for the appearance of a psychosis, but this is not to say that there is no hereditary component in the psychotic process. The failure of one theory to make its point does not strengthen the position of theories that take a different tack. The genetic and environmentalist positions are not mutually exclusive; they simply view common ground through different sets of eyes (Pastore, 1949).

Biochemistry and Psychosis

Biochemists have always dreamed of establishing control over man's behavior, but this dream has not yet been fulfilled (Himwich and Himwich, 1967). Biochemists have probed most aspects of human chemistry.

Since the patient's blood and urine are easily accessible to observation, they have frequently been subjected to study. Theorists assume that if psychopathology is a generalized physiological reaction it is reasonable to suppose that its presence ought to be reflected in some fashion in the fluid medium that surrounds the tissues of the body, in the body chemistry, or in human waste products. Study of the state of the body fluids seeks to discover the presence of substances that affect the brain, producing disordered patterns of behavior.

In this quest, pharmacologically active substances (drugs) have been introduced into the body to provoke reactions that may serve as models for those chemical-behavioral causes and effects produced naturally in the patient. A large number of drugs such as LSD (lysergic acid diethylamide) has been employed in research, and a great many tranquilizers, stimulants, and depressants have been used to alter the characteristic mood of the patient. It is, in fact, the promising response of patients to these mood-changing drugs that has recently encouraged researchers in their pursuit of other biochemical keys to behavior (Woolley, 1962).

Biochemical studies have explored the energy metabolism of patients—abnormalities of basal metabolism and glucose, carbohydrate, and phosphate utilization by the body—but have not managed, convincingly, to connect biochemical anomalies to human behavioral disorder. Most studies marked by initially glowing accounts of statistical significance simply fail to provide adequate experimental control (comparison with nondisordered persons) for other possible "causes" of the condition (Benjamin, 1958; Kety, 1959).

The discovery of a high correlation between catatonic schiozophrenia and some element of blood chemistry must, for example, demonstrate that the same chemical finding *cannot* be traced to the patient's diet or lack of physical exercise that occurs for all hospitalized patients. Bulle and Konchegul (1957), for example, found a substance very much like the compound serotonin in the cerebrospinal fluid of psychotics and a substance with the properties of adrenaline in manic-depressives. When dosages of these substances were administered to the patients, alterations in their symptoms appeared. A detailed theory of biochemical action in the psychoses was developed based on these findings, but the raw biochemical data were not enough to rule out the possibility of a great many other interacting events that could produce such chemical changes independent of the psychotic state of the patient. Biochemistry furnishes interesting *clues* to psychosis, but a careful appraisal of the data suggests that conclusions such as "Schizophrenia is regarded as starting with a failure to form enough serotonin in the brain" (Woolley, 1962, p. 183) are more than a little premature.

The list of possible biochemical "causes" investigated has included: amino acid and monoamine metabolism, endocrine gland excretions, and serum proteins. We know, for example, that the neuro hormones mediate the transmission of nerve impulses and that the primary neuro hormones (acetylocholine, histamine, noradrenalin, serotonin, and gamma amino butyric acid) make up a kind of internal "tide of life" that is thought to influence the direction of mental activity (Rubin, 1962). Experimental reactions produced in animals and the discovery of similar or related substances in the brain and nervous system of some of the victims of psychopathology encourage the biochemist's hope for the discovery of keys that will unlock some of the mystery of man's behavior (Bulle and Konchegul, 1957).

Biochemical study of the schizophrenias presents a wildly scattered set of findings—findings that do not always fit into a reasonable pattern. Reaction to reports in the professional literature depends, in great part, on the initial optimism or pessimism with which one approaches the field (Durell and Schildkraut, 1966). For a variety of reasons, significant and meaningful "breakthroughs" in biochemical research most often fail to be confirmed by the next researcher to try the experiment (Jackson, 1962). There is a close kinship of genetic and biochemical studies in this respect since a number of theorists have suggested that genetic or constitutional defects might take the form of biochemical disarray. Research to explore this possible connection is almost nonexistent.

Much of what we know of biochemistry and disorder comes from comparisons between normal and pathological groups. It is in the faulty comparisons of these that many errors are made. As Kety (1959) has noted, the concept of schizophrenia is so loose and incapable of definition that it is difficult to know if two geographically separated researchers are working on comparable populations. The easy availability of captive populations of schizophrenic patients in mental hospitals has always been seductive to researchers and has provoked a number of indiscretions in experimental design. As long as biochemical studies are carried out on patients who have been hospitalized for a great many years, it is impossible to determine whether findings relate to fundamental differences between normals and schizophrenics, or to hospital diets and chronic infections of the digestive tract, or to the consequences of prolonged courses of medication, drugs, or convulsive shock. Cause and effect relationship is the issue to be resolved, and this has most often been treated in a very cavalier and unscientific fashion.

In addition, diagnostic categories are woefully unreliable; control subjects are not easily available (volunteers cannot be used since they may have special psychological characteristics); normal chemical base lines may not be known (and these may wax and wane in unknown ways); and observed chemical changes may be a response to psychotic disorder rather than a cause of it. It is not a hopeless arena for scientific grappling with issues, but it is a demanding and challenging one. Refinements in theory and technique still hold promise, but researchers may one day be forced to make friends with the psychological enemy in order to achieve their aims.

Biochemists view psychosis as a disease, and it is reasonable, then, to suppose the "disease" is a function of body chemistry. It is interesting that the neuroses are seldom seen as disease in the same fashion as the psychoses. Perhaps the psychoses are so alien to our notions of normal human behavior that, for those who think "chemically," the psychotic population is a prime candidate for biochemical disorder.

The psychoses are obviously some mixture of mental and physical but they are not simply either/or. One form of causation does not automatically exclude the other. It is most reasonable to say that an interactive effect of the two is necessary to produce so serious a disorder in human kind. The question is, "How far do you reduce causes?" i.e., beginning with the demands of adult social life, how much distance must be travelled before we can achieve some understanding of the disorder? At what juncture do we declare that we have unearthed the true causes? Must we return, ultimately, to the level of the cell structure?

Horwitt (1956) in discussing schizophrenia and biology said, "The sum total of the differences reported [in the literature] would make the schizophrenic patient a sorry specimen indeed: his liver, brain, kidney, and circulatory functions are impaired; he is deficient in practically every vitamin; his hormones are out of balance, and his enzymes are askew" (p. 430). Claims of new chemical answers to schizophrenia come and go with time but it is unfortunate that so many generations of biologists must repeat the theoretical errors of those who went before them.

This is not to suggest that biochemistry has seen its heyday. It is still in its infancy and we would be presumptuous to expect that in biochemistry a single, simple answer to severe human disorder is soon to be found (Throne and Gowdey, 1967). If biochemical studies are to contribute to our understanding of the nature of the psychoses, they must mature to a point where they recognize the complicated nature of man and cease to treat him as though he were an uncomprehending vial of chemicals.

Physique and Psychosis

The assumption of a relationship between body type and behavior patterns has been popular with theorists since the earliest times. The theory was then, and is now, simply that the human physique must shape some part of the direction of the behavior of man. As long ago as five centuries before Christ, Hippocrates described a dual classification of physique in man (habitus apoplecticus—short, muscular, strong; habitus phthisicus—thin, tall, and delicate). Hippocrates matched these body types to a set of human temperaments, and for him this described the nature of man.

In the 1920's, Ernest Kretschmer (1888–1964) proposed the theory that tendencies toward certain forms of serious emotional disorder were associated with particular body types (Kretschmer, 1925). Schizophrenics, according to Kretschmer, tend to be somewhat smaller and thinner than the average person.

TABLE 3.1   BODY TYPE THEORIES

KRETSCHMER (1925)

Body Type Name	Description	Mental Disorder
Asthenic	Slight, slender, long-boned	Schizophrenic, schizoid
Pyknic	Round, stocky, heavy	Manic-depressive
Athletic	Strong, muscular	Schizophrenic

SHELDON (1940)

Body Type Name	Description	Temperament
Ectomorph	Delicate, fragile	Cerebrotonic (restrained, inhibited, withdrawn)
Endomorph	Fat, visceral	Viscerotonic (relaxed, comfort-loving, sociable)
Mesomorph	Muscled, athletic	Somatotonic (active, vigorous, assertive)

Sheldon (1940, 1954) divided human body types on a seven-point scale along three basic dimensions: ectomorph, mesomorph, and endomorph. In his system of rating physique the ectomorph is thin, long-boned, poorly muscled, and delicate; the mesomorph is well-muscled, athletically built; the endomorph is heavy and fat. Dysplasia, in which physical development shows a mixture of these types, makes up a fourth category. Body typing is accomplished by a rating system that gives each subject a "somatotype" reflecting the contribution of each of these dimentions to an overall description of his human structure. These body-type indexes reflected contributions from each of the three components, i.e. a body type of 444 reflected a balanced somatotype constructed equally of all three parts, and a 171 was used to designate a muscular type (mesomorph) with little if any ectomorphy or endomorphy in his make up. These were, of course, idealized types rarely discovered in nature.

Once a reliable means of describing physical attributes is devised, an equally dependable way of relating them to human temperament and psychological make up is needed. To describe man's temperament, Sheldon used the awkward terms cerebrotonia (inhibited expression of affect and energy), viscerotonia (uninhibited expression of feeling and emotion), and somatotonia (an open expression of action). The matching of physical and temperamental characteristics (ectomorph-cerebrotonia; mesomorph-somatotonia; endomorph-viscerotonia) constituted his system of relating body and mind. Body type was thought to be fashioned by heredity and glandular functioning in concert with early environmental experiences.

The early work of Sheldon and his associates was modified by a number of other researchers. Thus, Davidson *et al.* (1957) studied 7-year-old children, Parnell (1957) studied college students, and the Glueck's (1952) examined delinquents.

Kline and Tenney (1950) studied a military population that included hundreds of male schizophrenics and found them distributed by body type as follows: ectomorph, 26 per cent; mesomorph, 46 per cent; endomorph, 11 per cent. It was not possible to make an adequate classification for another 17 per cent of the subjects.

There is an obvious bias, of course, in studying the body types of those who serve in the military forces since the military insists on a high degree of physical fitness. Kline and Tenney concluded not only that schizophrenia was unequally distributed among body types but that mesomorphs were more often diagnosed paranoid schizophrenic and had a better prognosis (prediction of recovery) while endomorphs had a poorer prognosis. In a follow up two years later, Kline and Oppenheim (1952) could not confirm that mesomorphs had a good prognosis, although they accepted the hypothesis of a poor prognosis for endomorphs.

A great many studies of the relation of constitution to personality, involving a wide variety of subjects, have been completed over the years, but the findings are not very convincing. A number of researchers have criticized the constitutional approach (Cameron and Magaret, 1951; Humphreys, 1957; Rees, 1961) on methodological and statistical grounds. In general, these criticisms point out that researchers have yet to find fully reliable and meaningful relationships between body types and social behavior. Theoretical hypotheses—ectomorphs have schizophrenic break-downs at an earlier age than endomorphs; endomorphs are more susceptible to affective disorders, etc.—remain theoretical. To date, the statistical evidence of a relationship between body and behavior is slight and unreliable. The evidence that does exist might as easily be attributed to a variety of other possible variables.

PSYCHOGENIC VIEWS OF DISORDER

Weiner (1967) lists a great number of current versions of psychogenic theories about psychosis. His list is too long to recount here, but it reflects an exceptionally wide range of theorizing. Some theorists underscore the psychosomatic elements of disorder and believe that symptoms that are visible in the patient are the outcome of a complicated, circular interplay of mental life and human physiology. The person exposed to stress reacts with an alteration of his physiology or central nervous system that reduces his capacity to adjust to the very stress he is experiencing. This plunges him further into a set of emergency reactions that culminate, over time, in what is called schizophrenia. Other theorists start with the belief that some persons are extremely sensitive to stress or predisposed to inadequate management of life's daily problems.

Subgroups of theorists who accept this general premise are formed according to the weight each ascribes to some combination of genetic, physiological, psychological, or social events. A "pure" psychogenic point of view is represented by those who believe that the schizophrenic patient has experienced an arrested or warped psychosocial development. This kind of development, they assume, either progressively destroys the person's capacity to adapt or renders his personality prone to disintegration and decompensation when faced with adult stress.

While these theories rest on a common psychogenic base, they differ in the emphasis placed on various psychological events. Still, there is a rough correspondence between them based on a concern with the issues of stress, coping, and the functioning of that theoretical part of the self called the ego. We shall consider each of these elements in turn.

Stress

The concept of humans under psychological stress seems vital to our understanding of psychotic disorder in man. Lazarus (1963) is one of the most articulate spokesmen for this point of view, and his observations are worth recounting here.

Lazarus assumes that the schizophrenic is one who has reacted inadequately to, or failed to cope with life's stresses. His concept of stress is sufficiently all-enveloping to encompass many subdivisions, i.e., conflict, anxiety, frustration, emotion, and psychological defense. Stress, as Lazarus (1963) indicates, is "a universal human . . . phenomenon, [that] results in intense and distressing experience and appears to be a tremendous influence in behavior" (p. 2). Stress is the outcome of the perceived threat to one's life or well-being.

Stress is a fundamental consideration in the study of psychopathology since many theorists assume that the symptoms of schizophrenia are behavioral examples of response to severe stress in the patient's life. By the same token, we need to explain how stress can be evident in the life of a healthy person without producing schizophrenia symptoms. Much of the research on psychosis has directed its attention to a delineation and specification of the relationship between individuals and stressful situations, but a great deal remains to be done before we can reach firm conclusions.

Specific forms of stress have been explored, and one of the classic studies was done by Grinker and Spiegel (1945) who treated World War II soldiers suffering from severely traumatic battle experiences. Many of the soldiers' reactions to stress bore all the symptomatic characteristics of full-blown psychosis. Using narcosynthesis and narcoanalysis (interviews with patients under the influence of barbiturates such as Amytal or Sodium Pentothal), they were able to have the soldiers relive their traumatic combat experiences psychologically in order to discharge the tension associated with them. These stress-associated experiences were then "resynthesized" or assimilated into consciousness with the help of a therapist.

Much of the clinical work with psychoses has relied on a retrospective, or historical, account of possible stresses in the patient's early life and, unlike the visible stress of combat, these case histories may be only rough guesses. As Lazarus (1963) indicated, "Psychological structure is by no means the same in the infant, young child, and mature adult, and we should expect that important details of psychological-stress production and reduction will be different at these developmental levels" (p. 22). In retrospect the clinician can only speculate about first causes and the psychological state of the patient at that moment in early life when it seemed stress was an important part of his environment. We know too little about what constitutes destructive stress in an individual's life and even less about judging who among us can cope with it in a healthy and productive fashion.

For Lazarus (1963), a vital aspect of stress is that the individual continually anticipates confrontation with some harmful condition. Threat becomes stress when it is appraised as an event that is imminent, that will be harmful, and that might be beyond the individual's coping resources. Researchers intent on measuring and appraising the relationship of stress and the psychoses, then, need access to the personal psychological experience of the patient to determine what has and has not been viewed as threatening and stressful throughout his life.

The key to psychosis may not be in the concepts of threat and stress so much as in how one manages to cope with these elements.

Coping with Stress

Children raised in Western society are exposed to roughly similar patterns of child rearing in which basic strategies of coping with life are learned. The strategies the child learns that are suitable for one age must be modified or abandoned as the child grows older and faces new developmental tasks. If the child fails to learn adequate coping strategies, or uses strategies inappropriate to the time and place, he will fail to solve the problems life presents. He will experience the very stress these coping mechanisms were designed to avoid. Learning to cope is a continuous process—a process that concerns the adult as well as the child (Torrance, 1965).

Few studies exist of coping in children. But, one study, by Lois Murphy (1957), describes eight basic strategies that may be used by children. Unfortunately, these childish strategies all too often become the essential components of adult behavior.

In potentially stressful situations—separation from the mother, new challenges, demands to comply, or competition with siblings and peers—coping refers to learned ways of managing the environment and the tensions aroused by stress. Murphy distinguishes primary coping (the attempt to deal with problems in the first place) from secondary coping (the attempt to manage the consequences of having made an inadequate initial mastery of problems). If the problem that was failed the first time is solved the second time around, the child is free to confront future problems unhampered. When the child fails to solve the problem for the second time, he has to make frenzied attempts to restore his equilibrium despite the crippling effects of previous failure.

Strategies of Coping

Murphy's (1957) description of strategies of coping and adjustment include the following:

1. *Children react to their environment by choosing those situations*

that can reasonably be coped with and comfortably handled. She recalls, for example, bringing children into a testing situation and offering them large paper cups of juice. For some children this new situation was greeted without fear or concern; they gulped down the juice and darted into the play environment to explore its pleasures. Apprehensive children prolonged their juice-drinking by sipping the beverage slowly as they surveyed their surroundings and calculated how best to manage them. Delay in entering the play setting was a device for selecting those features of the environment most pleasurable and manageable.

2. *Fantasy and denial of reality can make what is real not real.* Children retreat easily and comfortably into a fantasy world free of the painful limitations of the real world. In this way, the pain of stress is escaped for brief periods of time.

3. *Escape is a way of coping with the environment.* Feigning illness, sleep, or stupidity may protect the child from highly stimulating social situations. When strangers are present children may hide behind parents to control the amount of stimulation to which they will be exposed.

4. *An unenthusiastic acceptance and reluctant tolerance of the anxiety-provoking situation is an additional way to cope with stress.* Realizing that the confrontation is inevitable, children may resign themselves to it and try to brazen it out as best they can since they have no other choice.

5. *The mobilization of extra effort and/or compulsive repetition may be used to face stress.* Compulsive repetition of an act is, in the long run, self-destructive because it leaves the child little energy to cope with the ever-present new demands of living. But, as Hans Selye (1956) has observed, each of us possesses a reserve of *adaptation energy* which is used to meet unusual circumstances. When this adaptation energy is exhausted, we break down under stress and may be forced to revert to more primitive and psychologically debilitating means of meeting stress.

6. *Children protect themselves from stress by "cushioning" or taking advantage of available gratifications.* Reassurance, in this case, can support the child's attempt to deal with stress. Children will seize ways out of situations by seeking help from others, even if these exits offer only a temporary escape from pressure.

7. *Temporary regression to previously successful means of adaptation or to inappropriate patterns of response may be a last resort.* Under tension, both children and adults may revert to patterns of action that were workable in the past but are ineffective in the present. Regression doesn't solve problems, but it gives the problem solver relief from an otherwise unbearable situation.

8. *Restructuring situations into more manageable form may be all the*

child can accomplish. Unwilling or unable to deal with the situation as it is, a child may redefine the problem, making it one that can more easily be handled. Unable to attain what he wishes, he may restructure the situation and insist he didn't want it in the first place.

SHIRLEY R.

Shirley R. was an only child, and her parents were slow to realize that she was not exactly like other children. In her preschool years she was considered unusually shy, but this was a gross understatement—she was terrified of everyone but her parents. Whenever the doorbell rang she would bolt for her bedroom and hide till the visitors had left the house. At those times when she had to confront strangers (the doctor, the dentist) the event would be commemorated by the seemingly senseless constant repetition of some phrase ("How are you little girl?") that caught her attention at the time. The traumatic situation was acted out endlessly in play until her parents, wearying of the repetitious game, began to punish her until she stopped. Punishment always worked, and it was always followed by a week of baby talk, crying out for her mother during the night, playing with her food in a baby-like fashion, or occasional toilet "accidents" in which she would soil herself. She was removed from nursery school following a series of screaming tantrums and was referred to the clinic a year later when she repeated this behavior in kindergarten. She is in the first grade now but she sits silently, apprehensively, and miserably in the back of the room.

These child-like means of coping with conflict and stress may be carried over to adult response to pressure.

In the view of Robert White (1964), both psychosis and schizophrenia should be considered developmental disorders in which the child's defensive withdrawal from life produces a seriously disturbed pattern of adjustment. The child who avoids the risk of contact with others eliminates the possibility of learning the social skills that will free him from the need for continued withdrawal. The withdrawn child ceases to cope and becomes more and more threatened by social stimuli and less and less capable of managing it. By the time of early adulthood, the withdrawal may be so complete that the schizophrenic is completely estranged from his fellow human beings.

The nature and degree of stress to which the child is exposed and the adequacy or inadequacy of his ability to cope with it will establish the foundation on which the adult structure will rise. Development is cumulative in that each successive step requires successful accomplishment of the one that precedes it. The single most demanding task for the growing child is to succeed in the world of interpersonal relations. If he fails with his fellow human beings, he is liable to be excluded from the society.

The Ego and Defense Mechanisms

Contained within the broad grouping of psychogenic theories is a current emphasis on the functions of what Freud labeled the ego. The ego is described as that part of the organization of the self that has as its task making adjustments between one's impulse system (id, or basic urges and desires), one's "super ego" (conscience, values, standards of behavior), and the demands of the real world. Since the ego is essentially what makes one recognizably human and civilized, defects in its functioning would be disastrous to the attempt to adjust to life.

It is the ego that is called upon to manage stress and to cope with problems, and when the "executive" part of the self is incapable of managing the pressures that impinge upon it, we are witness to the destruction of the individual as schizophrenia becomes the best adjustment he can manage. Ego disturbances may encompass the whole person or only significant parts of the self. The ego regulates the capacity to know about the real world (cognition), to react adaptively to it (intelligence), to experience it accurately (sensation), to interpret it reasonably (perception), to respond to it appropriately (emotion). Hallucinations, delusions, withdrawal, confused communications, and inappropriate responses may all reflect the inability of the ego to function adequately.

How the ego comes to perform less well than it ought to is a prime issue in theorizing about the psychoses. One description of the work of the ego is contained in the concept of defense mechanisms—mechanisms to defend the self against anxiety. Ideally, the ego ought to meet frustrations and resolve conflicts by making the best possible decisions in a given set of circumstances.

Our society has a great many prescriptions for proper behavior and these become a part of the growing child's value system and conscience (super ego) and determine the pattern of his psychological responses. The child must learn, for example, to think and feel in acceptable ways, and if life's stress seems too great for him to cope with, he must learn to manipulate his psychic world to make it bearable. The ego is sometimes driven to employ defense mechanisms to retain psychological stability:

> How can the child avoid being caught, by himself or others, with contraband feelings? There are four elements or dimensions of the forbidden situation that he can alter to bring about a new situation more in keeping with society's dictates and his own anxieties. Momentarily, he feels that he hates his mother and wants to kill her. There is the source (himself) of the feeling, the impulse (hate), the object (mother) toward which it is directed, and the aim (kill)

of the impulse. Alteration of any one of these aspects will produce a formula which is no longer threatening to his self-esteem or
to the esteem others have for him. He can, for example, change the
source in some fashion and not tamper with the other elements;
now *he* doesn't hate his mother and want to kill her. Or he can alter
the *impulse* so that he *loves* his mother, not hates her. The *object*
can be transformed so that he hates *school* but not his mother.
Another compromise that will solve his dilemma is to admit that he
hates his mother but merely wishes to *reprimand* her rather than
kill her. In each instance, a slight change in his perception of the
reality of hating his mother cleans up the thought and makes it
presentable. In extreme circumstances the whole thought must be
changed, leaving no element unaltered; in less threatening situations
it is necessary only to reduce the intensity of each element of the
sequence. This means that the kind, quality, and degree of distortion will always be dependent upon the demands made by the
environment and the internal psychic resources he has available
to him. In one family a child must see, hear, speak, and think no
evil, while in another an aggressive outburst is a natural event
which must be managed but is viewed as a reasonable consequence of the frustrations of living with other people.

At first, mechanisms for managing hostile feelings are practiced
in a conscious form by the child. He will, for example, retain his
feelings but suppress the overt attack on the mother to insure her
continued acceptance of him. Such feelings, as well as the act of
altering a prohibited situation, must be hidden from both the self
and others (after all, the best-adjusted adult could not be comfortable thinking murderous thoughts about others all day). Through
a process we can label, but not fully understand, the effort that the
child once made wilfully and consciously becomes an event which
occurs in so subtle a fashion that no one is the wiser.

This description of perceptual maneuvering to escape experiencing anxiety is particularly relevant to aggressive impulses which,
because of their potential destructiveness, must be highly regulated
and controlled. The average person in our society is made quite uncomfortable by the sight of naked hostility in himself or in others,
since one of the hallmarks of maturity is control over aggression.
The description of the need to defend one's self makes it appear
that this is a consciously willed, mechanical process—something
like a bag of tricks used when appropriate to the emergency. A more
apt description would be that normal persons *cope* with frustrations

and forbidden impulses and only *defend* against them when no other alternative remains. When defensive tactics relieve anxiety, this very relief will reinforce the defensive behavior and tend to solidify it into a habitual and characteristic pattern of reaction when faced with conflict in the future. When this occurs, they no longer act as emergency reactions but become predictable character traits that distinguish the individual for life. Since a variety of defense mechanisms is available to the individual, he usually proceeds by trial and error to select those that are the most effective in freeing him from guilt and anxiety. A mechanism that proves to be effective in one situation is tried in another and its use continued until it fails to accomplish its purpose. Highly flexible individuals may acquire a set of defenses which are adapted specifically to each situation; rigid or less resourceful persons may become general defenders who find one dramatic mechanism that works (such as thorough-going repression) and use it for a variety of situations and with all kinds of impulses.

Using hostility as the model of impulses to be dealt with, what are the ways in which it can be managed defensively? At a broad level, the choices of the individual are restricted to *changing the situation* through the process of conscious problem solving and working out a new relationship with the person toward whom he is hostile; *escaping from the situation* by running away or retreating into a fantasy life, where the problems do not exist; or *changing his perception of the hostile situation* through defense mechanisms which render it innocuous (McNeil, 1959) p. 210–11.

Defense mechanisms are necessary when all other attempts at solution have failed or are barred from use by the peculiarities of the individual's environment. Defenses involve an unhealthy distortion of the world as it really is and exact an enormous toll on the integrity of the personality. Defenses cripple, but they do not destroy in the way that feelings of anxiety and worthlessness might if defenses were not available. As drastic as defensive steps may seem, they may fail to be adequate, and a total destruction of the personality may occur in the form of psychosis.

Interpersonal, Motivational and
Cognitive Theories

Why does the schizophrenic have poor contact with other human beings, and why is he insecure and socially withdrawn? Why, as Whitehorn (1960) asks, is the schizophrenic's attitude "manifested in passivity, lack of initiative, lack of hopeful expectation for the future, withdrawal, negativism, and resistance? Relationships with others tend to be reduced to watchful waiting" (p. 76).

For interpersonal theorists, it is because the newborn human organism cannot escape being shaped by his fellow man. People must care for him if he is to survive, and people leave their imprint on him. If the child learns inadequately or learns inappropriate and distorted responses to others, he begins a life of alienation from his fellow man. What, then, is needed to succeed with one's fellow man?

Buss (1966) maintains that the quality of interpersonal relationships depends on success in the twin tasks of 1. forming a stable identity (trust of self and others and learning proper societal roles), and 2. fashioning accurate perceptions of others and of reality, and the ability to communicate with others. For Buss, the learning of proper role playing is essential to successful interpersonal relations. Both are forged in the interplay of family life and if either is learned imperfectly, the consequence (if severe) is described as schizophrenia. Witness the damaging conclusion of Fleck, Lidz, and Cornelison (1963) that "schizophrenic males often come from . . . families with passive, ineffectual fathers and disturbed, engulfing mothers, whereas schizophrenic girls typically grew up in . . . families with narcissistic fathers who were paranoid and disparaging of women, and with mothers who were unempathic and emotionally distant" (p. 6).

A related body of theory has to do with cognitive and motivational explanations of disturbance. Motivational theories assume that the distorted individual suffers psychological deficit (Buss and Lang [1965]; Lang and Buss [1965]). Psychological deficit can occur if the schizophrenic is without enough motivation, i.e., without the drive to interact with others or overly sensitive to the reactions of others, seeing everywhere threat to personal well-being. When avoidance is a natural response to threat and anxiety, motivation may suffer accordingly. Schizophrenics seem to evolve to a stage in which any stimuli delivered by others seems threatening and unmanageable.

Cognitive theories describe a model of psychopathology in which the abnormal learning of perceptions, associations, and concepts accounts for the structural disorganization of thinking of the schizophrenic. If the process of seeing the world and interpreting its meaning gets disordered early in life, distorted social and interpersonal development are subsequently produced. The disorganization of the senses and the attendant disruption of life are what cognitive theorists think schizophrenia is made of.

Suppose, cognitive theorists say, you could not sort ideas, stimuli, and thoughts into proper and meaningful categories. Suppose your memories were chaotic collections of unrelated bits and pieces of experience. Suppose this confusion applied not only to the physical world (things looked strange or distorted) but to social relationships as well. What if the conversation of other people continuously seemed evil and threatening, and provoked anxiety in you? What if "Hello, how are you?" had deep, symbolic, complex meanings that no one else would understand? These cognitive distortions would make normal life impossible.

How could such cognitive distortion come about? Shakow (1963) suggests that there is interference with cognition during development and that the schizophrenic cannot focus on the relevant aspects of a social situation because he is overly susceptible to peripheral stimulation. The schizophrenic thus fails to habituate to usual situations, i.e., each situation seems new to him but he fails to treat new situations with new responses. He perseverates (repeating old responses to new situations), and he responds inappropriately to the situation with which he is confronted.

Schizophrenics—according to this theory—process information improperly, and they inappropriately "filter" the vagaries of a constantly changing environment. Children must learn to make sense of the world about them and react to it in a way acceptable to others in the society. If, beyond infancy, an individual sees the world as confused, contradictory, and incomprehensible, his adjustment to society is rendered nearly impossible. Each of us must learn to select from, attend to, and differentially respond to an incredible mass of stimuli. Without this basic capacity, psychological growth becomes stunted and chaotic.

A SOCIAL VIEW OF DISORDER

At this point the observant reader has become aware that no one of the theories described was touched upon in sufficient detail to allow more than a casual acquaintance. It is also true that no two theories were laid side by side to offer comparison and contrast in their approach to common issues. The decision to present only a descriptive and eclectic account of the variety of theories was deliberate. We have not yet been able to arrange our theories to correspond with the obvious unity that is individual man. Somehow he manages to assemble his life into a workable form at the very moment theorists busy themselves with weighing and measuring the components that make it up. Hopefully, one day, we will draw together these disparate theoretical views into a single, unified conception of the psychic life of man. Meanwhile, we need only indicate that theory is currently broken into partisan segments none of which answers all the questions or speaks to all the issues. We might now add a social or sociocultural view of man in disorder to complete our cursory account of psychogenic theories.

Severe emotional disorder is a two-way cultural street—it may be an individual's response to the expectations the society sets for him as well as an example of society's reaction to those who fail to meet its demands. And, mental disturbance may be a symptom of pervasive cultural diffi- culties as much as it is a personal, internal psychic reaction. Leslie Phillips (1968) expresses this thought most succinctly: "Sometimes failures in living are expressed in the ostensibly aimless, bizarre, and socially inappropriate behaviors of psychiatric disorder. Sometimes the difficulties of life are expressed in the distorted human relationships of delinquency and crime and at others, in the bodily dysfunctions known as psychosomatic disorders. There is increasing evidence that some pro- portion of the wide range of misfortunes seen in social welfare agencies —mental disorder, mental retardation, delinquency or crime, and physical disorders—may be regarded as diverse expressions of a deficiency in meet- ing social expectations. Certainly, many forms of psychological, social, and physical pathology tend to cluster in one relatively small segment of the total population which fails to cope effectively with the complex problems of urban living" (p. 452).

As Phillips points out, the categories of symptoms that we have used for so long and that seem roughly to correspond to the current patterns of human disorder may fit at all, simply because they reflect "common elements of human experience which mark a particular historical period and society" (p. 453).

The social impact of emotional disorders is enormous if measured along any dimension. The number of citizens who must be confined to institutions constructed just for them (mental hospitals, prisons), the percent of our population who kill themselves or assault, rape, and murder others, and those chronically ill with psychosomatic disorders only begin the list. An even larger group might be composed of those whose daily life brings despair rather than joy or satisfaction and those whose potential was never achieved in a society not suited to their par- ticular needs.

The basic question is, "If the society is sick, how can its citizens be well?" What we take to be symptoms of disorder might be perceived as facets of adjustment in one setting but considered inappropriate in another. Symptoms of schizophrenia, for example, are not fixed, immutable behavioral displays that resemble the spots of measles or the swollen glands of mumps. Symptoms are expressed in differing styles and combinations, as well as in differing degrees. Thus, the socioculturalists point out, evidence at hand makes the conclusion inescapable that persons sharing similar styles of life display similar patterns in their psychopathology. If this similarity is defined in terms of sex, social class, age, race, marital status, and the like, then we begin to see patterns that could account for part (but not all) of the symptoms of schizophrenia.

Sociocultural theory is one step removed from the personal experience of psychogenesis of disorder in the individual, of course. But, it points

TABLE 3.2   THE DETERMINANTS OF PATHOLOGY—A SUMMARY

HEREDITARY	BIOLOGICAL
1. Behavior is a consequence both of heredity and environment.	1. Noxious agents (poisons) or biological deprivations can precipitate disorder.
2. Heredity can predispose the individual to breakdown; nonheredity can predispose *or* precipitate breakdown.	2. Injury or deprivation in a young organism produces more severe effects than in an older organism.
3. Specific hereditary causes have not yet been established for most disorders, and the exact proportion of the hereditary contribution is unknown.	3. Severe biological distress leads to physiological reactions that become pathological disorders.
4. Evidence for hereditary factors in psychosis is stronger than for neurosis.	
PSYCHOLOGICAL	SOCIOLOGICAL
1. Abnormal behavior can be learned.	1. Culture shapes the normal and abnormal person but civilization, in itself, does not produce disorder.
2. Conflict, threat, and frustration and extremes of frustration or gratification can produce disordered behavior.	2. Psychosis has not increased, but the frequency of certain syndromes has changed over time.
3. Maternal deprivation is an important source of adult disorder.	3. Social status—lower class, minority group membership, and exposure to cultural disorganization—can influence the rate and form of disorder.
	4. Social stress (war, unemployment, death, divorce, etc.) can contribute to disorder.

Adapted from E. Rosen and I. Gregory, *Abnormal Psychology*. Philadelphia: W. B. Saunders Co., 1965.

to a vital contributor to the nature of that experience and allows us to see more clearly how the psychotic got that way, how little he was able to cope with the demands of life, and how long will be his path back to readmission into the society. Cultural and community disorganization, wars, economic displacements, and the personal-social fate one experiences all contribute to the pathology we find in those who cannot adjust and adapt.

There is a reason for presenting this viewpoint in more detail than some other theories. First, it reflects a preference of the author. Second, it seems to be an essential ingredient in any understanding of first causes or sources of pathology. Finally, it is an aspect of psychopathology that is least incompatible and most congruent with any of the varieties of other theoretical views. It seems reasonable to conclude that culture plus some collection of other theories will be needed to understand disordered man.

SUMMARY

A summary of theories of the source of psychosis can best and most graphically be presented in tabular form. Table 3.2 is a simplified summary of some of the basic principles of hereditary, biological, psychological and sociological viewpoints.

THE FORMS OF PSYCHOSIS III

The Child and 4
Psychosis

Even without evident pathology, that which is called family *schism* is of great importance to normal and pathological development. The overtly or covertly divided family riddled with conflict forces the child to take sides in the combat while his personality development suffers. And, *skewed* families in which father and mother roles get scrambled or one disturbed parent dominates the marital relationship leads the child to acquire a distorted view of life. As Fleck (1967) said, "almost any form of neurosis or psychosis in one parent is apt to produce a defective parental coalition, which in turn will handicap the nurturant and en-culturating tasks on which children depend" (p. 222). It is to these and other variants in family life we will first turn our attention.

PSYCHOSIS AND FAMILY LIFE

Studies of the family structure of schizophrenic children are more often a source of puzzlement than insight. Studies are relatively few, and the conclusions they reach are not always based on equivalent kinds of data.

John Clausen (1966) has made the clearest statement of the inherent difficulty of penetrating to the core of family life. The social matrix of the family is so complicated by the interplay of an enormous number of personal and cultural factors, that any single formula to "explain" it must certainly be inadequate to the task. Clausen lists, as relevant variables for exploring family structure: family composition (involvement of relatives in child rearing, number of children in the family, birth order of the

75

child, and the role of siblings in socialization); the structure of family relationships (parental power over children, power and authority in the marital relationship, the allocation of role functions, and the division of labor); parental personalities and values; and family processes (the negotiations between parent and child).

The study of psychosis and family life, then, remains a thing of bits and pieces. But, this is as far as we have been able to advance, and the interpretations of existing data are worth examining.

Kaufman and his coworkers (1960), for example, speculated that there was a uniform psychotic-like set of defensive patterns which characterized the mothers of 80 schizophrenic young people they studied. The quality of mother-son relationships, as you might imagine, was less than healthy and a prime contributor to the anxious, distorted, handicapped reaction to the world the sons finally displayed.

The studies of the fathers of schizophrenics are even less reassuring (see Figure 4-1). They regularly report the presence of a variety of paternal pathological features. The personal inadequacy, indifference, coldness, and detachedness of such fathers offers little in the way of correction or balance to the psychologically unhealthy features of the mother of the soon-to-be schizophrenic child (Farina and Holzberg, 1967). The potential for lasting parent-child conflict can be enormous in such a family, and its outcome is visible in the schizophrenic condition of the children. What else might we expect from this set of mothers and fathers (Fleck, Lidz, and Cornelison, 1963)?

The internal pathology of such disturbed fathers and mothers is a highly complex phenomenon that must resemble a snake-pit of twisted relationships and destructive interpersonal exchanges for the developing child. In a study of fourteen married couples with schizophrenic offspring, Lidz et al (1958) found at least eight families living in a condition of marital schism—a hostile interaction founded in hatred and mistrust. The remaining six family structures had little to recommend them. In these families, equilibrium of a crude sort had been achieved, but the balance was a costly one.

Both Bateson (1960) and Coleman (1966) make reference to what has been called the "double bind" hypothesis in the family life of the schizophrenic. This concept refers to the contradictory demands—the push and pull conflict—facing the potentially schizophrenic child in an unstable home. The child caught in the middle between warring parents (McNeil, 1967), is an appropriate example. He can't win whatever course of action he decides upon. Caught in a bind in which he can't win and he can't break even (the mother who gives the child two neckties and feels hurt if he wears one rather than the other), the child may see life as a

FIGURE 4.1   THE ROLE OF THE FATHERS OF SCHIZOPHRENICS *

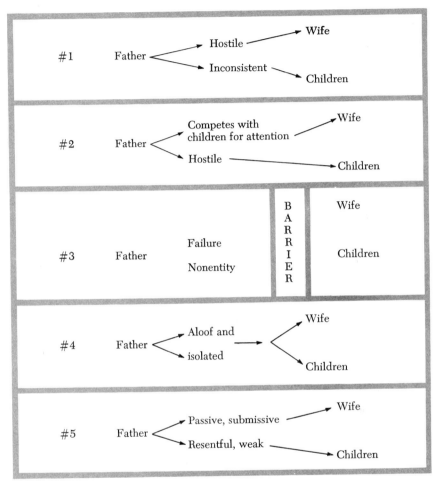

* This study reports judgments of the fathers of schizophrenics, but it does not compare its findings with those that might be obtained from the study of "normal" fathers.

Based on T. Lidz, Alice R. Cornelison, Dorothy Terry, and S. Fleck. The intrafamilial environment of the schizophrenic patient. I. The father. *Psychiat.*, 1957, **20**, 329–42.

dangerous assault on his personal integrity and well-being and react accordingly.

Schizophrenia is, of course, a complex disorder not easily reducible to the simple formula of "like parents like child." Some theorists, however, have attempted to describe a broad set of conditions conducive to the production of schizophrenic children.

Harvey, Hunt, and Schroder (1961), for example, have outlined some of the antecedents of the formation of schizophrenia by indicating that the destructive training environment might include:

a. absolute parental demands for specific forms of behavior.
b. no provision for alternative or substitute patterns of thought or behavior.
c. one dominant parent who establishes the nature of the parent-child relationship—usually restrictive and severely controlling.
d. conflicting demands made on the child such that he is "damned if he does and damned if he doesn't."

Socialization and Schizophrenia—Life History

Some forms of socialization produce socially positive results while others confront us with the specter of severe disorder. If socialization is vital to deviant forms of adult adjustment, it would seem a simple task to study rearing practices and experiences that distort later life. The life history of a group of schizophrenic patients, for example, could be compared with that of normals, i.e. nonpsychiatric cases. Such an exploration ought to reveal a number of events we could avoid if we wished to eliminate the entry of disturbed adults into our culture.

In theory, socialization during the early years has long been considered crucial to later emotional health or illness. In the past, three kinds of possibilities have been considered: 1. At a critical time in the life of the child he is exposed to some traumatic incident, an event so incapable of being assimilated psychologically that further attempts to socialize the child produce negative results and a deepening of the distortion of his behavior. This theory is less in vogue today than it was in the very early days of the study of socialization since single causes are rarely found for any kind of disturbance. 2. The failure of socialization is attributed to accumulated trauma. If not a single trauma, then certainly a piling-up of blows or a collection of straws-that-broke-the-camel's-back would account for deviation. A personal history studded by a series of traumatic experiences ought then produce an adult unable to adjust to life. This is a popular view. 3. The cause of deviation is located in the learning of maladaptive responses as the child develops. Keeping these three possibilities in mind, let us look at a critical exploration, by Schofield and Balian (1959), of the life histories of schizophrenic and normal adults.

They sought to determine whether the early life histories of these two groups were distinguishable in the ways theory said they ought to be.

They chose 150 "normal" subjects and 178 schizophrenics who were matched to the normal group for age, sex, and marital status. Comparisons were made along a wide range of life-history dimensions thought to be relevant to adult maladjustment. The findings are startling because they suggest we must be cautious about making the easy and glib assumption that the early life of the schizophrenic will reveal an unmistakably warped history of socialization clearly distinct from that of "normals."

Thus, the relationship of both the parents of schizophrenic patients and normal subjects appeared to be one of affection. In fact, parent-to-parent relationships described as ambivalent, indifferent, or hostile appeared more frequently among parents of normals than parents of schizophrenics. Mothers and fathers of schizophrenics did not lack affection for their children. The dominating, overprotective mother thought by some theorists to be characteristic of parents of schizophrenics appeared in fewer than 25 per cent of the mothers of the schizophrenics in this study.

The schizophrenic subjects did report greater academic difficulty than the normals, but here cause may be indistinguishable from effect. The prepsychotic personality of the schizophrenic is notably passive and little capable of mustering the concentration needed for good academic habits. Thus, while 90 per cent of the schizophrenics had records of good deportment in school (as compared with 50 per cent of the normals), 85 per cent of the normals had satisfactory or superior records of academic achievement at the same time that nearly one-fourth of the schizophrenics experienced failure or difficulty with their school work. The schizophrenics were well-behaved but unable to achieve academic proficiency.

Additional unexpected findings appeared when occupational success, religious belief and church attendance, dating history, and marital or sexual adjustment were considered. The details are of less interest here than the observation of the sizable overlap of personal history in the life history of schizophrenics and normals. The conclusion reached by Schofield and Balian was that the data seemed to cast serious doubt on the etiological significance of some early life factors for which a great deal of import has frequently been claimed. They suggested that it is the patterning or chaining of experiences rather than occurrence or absence which must be examined in future studies. If so many forms of experience appear as prominent features in the life histories of normals, it is evident that more consideration should be given to the study of what prevents these experiences from warping the adult lives of those we call "normal."

Life History—A Comment

The findings in the Schofield and Balian research need careful interpretation if the reader is to avoid jumping to the conclusion that this investigation has laid waste all the previous years of theorizing by so many professionals. While those long in the field are tempted to attack this research (which runs counter to most clinical experience with severely disturbed patients) on methodological grounds and dwell at length on the serious unreliability of the case-history technique as a true representation of what really took place in the patient's life, a more constructive task would be to underscore the core problem in the schizophrenic experience.

If we were to interpret the findings of Schofield and Balian literally and directly we would have to conclude that the family and social factors long felt to be important in schizophrenia are *not* true. No professional really believes this. The feeling would be that a simple after-the-fact recital of recollections of what happened in the life of the schizophrenic is not only likely to be inaccurate but would probably not record the most vital features of events in family life—critical psychological incidents and the total context in which the incident took place.

The clear fact is that we are not yet sufficiently sophisticated to measure so complex an interpersonal affair as a multi-membered family dealing with the stresses and strains of living together. For example, the notation in a life history "father drinks excessively" is meaningless until we know when he drinks and how and what he does, when drunk, to his relationships with his wife and children. We will never find something so simple as a skeleton-in-the-closet to explain schizophrenia.

What, then, should parents do to assure the formation of socially acceptable adults? A cookbook of specific methods and techniques will probably never be feasible since human beings are not inert substances that can be altered chemically in a predictable manner. And, most prescriptions for child rearing tend to be vague, general, and of little help to the parent. Perhaps we will never be able to be much more specific, and child rearing may always remain an art rather than a science.

PSYCHOSIS IN THE CHILD

Up to this point we have dealt exclusively with theories of the etiology of psychosis, the conditions of the growth of psychosis, and the forces that shape it. We have said little about the form psychosis takes when it occurs in childhood rather than in early adulthood.

Some children fail to survive the socialization process intact, and the schizophrenic process makes it presence known when these children finally try to respond to demands for adult behavior. We have not been very effective in prevention of, detection of, or early intervention in serious disorders in children (Augenbraun, Reid, and Friedman, 1967; Cary and Reveal, 1967). We have, at best, a broad set of principles we feel apply to the acquisition of abnormality in children. These principles are only rough guides to the hazards of the socialization process.

PSYCHOLOGICAL PREDISPOSITION TO ABNORMALITY: PRINCIPLES [*]

1. Psychopathology can be learned under conditions of deprivation, frustration, and conflict.
2. Early experience may produce irreversible damage.
3. There are critical periods of stimulation and experience in childhood.
4. A single traumatic event is less likely than prolonged stress to produce psychopathology.
5. Children need close and enduring relationships with parents and peers for normal development.
6. Negative parental attitudes—rejection, domination, inconsistency, perfectionism—make an emotional disorder more likely.

The history of theoretical and clinical concern with childhood psychosis is surprisingly recent. Kessler (1966) observed that literature specifically addressed to this topic was scant prior to 1941 and has burgeoned despite the fact that childhood psychosis is a rare phenomenon afflicting only 1 to 2 per cent of all children seen for psychotherapeutic treatment. An accurate estimate of the total number of such children is impossible to achieve since this syndrome is frequently mistaken for mental retardation, severe neurosis, organic disorder, or some other form of emotional disturbance. Scientific concern is evident, however. The literature addressed to childhood schizophrenia seems to increase tenfold with each decade (Kanner, 1967).

There are several reasons for this state of affairs. First, childhood is now recognized as a distinct period of existence—one with unique developmental problems. Second, the hypothesis that *all* emotional disorder has organic malfunctioning at its base has been abandoned. And, finally, therapists have reluctantly recognized that severe childhood disorders are congruent with but not identical to the classic psychotic and schizophrenic disorders of adult life. Children have not had time to consolidate

[*] After E. Rosen and I. Gregory. *Abnormal Psychology*. Philadelphia: W. B. Saunders Co., 1965.

patterns of extremely disordered behavior and can, thus, only approximate the full blown psychosis of the adult (Eisenberg, 1967). Thus, the organic psychoses of childhood should resemble their counterpart in the adult tempered by allowance for the developmental stage of the child.

For Kessler (1966) two forms of psychosis can exist for children— regressive and developmental. This is to say that some children "regress" following a period of normal development and return to primitive, infantile, or deteriorated patterns of relating to the world. The so-called "normal" development preceding regression to psychosis may be only a comforting myth spawned in the mind of the parent, of course. It may be a myth based on selective observation, distorted recollection, or biased interpretation on the part of parents unwilling to face the reality of having raised a seriously disturbed child.

Psychosis of the developmental sort presents a different problem to the clinician. These children may simply never accomplish a level of social adjustment appropriate to their age—they may never develop typical or average patterns of growth and mastery of the world. Developmental psychosis is usually visible to the parents, but it is most often mistaken for some other problem. Parental inclination to compare developmental progress of their own children to that of children of similar age is so widespread that parents must deny reality to be unaware that their child fails to measure up to expectations. Autism is a case in point.

Autism

A fascinating variant of childhood psychosis is that discussed in the work of Kanner (1949) who described a special form of childhood psychosis labeled "early infantile autism." He outlined a new subtype of the schizophrenias (based initially on the observation of 11 children) and concluded that this disorder reflected an innate inability of some children to relate to people in the ordinary ways. Kanner has since modified his original view and abandoned his original conclusion that these symptoms were constitutionally formed. Kanner and others now stress the conviction that this syndrome occurs as a result of a combination of innate and experiential events that merge to produce the autistic child.

Not all theorists are so willing to go along with this point of view, however. Rimland (1964), for example, did a careful examination of the clinical literature on autism and concluded that while infantile autism and childhood schizophrenia are "separate and quite unrelated disease entities" (p. 76), the descriptive term "autism" should be limited to children whose disordered behavior appeared following a beginning, normal period of development. Rimland also came to believe that a genetic flaw or predisposition would eventually be discovered to account for this condition.

Despite some feelings of optimism on the part of certain theorists, it is probably an accurate appraisal of current points of view to state that the clinical views of autism reflect a severe organic bias at the moment. Most theorists report the conviction that this pattern of symptoms has an organic base rather than a base in interpersonal relations.

FIGURE 4.2   A GUIDE TO EVALUATION OF PERSONAL
RELATIONSHIPS IN CHILDREN

	LEVEL		
	1	Infant responds to physical contact	(Infant)
	2	Visibly attentive to others, aware, responds	(3 months)
Limit of	3	Selective response to people; anxious with strangers	(6–12 months)
develop-	4	Imitates others, incorporates parts of others, becomes active	(6–12 months)
ment of	5	Attached to mother; seeks comfort and reassurance	(Toddler)
autistic			
child	6	Modifies behavior to please others; responds to influence	(Toddler)
	7	Communicates verbally with others; shares thoughts and feelings	(3 yrs.)
	8	Demands attention; shows jealousy and resentment	(3 yrs.)
	9	Demands for attention include fantasy life, e.g., wish to be husband or mother	(3–4 yrs.)
	10	Identifies with parents; behavior based on learning	(6–8 yrs.)
	11	Interested in children of his age, acts like them, aware of their response to him, and can share feelings with them	

Modified from Jane W. Kessler. *Psychopathology of Childhood.* New York: Prentice-Hall, Inc., 1966.

Since the original description of this syndrome nearly three decades ago, clinicians addicted to fad and fashion have over-reacted to this diagnostic category. Children who would once have been designated schizophrenics have now been classified autistic. There is perhaps some poetic justice here. The label schizophrenia—through long and despairing usage—has come to spell hopelessness and serves to relegate the patient so labeled to the back wards of our mental institutions where the likelihood of adequate treatment is slim indeed. Childhood autism is "overdiagnosed" today, but it may be socially useful to describe disturbed children with a term that implies less hopelessness than has been the case in the past.

The autistic child has been described by some theorists as aloof from interpersonal contact rather than regressed from a previous level of successful relations with others. Autistic children are identifiably pathological in their lack of relatedness to others. The autistic child does not interact with his environment or respond to stimulation as the normal child does.

Separated emotionally from the world of others, autistic children are unresponsive in early life; alienated from contact with others, they usually fail to communicate verbally at a proper age and their language, when present, has an unusual quality to it. Inanimate objects, rather than people, may hold great fascination for such children, e.g. one child in treatment would hug the still-warm hoods of automobiles and preferred machines to people.

These children are frequently mistaken for retardates or those suffering brain damage (Kanner, 1957), but they have traits not common to retarded or brain damaged children. An example of these traits can be found in their distress at disruption of the sameness of their environment. Their possessive need for a permanent and exact order of familiar objects is remarkable.

FLOYD M.

Floyd's parents sent him to a special summer camp for boys with emotional problems, but even in this setting his conduct was "too far out." His fellow campers called him "Dummy," ignored him most of the time, and teased him when they were bored. Floyd was 11 years old, looked no more than 6, and acted like a toddler. Sand occupied most of his attention, and he endlessly poked twigs into the beach in seemingly senseless patterns. When other children approached him he would close his eyes and scream till they left the vicinity. Beyond screaming, his communication repertory included only grunts, whines, and animal-like cries of distress. He clearly comprehended the world about him and was exceptionally alert and sensitive to the moods and motives of others. He was a neat camper whose carefully folded clothes were both immaculate and arranged in a precise and never altered order—a virtue unappreciated by his peers. His summer's sojourn seemed to make little impression on him; he returned to his parents much as he had left them, bearing only the newly acquired label "autistic."

Autism is an almost rare phenomenon. In nearly 20 years of active practice involving approximately 20,000 children, Kanner reports only 150 cases that fit the criteria he established for such a diagnosis. The study of autistic children has a significance that extends beyond their numbers, however, since it may reveal factors in distorted development applicable to the childhood schizophrenias. Theorists and practitioners have yet to decide whether infantile autism is a specific form of severe emotional disorder or only a collection of various symptoms of schizophrenia finding a unique form of expression in the developing child.

Family Life and Thought Disorder
in Children

A bright hope for access to the secrets of family life and thought disorder in children is contained in the carefully designed and executed work of Wynne and Singer (Wynne and Singer, 1963; Singer and Wynne, 1963; Singer and Wynne, 1965a; Singer and Wynne, 1965b). They have tried, successfully, to predict the diagnosis, formal qualities of thought, and severity of disorders of thinking in children based only on data from projective tests taken from members of their family.

In keeping with the best of scientific protocol, these researchers regard their findings as tentative. They conclude that there is a close correspondence, among family members, of the kind of formal thought disorders of adults to those of children. Treating the relationship between parent and child as an interpersonal transaction that has important cognitive, emotional, and intellectual elements, they feel it is vital to determine not only how parents influence children but how children contribute to this interaction by influencing parents. The child disturbed early in life may force a pattern of parental response that may deepen the child's disturbance.

For Singer and Wynne, the essential familial transaction involves, theoretically, a *style* of communicating and interacting with children that works to produce disturbances in the cognitive development of the child. This is to say that what a child thinks, how he thinks about it, what he accepts as real and unreal or true and not-true, are determined by the family setting.

For example, the objects and events a child is taught to pay attention to and the meaning he will attach to these objects and events may all be subtly prescribed by his interaction with other members of the family.

Does the child learn, for example, to attend more closely to external events or to internal experiences? Is he taught to focus his attention, or does it remain diffuse, random, and haphazard? How close or distant an attachment is he taught to form to animate rather than inanimate objects? How literally or symbolically is he to interpret his world? How meaningful or meaningless is the world as he is taught, consciously or unconsciously, to see it? How vital is it to communicate clearly to other people?

Singer and Wynne suggest that it is possible for parents to "pass on" to their children the style, distortions, deviations, and inadequacies of cognitive and communicative skills to their offspring. The question we must ask is, how can the child learn to establish a separate identity, establish mutual relationships with others, and communicate reasonably to his fellow human beings if his intellectual, cognitive, and emotional skills are limited by the parental patterns of response he is exposed to early in life?

The highly verbal, abstract, and symbolic communications of the bright children of affluent, well-educated members of the middle-class may promise a kind of success in our culture that is regularly denied to their rural-mountain or slum-ghetto counterparts. In this way, suggest Singer and Wynne, the foundation for inadequate adjustment to our society may be constructed.

The search Singer and Wynne launched was for the source of the amorphous and fragmented styles of thinking and communicating that are prominent parts of the symptom pictures that characterize the childhood schizophrenic disorders. While this research failed to include equally careful studies of families and communication patterns in non-schizophrenic family groups, this approach to distorted and deviant child-parent interaction remains an important area for future study. Retrospective studies must one day give way to longitudinal explorations that detect such patterns early and pursue them throughout the period of growth of the child.

The Diagnosis of Psychosis in Children

The diagnosis of psychosis in infants or young children is based on a broad collection of loosely defined patterns of symptoms (Bradley, 1941; Bradley and Bowen, 1941; Eisenberg, 1967) ranging from irritability, daydreaming, seclusiveness, and physical inactivity, to bizarre behavior, sensitivity to criticism, and regression.

When psychosis is developmental it is likely to be apparent by five years of age either in a failure to develop or a development in distorted or deviant directions. The regressive forms of psychosis occur later in life and represent failure to navigate successfully through the tasks of young adulthood. Unable to meet the demands for increasingly refined and self-controlled behavior, the young person simply refuses the challenge and returns to the safer ground of child-like adjustment. Distinction between these two conditions obviously relies heavily on the information gained from a carefully assembled life history.

With less than perfect agreement about what does or does not constitute childhood psychosis, there has been a proliferation of subtypes within it. These childhood distortions of life are free of many of the adult symptoms of psychosis, i.e. full-fledged delusions and hallucinations are rare in children. Childhood patterns of distortion are most often faint resemblances of the adult forms of pathology.

In addition, it is particularly difficult to distinguish children suffering from a severe and massive neurosis from children whose pathology is psychotic in nature. In childhood a linked continuum of neurosis and psychosis seems theoretically defensible. It is not simply that the neurotic child may become psychotic, it is rather that the primitive form of response available to all children confuses the diagnostic process. Little of the child's internal psychic life is available, via language, for careful inspection, and there are special difficulties in making an accurate appraisal of the exact contribution of organic or physiological factors to pathological behavior.

Kessler (1966) maintains that all diagnosis of childhood psychosis should focus on the kind, quantity, and quality of the disturbance the child displays in relationships to other people. The child grossly disinterested in others, unaware of them, unable to distinguish between them, or incapable of communicating with them is in such serious personal and social trouble that the diagnostic category to which he is assigned is less relevant than the conclusion that he is little likely to achieve an intact adult status.

The problem of descriptive categorization of severely disturbed children has forced us to have recourse to terms such as autistic, atypical, symbiotic, etc., and we have yet to determine the proper theoretical relationship between adult and child forms of psychosis. Are they forms of the same process or distinct and unrelated kinds of pathology?

Perhaps a "down beat" summary is called for in our consideration of psychosis in childhood with the conclusion that the game of nosology and labeling is self-defeating and amounts to a side-stepping of the issue of what can be done to restore such children to relative freedom from distress. The various psychotic-like disturbances of childhood might better be considered more different than similar and treated as unique events

explainable only in light of the individual's particular developmental experience with life. Judging by the increased theoretical interest in the
problems of childhood, the next decades ought to be a productive era for
insight into the nature of psychosis in childhood.

DEPRIVATION IN INFANCY

Deprivation in early infancy is one of the most dramatic means of dis-
torting the process of socialization; the absence of a warm, supportive
relationship between mother and infant seems to be disastrous for normal
growth. There are different kinds of separation from the mother, of
course, separations over different spans of time and separations that
have different implications to the child. A simple notation of "infant
minus mother" is not adequate, since separation does not always mean
deprivation.

In the days when the terms separation and deprivation were used in-
terchangeably, a great many errors of oversimplification were made. Leon
Yarrow (1964) noted that maternal deprivation has both a quantitative
and qualitative element. That is, one must ask both "how much" and
"what kind of" depriviation is involved. An infant may lose its mother
and then be subjected to a series of mother substitutes who may be good
or bad, consistent or inconsistent, accepting or rejecting. Another infant
might lose its mother and be cared for consistently and well by one long-
term mother substitute.

We must refer to particular children separated from particular
mothers (Yarrow, 1967). Separation can be sudden, explosive, unpre-
meditated, and accidental. Or, it can be the culmination of a long series
of slow-motion violences, in which it is only the final blow. Separation
can be brief and followed by reunion with the parents (parental trips,
child hospitalization, school, etc.); it can be a single, permanent separation (death or permanent parental disability) in which the child is for-
ever removed from the maternal home; or it can be a series of repeated
separations (a succession of foster homes where emotional bonds are
established only to be destroyed once more).

As Yarrow indicates, some theoretical distinction should be made between the immediate and long-term effects of separation in infants and
children. The immediate reaction reported in children for whom the
separation came under two years of age (if the children were placed in
institutional settings) has a highly regular consequence. The sequence,
usually, is one of violent crying followed by a steady and progressive
withdrawal from people and surroundings. This first stage has been described as apathy, despair, or resignation.

Disturbance apparently occurs in almost all dimensions of development. Although psychological damage is a predictable outcome, the physical devastation (slow development, below average weight, height, etc.) experienced by such children is less simply explained. Spitz (1945, 1946) concluded that this damage is progressive and that after five months of separation the damage cannot be reversed. Interestingly, children separated from mothers in the first place showed much less disturbance. Infants who were rapidly provided with a good substitute mother also showed less severe reactions.

Bowlby (1951) studied 14 juvenile thieves diagnosed as "affectionless characters." When he searched their life histories, he discovered that at least 12 of them had suffered separation from their mothers in infancy. They had been hospitalized for unusual periods, some were institutionalized, many had a number of changes in their foster homes. The conclusion reached was that institutional life seems to produce psychopathic behavior, inadequate control over one's impulses, and a basic inability to relate to others with the kind and quality of emotion we normally expect. Yet, the connection between early experience and later behavior is difficult to demonstrate in a clean and crisp manner, and it remains unclear today. Age of child, institutionalization, condition of the environment, and the interpersonal bond of mother and child all seem vital to the final explanation of deviation (Ballard, Glaser, Heagarty, Pivchik, 1967).

Monkeys and Mothers

The closest researchers have come to true experimental control of the conditions of child-rearing has been in experiments with the rhesus monkey. In a series of carefully designed experiments, Harry and Margaret Harlow (Harlow, 1958; Harlow, 1959; Harlow and Harlow, 1961; Harlow and Harlow, 1962; Harlow and Harlow, 1965) explored facets of one of the most basic tenets of the effect of child-rearing on later behavior.

A mixture of common sense and clinical evidence has long suggested that human children who lack proper maternal care suffer critical disturbances or damage to later personal and social development. At various times theorists have, as Harlow and Harlow (1962) report, suggested that syndromes such as autism, marasmus, sexual deviation, and other disorders of infancy can be traced to the earliest years.

The human mother-child relationship cannot be exploited experimentally to reveal those conditions which produce psychological damage of a severe sort. Monkeys, however, can be 1. raised in isolation, 2. provided with inadequate mothers, 3. deprived of mothers completely, or 4. "issued" siblings as the experimental conditions dictate. Harlow raised monkeys without mothers, monkeys with inadequate mothers, and monkeys without siblings and studied the effect of these conditions on the development of the affectional system of the monkey.

First, Harlow (1958) raised male and female rhesus monkeys in conditions of total social deprivation in their first two years of life. Each of the monkeys was isolated from all other forms of life, and as they grew and developed (slowly), it became apparent that they were unable to make a successful adjustment to other monkeys. They were frightened, interacted little with other monkeys, were uninterested in sex, and remained unable to defend themselves from smaller and weaker monkeys for as long as two years after the isolation experience. The longer the deprivation and isolation lasts in the early life of the monkey, the greater the social damage that follows. Contact with human beings (the experimenters) does seem to help adjustment even if monkey companionship is denied the infant.

One group of 56 monkeys was reared in wire cages from which they could see and hear, but not touch, other monkeys. Two other groups of monkeys were raised in similar conditions but one group had access to a wire surrogate mother (a cylindrical wire monkey, of appropriate size, welded in a semi-upright position, and topped by a crude wooden head) while the other group had a terry cloth covered surrogate mother. Monkeys in all three of the groups grew to develop abnormal patterns of behavior such as fixed staring into space, self-injury, rocking motions, and the inability to mate sexually.

In mechanical terms, the terry cloth mother surrogates were ideal "mothers." They always provided milk, warmth (a light bulb inside), and softness. They never scolded or hurt the young and were available 24 hours a day. But, these soft figures could not interact with their "offspring." When the young raised by surrogate mothers played with young raised by monkey mothers, the surrogate-reared monkeys were obviously socially inferior in a variety of ways. And, most of the young proved to be, in adulthood, incapable of appropriate sexual response (Harlow and Harlow, 1965).

When a few of the surrogate-raised females had babies of their own, they proved to be totally inadequate mothers and failed to display proper maternal responses. Either the babies were ignored and rejected or they were attacked and beaten by the inadequate mothers. Interestingly, the abused infants returned again and again to seek physical comfort even from these angry, hurting mothers.

There is no fully trustworthy, easy translation of these observations of monkey behavior into theories of human parent-child relationships. It may be that at birth the human infant is much more dependent that the monkey and thus much more susceptible to psychic and developmental damage. An inadequate, cruel, or rejecting mother may distort the child's capacity to learn the lessons of socialization in a manner even more devastating than that displayed in monkeys.

This pioneering research of the Harlows is highly provocative since it may shed light on the crucial elements of early socialization and the critical questions of the timing of proper stimulation in producing appropriate emotional response in the young.

Our understanding of childhood psychosis owes much to the works of Spitz (1945, 1946) and Goldfarb (1943, 1947). Both researchers studied the effects of emotional, sensory, and cognitive deprivation in early childhood and concluded that the consequences are a progressive deterioration in most developmental indices. The essential observation is that there seem to be critical periods in life and critical human relationships necessary to healthy psychic development in growing human organisms. As Goldfarb (1947) reports, early deprivation clearly marks the individual in ways that make later adjustment difficult if not impossible.

Even in so-called "normal" parent-child relationships, something akin to the institutional syndrome of hospitalism (once called marasmus, a condition in which the child "wastes away," i.e., becomes physically debilitated for no apparent reason) may occur. A disturbed mother may establish as distorted a relationship with her newborn child as that manufactured in institutions in which individual attention is simply impossible. Research on the effects of sensory deprivation in experiments with adults have demonstrated again and again that man's grasp of consciousness and personal identity is tenuous indeed. If adults can suffer psychic distortion through the simple process of manipulating cognitive and sensory stimuli that would normally flood the senses, we may have a clue to understanding psychic distortion in the complexities of parent-child relationships.

SUMMARY

It is to the intimate confines of the family that most modern theorists look for clues to the factors that produce psychosis. Cases in which there is transmission of distorted and disorganized perceptual, congitive, and emotional values from parent to child are superficially easier to understand when one or both of the parents are psychotic. Yet, we have a great deal to discover about the exact transaction between parent and child.

Attempts to unravel the nature of the life experience of schizophrenics using retrospective life history accounts have proved insufficient to the task, since descriptive reports of mile posts on the road of life are not the same as taking the trip itself. It is the total context of family life in which critical incidents occur in the life of the child that may be the crucial variable in the formation of a disturbed psychic structure. Preliminary studies of the communication of thought disorder in the parent-child transaction point to a *style* of family interaction and communication that gets learned by the child.

Current theory suggests psychopathology can be learned under conditions of severe deprivation and stress that can range from negative parental attitudes—rejection, inconsistency—to absence of properly supportive, close parent-child relations early in life. In childhood psychosis and autism, we have prime examples of distortion of the ability to relate to others in a mutually meaningful way.

Deprivation in infancy remains a special case in which the outcome is regularly destructive to human existence. Experimental work with monkeys has begun a detailed exploration of the effects of early deprivation in an attempt to untangle this complex web. We must one day get a better view of the day-by-day parent-child transaction and devise the theoretical yardstick with which to measure it if we are to understand the formation of the psychotic process.

The Schizophrenic Reactions

Our current procedures for describing the schizophrenic reactions have changed remarkably little in the last 75 years. We have made a few modern additions but they seem minor when placed alongside the major systematic categorizations of Kraepelin and Bleuler at the turn of the century.

The Classic Descriptions

In the middle of the last century, the Belgian psychiatrist Benedict Augustin Morel (1809–1873), caught up in the organic bias of his time, described a condition he labeled "demence precoce." For Morel, this was a hereditary disease that unfailingly led to deterioration and degeneracy after its first appearance in the adolescent years. Morel's observations in 1860 of intellectual and personality deterioration in an apparently normal 14-year-old boy seemed sufficient "proof" that dementia could appear precociously, i.e. at a very tender age, and thus must be inherited.

Emil Kraepelin (1856–1926) was a German psychiatrist whose personality and style of life were precisely suited to describing in monumental detail the clinical picture of decay of the normal personality into dementia. He was once described as the father of "Imperial German Psychiatry," and his system was a model of exactness and order that fitted this unofficial title exactly. Kraepelin conscientiously gathered thousands of case histories and from these developed a descriptive system of classification that distinguished three major kinds of dementia praecox (hebe-

93

phrenia, catatonia, and paranoia). Kraepelin considered them organic illnesses even though he described them in psychological terms.

Eugene Bleuler (1857–1939) then added a fourth form of dementia (simple type) to the Kraepelinian system and coined the term schizophrenia (divided or split mind) to describe the disease process. For Bleuler, schizophrenia was less a physiologically degenerative and deteriorating illness than it was a disturbance of the capacity of association and an autistic retreat from reality—a disorganization of the self. Bleuler wrote his monograph in 1911, and modern theorists have strived valiantly since then to live with a system that reflects too much of the organic period in the history of mental disorder and too little of the social-interpersonal approach to human disease.

Schizophrenia's Common Denominators

We shall discuss each of today's types of schizophrenia in turn but, in so doing, we must be aware that it is assumed they share a general, common denominator. There is a presumed "essence" of schizophrenia. This essence is described by Fredrick Redlich and Daniel Freedman (1966) as a cardinal disturbance of the patient's "organization of communications, resulting in profound alteration of the patient's self-experience and his experience of the world" (p. 463). This implies for all schizophrenics a basic dysfunction in the psychobiological equipment that receives, codes, and responds to information and communications. Once the schizophrenic has abandoned meaningful contact with the outside world, he becomes absorbed with the self and displays the symptoms of withdrawal, unstable behavior, delusion, hallucination, and loss of the usual boundaries of perception of the self, others, and the real world. It is as if the schizophrenic unlearns all the things that made him a civilized, social being as he grew to maturity.

What may sometimes appear to others to be a sudden transformation from normality to schizophrenia is in actuality the final stage of an intricate series of events in the individual's life (Arieti, 1967). Beginning life in a family that cannot provide him with a needed sense of security and basic trust, he embarks on the process of acquiring a set of distorted and disorganized interpersonal relations marked by anxiety, hostility, and inadequate perception of the real world and the motives and feelings of those who populate it. Compensatory and inhibitory psychological mechanisms do the best they can to integrate the personality and make of it a socially acceptable, functioning organism that can stay assembled and undetected through childhood. Depending on the demands made by the culture, the ineptly organized child may find the stress of puberty too much for his defenses and begin the psychological decline and disintegration that will finally identify him as schizophrenic.

Finding his resources incapable of managing the tasks that confront him and forced to an awareness that his adjustmental world is crumbling about him, the preschizophrenic retreats into full schizophrenia. Schizophrenics have in common, then, severe disturbance in the cognitive, emotional, intellectual, and perceptual sense of the self and of the world. We can now examine the variety of ways in which this distorted experience is expressed in overt and covert behavior.

SIMPLE SCHIZOPHRENIA

It is the absence of bizarre forms of behavior, hallucinations, or delusions that, almost by subtraction, suggest the diagnosis simple schizophrenia. Between 3 to 7 per cent of hospitalized schizophrenic patients are tagged with the label "simple." Simple schizophrenics are described as 1. apathetic, 2. seclusive, and 3. in minimal social and interpersonal contact with other human beings. Their symptoms are often underscored by regression to illogical forms and modes of thinking and by general dulling or flattening of emotional response to people and objects.

Without the floridly visible, dramatic symptoms typical of the other syndromes, it is difficult to make a clear diagnosis of simple schizophrenia. The limited level of social interest and public activity of simple schizophrenics may become apparent quite gradually, and this way of living can be so typical of the patient for such a long period of time that even close friends shrug and dismiss the pattern of behavior as "the way way he is; he has always been that way."

This motif of turning away from others and withdrawing from the world may appear unusual only when an exceptional number of contacts with reality are severed or when the patient begins to be markedly uncommunicative, incredibly sloppy in his personal habits, and excessively absorbed in fantasy and daydreaming. It is not that there is an unmistakable intellectual impairment, it is rather that a subtle quality of dullness and indifference, an absence of motivation, and a scatter in attention become predominant. Sometimes it looks like mental retardation and sometimes it looks like the development of a personality inadequate to cope with the complexities of modern life. Yet, both retardates and inadequate personalities make some attempt to cope with their environment without excessive apathy and withdrawal.

In simple schizophrenia the promise of early childhood slowly dwindles into a disconnection from the rest of humanity that, painfully, kills parental hopes and ambitions. When the process finally runs its course and stabilizes in a disappointing adaptation to the world, the patient usually leaves school to seek an occupation suited to his diminished personal resources.

For some simple schizophrenics, the path of least resistance is vagabondage and an aimless wandering from place to place. The ranks of hobos, tramps, bums, and prostitutes are swelled by simple schizophrenics who are seldom detected or diagnosed as they live lives of minimal responsibility that provoke only occasional social concern. Our prisons contain a fair number of simple schizophrenics who, alone in a prison cell, devote themselves to a world of fantasy from which they seldom depart. An educated guess would suggest that many more simple schizophrenics roam the outside world than are hospitalized or given appropriate treatment.

LORRAINE N.

Lorraine has been a prostitute since she was 16. Although she is the virtual prisoner of her employer, she is no more distressed by her bondage than by her daily labors of love. Nothing much distresses her and very little interests her. She keeps pretty much to herself and rarely joins in the endless stream of gossip and small talk of the other girls. She plays her professional sexual role with well rehearsed gusto, but it is tedious make believe. As Lorraine reports, "I don't even think about it when I'm doing it. It's like he's doing it to somebody else." Nothing seems to bother Lorraine. She feels nothing about her past life, accepts life day by day, and hardly thinks about tomorrow. She can not quite comprehend what life is all about but she doesn't worry about it.

The homes that disgorge such persons into the general population are psychologically borderline by any standards, with one third of the families displaying clear cut evidence of some form of functional psychosis. The early form of simple schizophrenia is marked by shyness and hypersensitivity, and its victims display, typically, a poor sexual adjustment and an unaggressive personality. In general, the symptoms of simple schizophrenia make their first appearance around age 17. When simple schizophrenics come to the attention of social and legal authorities it is most often as a result of an "opening up" of the personality via the appearance of deviant sexual behavior (child accosting, rape, voyeurism, prostitution) or through assault on others, destruction of property, or some other form of anti-social behavior.

The slums of major cities and the back-country farms of rural communities are either exceptionally forgiving of personality disorders or sufficiently depersonalized in the relations of one person to another to afford a shelter to those with such afflictions. Simple schizophrenics exist in uncounted numbers simply because the pattern of their adjustment to life makes them undemanding and unthreatening to others in our society. As we will see, more involved conformations of symptoms are reacted to with greater concern in our culture.

HEBEPHRENIC SCHIZOPHRENIA

From the Greek, and literally meaning youthful mind, hebephrenic behavior is what people popularly associate with the stereotype of insanity or craziness. This form of disorder appears, typically, at an earlier age than simple schizophrenia and represents a most severe disintegration and disorganization of personality. While its appearance may seem sudden and unannounced (overnight, a week, a month), it most often runs a slow and insidious course of development including the following symptoms:

1. The hebephrenic's speech is often incoherent, unintelligible, and punctuated with inappropriate giggling, smiling, or open laughter.
2. Suffering from intense delusions and hallucinations, he is effectively cut off from the accepted views of human reality as he substitutes for them a personal and private world that may be comprehensible only to himself.
3. The signals he emits from this inner world are strange since they include grimaces, odd posturing, unusual mannerisms and gestures, and alterations of voice and rhythms of speech.

The hebephrenic has been described as "silly" and "childish" because his behavior is cryptic, untranslatable, and thought to be an outward manifestation of preoccupation with an internal life organized according to alien rules. The degree of psychic distortion suffered by the patient is perhaps best revealed by the bizarre quality of his delusions and hallucinations. He may be convinced that he is some famous person, that he has a live rat inside himself chewing up his entrails, that he is dead and still ambulatory, that he has X-ray eyes, or that he is invisible. These patients can be dangerous since they view the real world in a distorted perceptual, emotional, and cognitive fashion, e.g. the hebephrenic convinced that he is Robin Hood may attack a ward attendant who appears to resemble the Sheriff of Nottingham.

This disconnection from the real world may become so complete that the hebephrenic abandons most of the responses to civilization learned in his childhood. He may lose bowel and bladder control, indulge unselfconsciously in obscene and exhibitionistic behavior, smear urine and feces, or act like a quite young infant. The emotional blunting typical of the hebephrenic makes him unresponsive to events or scenes that would revolt or horrify most of us. Coupled with this inappropriate emotional reaction is a deterioration of the ability to cope with reality.

The hebephrenic schizophrenic admitted to a mental hospital is often diagnosed as a chronic, undifferentiated, simple, or paranoid type. As the true form of the disorder becomes manifest, the diagnosis is altered and the prognosis becomes less favorable. The case of Sam P. is illustrative of this point. Sam was hospitalized with a diagnosis of schizophrenic reaction—chronic, undifferentiated type. While hospitalized, he was re-diagnosed as a hebephrenic schizophrenic.

EVERYBODY HAS NIGHTMARES DON'T THEY?

SAM P.

Doris, Sam's wife, reported that she was bothered by his behavior at times but she attributed it to the pressure of business and the series of disasters that befell him. As Doris said, "What hurt me most was the feeling I began to get more and more of the time that I was losing contact with him. It was as if he were drifting away from me and I didn't know what to do about it. I would talk to him for a while, but when I looked at him, I would realize he wasn't listening. He was off somewhere lost in thought and never heard a word I said. Then he began to do scary things and creepy things. I would wake up in the middle of the night and he would be gone. Once I found him sitting on the grass in the middle of the backyard at 4:00 A.M. and he didn't seem to know where he was or what was going on. He was confused, but he was all right the next day and never mentioned what had happened the night before. . . ."

About three weeks later, Sam was arrested at 3:00 A.M. in a small town about 40 miles from where he lived. The police report said that he was driving through town at nearly 85 miles an hour when he was stopped and that he told the arresting officers that he was trying to "get up escape velocity for a trip to Mars."

.   .   .

Some of the ideas Sam spoke about freely to doctors and fellow patients were extremely bizarre. At one time he was convinced he was Robin Hood, for example. He had not notified anyone of this sudden shift in his identity and it was discovered only when he leaped from a perch atop a door and landed on the back of an unsuspecting attendant who had just entered the room.[*]

The hebephrenic's symptoms may begin early in childhood when only a certain oddness or strangeness is apparent and parents report no more than an increasing preoccupation with the self and a seclusiveness from

[*] From E. B. McNeil. *The Quiet Furies.* Englewood Cliffs, N.J.: Prentice-Hall, Inc., © 1967, pp. 177–78. Reprinted by permission of the publishers.

others. The end point is a massive and dehumanizing departure from the social model of a normal human being. The regressed hebephrenic has suffered such severe damage that reasonable hope for his recovery is rarely justified. A total reeductational process must be instituted—literally to build a new human being—if expectations of recovery are to be realistic. The patient is rarely able to cooperate in such an endeavor and the odds are mightily against him. Hebephrenics are the patients who become "old timers" in every mental hospital, the patients who live most of their lives in a hospital setting.

The language of the hebephrenic—studded as it is with "almost-words" —is associated with a feeling that words have power and magic, power to influence others and magic for protection from many enemies. Words that have meaning only to the patient are one means of disconnecting the self from unpleasant reality. Indifferent to whether others understand him, he finds little reason to communicate in a coherent fashion. As his gestures and posture become symbolic of purely personal feelings and experiences, his language dissolves into an unrecognizable form. Each attempt to communicate with the hebephrenic may be greeted by acts and words that reflect the flagrant distortions of reality of a twisted psychic structure.

There is no exact replica of the hebephrenic experience in normal existence. Probably the closest match is the occasional bizarre, frightening, nonsensical nightmare that sometimes awakens us in a cold sweat in the dark of night. In a nightmare we are entangled in delusions, hallucinations, and distorted logic. But, we wake up to a rational, ordered life. The hebephrenic is caught in a nightmare from which he may never awaken.

CATATONIC SCHIZOPHRENIA

The capacity of catatonic patients to endure pain and to ignore the uncomfortable circumstances in which they find themselves may well have been the basis for a great many historical events that seem beyond belief today. It is very possible that some of the early martyrs could endure what they did because they were catatonic at the moment of great physical or social travail. Patients chained to a wall and living in filth in the early asylums may never have uttered a complaint because they were engrossed with their own internal conflicts.

Catatonic schizophrenia is undoubtedly the disorder most visible at a distance in a typical mental hospital ward, since it is marked by motor disturbances that are not evident in other schizophrenic reactions. The catatonic may inhibit most aspects of his expressive behavior and be stuporous, retarded in movement, or mute and unresponsive. He may express passive aggression by his refusal to comply with social demands made on him, but this may be the sole indication that he is aware of the world outside of his own vigorous fantasy life.

When the catatonic becomes agitated, negativism and resistance takes a much more active form. He can become assaultive and communicate his aggressive feelings in an explosive and destructive form. Some patients vascillate unpredictably between tight inhibition of movement and sudden, overt, aggressive response to stimulation. These inhibitory and expressive phases are probably opposite sides of the same coin.

The inhibition of the catatonic is not of the passive variety. It is, rather, an active, forceful controlling of one's self—a willful construction of an inhibited, noncooperative facade. It is as if the catatonic fears making a voluntary or willful mistake that would further jeopardize his already anxiety-ridden and dangerous situation. The stuporous, malleable posture these patients can maintain for hours (waxy flexibility) requires some force of will on their part and, if the position rigidly held to is a painful or exhausting one, the expenditure of physical energy must be extraordinary.

The stuporous catatonic patient resembles the seriously depressed patient just as the excited catatonic may, superficially, seem similar to the manic patient. On close and sophisticated inspection, however, these behaviors and emotional states will not be found identical. The catatonic is often the victim of strenuously active hallucinations and delusions of a mystical or persecutory nature. Caught up in the mystery of alien voices, visions, and visitations, the catatonic is preoccupied with an invisible world that fully absorbs his attention and energy. The depressive, on the other hand, worries about the outside world.

Catatonia—since it seems to involve severe emergency adjustments—bears a more favorable prognosis than do other types of schizophrenia. When the onset is acute, there is a greater likelihood of recovery since a sudden catatonic condition is, in many ways, the least complicated of the classic types of schizophrenia.

MR. ALEX

Addressing him as Mr. Alex always brought a shy, childlike smile to his face during those brief periods in which he was between the stuporous, unresponsive phase of his disorder and its opposite composed of panic, rage, and targetless assault. He was 48 years old but acted like a preadolescent at those rare times when he was in communication with the outside world. He had been hospitalized most of his adult life and there seemed little hope for his return to society. When he was in a stuporous state his disconnection from the real world was nearly complete. More than once he spent part of the night huddled in a painfully awkward position in a corner of the ward room when the overworked ward attendant failed to notice him. Swinging irregularly and unpredictably between stuporous and agitated states, he remains a management problem on his ward in the state hospital.

Spontaneous remission of symptoms—a sudden and inexplicable disappearance of one pattern of behavior and the substitution of a more normal, coherent one—is not infrequent in catatonia. At times an unexpected lucidity signals the midpoint in a shift from stuporous to agitated phases of the disorder. For some patients, the experience of catatonia will be episodic, i.e., brief instances of relatively short duration followed by remission of symptoms and an absence of apparent disorder for the remainder of the patient's life.

Catatonic schizophrenia is dramatic. It is a visible involvement of the body in an attempt to defend against a crushing and overwhelming set of experiences, events, or perceptions. As if on a battlefield, the patient freezes at the moment when constructive action is called for, and his immobilization is mute testimony to the inadequacy of his resources to cope with the threat that engulfs him. Catatonia is an almost complete collapse and withdrawal in the face of what appear to be insurmountable obstacles. We don't know why some individuals "choose" this form of reaction to distress or why others suddenly and spontaneously abandon it in a dramatic return to a more normal form of adjustment. Alert but immobilized, the catatonic crouches within himself unable to decide which way to turn.

In many respects, the behavior of the catatonic resembles that of a cornered animal. Seeing no means of escape, he immobilizes himself in order to survive. The human catatonic may accept his terrified, helpless state rather than worsen his chances for survival by taking positive action to change it.

PARANOID SCHIZOPHRENIA

On the surface, the paranoid schizophrenic appears the most normal and least disturbed patient on the ward. On closer contact, his accusatory and threatening delusions and hallucinations become apparent. Such patients make up more than half of all the first admissions for schizophrenia, and they remain hospitalized for so long that they shortly become a majority of all hospitalized schizophrenics (Cameron, 1967).

The potential paranoid schizophrenic lives with fear, suspicion, and

fragile interpersonal relations for many years before his delusional system becomes fixed, exact, and visible to others. Until his schizophrenic
deterioration becomes too massive, he may still maintain a fair orientation to reality in those few phases of his life not relevant to his suspicions,
and he may maintain a marginal social adjustment for a number of years.
A mixture of rational and irrational social interactions is deceptive to
the untutored observer, and the paranoid schizophrenic may escape detection until his late twenties or early thirties.

The paranoid schizophrenic reacts to life like a threatened, hunted
animal. He survives a dangerous environment through tense alertness and
carefully designed defensive measures to anticipate and thwart attack.
None of us trusts everyone in all circumstances, but few of us subscribe
to the doctrine of the paranoid schizophrenic—you can trust none of
the people none of the time.

The paranoid is grandiose and egocentric in his insistence that everyone is watching him, plotting against him, and trying to get things from
him. Underneath these feelings of persecution must lie a belief that only
unusually talented or important persons would be so hounded by the
majority of the inhabitants of this planet. The justification for such massive persecution is that others are jealous of the patient's superior ability,
talent, or knowledge. Persecution, thus, produces a mixed emotional state.
It is, simultaneously, painful and gratifying, frightening and reassuring.
In the case of Bob H. the deterioration that accompanies paranoid
schizophrenia is cast in sharp relief.

"You Can't Trust Anybody Nowadays."
BOB H.

During . . . [an extended] period of psychological decline, Bob was
totally humorless. The elasticity of life had gone out of him. Everything
worried him, the smallest things had great significance, and he began
to lose weight rather markedly. He was eating only one meal a day,
and he chose the meal he would eat by a system designed to outwit
anyone studying his personal habits. . . .

After an explosive scene in the office one day, he became quite
agitated and could not be reassured or calmed down. His superior told
him to take several days off and get some rest. The fear that prompted
this action communicated itself to Bob, so he left that day and never
returned. His wife reported that he came home in a rage, went to his
room, locked the door, and wrote a detailed account of the day's events.
Bob did not sleep that night. He wandered the house mumbling incoherently and woke his wife and children early to help him do what
was needed. He kept the children home from school that day, locked

all the windows and doors, and pulled the shades down at every window. Bob's vigil was kept all day and night and he allowed no one to turn on the radio or television set since it was necessary for him to hear everything going on outside the house. He armed himself and by 4:00 A.M. was so agitated that he roared out of the house firing shots in the air and daring his enemies to come and get him.*

The paranoid schizophrenias are a mixture of paranoid thought content and the cognitive, intellectual, and affective disorganization of schizophrenia. In some cases the patient regresses and withdraws into a private delusional and hallucinatory world housing a disconnected collection of suspicions and fears. Behavior is erratic and unpredictable since it is rooted in a private and inaccessible system.

THE PARANOID DISORDERS

In "pure" paranoia, or its lesser form the paranoid state, many personality functions are reasonably intact and deceptively normal. This apparent insulation of some parts of the psychic self from others seems remarkable at first glance, but on closer inspection it is evident that paranoid persons only *seem* successfully to be performing the everyday tasks of living. There is actually little of their conscious life that is not obsessively preoccupied with the fine points of an intricate delusional system. Paranoia is a poison of suspicion that infuses the total psychic life of its victim; in paranoia we see mistrust that in a less intense form is familiar to all of us.

The frequency of pure paranoia in the patient population of the typical hospital is small indeed. Such patients are hospitalized later in life (the average age is 50 at first admission), and they make up fewer than 1 per cent of all hospitalized cases. This low figure is not dependable since the intactness referred to earlier obviously contributes to their ability to avoid hospitalization.

Except in extreme cases, they are a mixture of seemingly normal and seemingly disturbed. It is this oscillation of normal and pathological behavior that delays hospitalization and fends off social action. Too, paranoid symptoms are not all of one kind or all of the same degree of severity. They may range from a more normal "hostile attitude" to a severe state marked by delusional ideas of "Divine Mission" as in Figure 5.1.

* From E. B. McNeil. *The Quiet Furies.* Englewood Cliffs, N.J.: Prentice-Hall, Inc., © 1967, pp. 168–71. Reprinted by permission of the publishers.

FIGURE 5.1   SEVERITY IN PARANOID SYMPTOMS AS RANKED BY CLINICIANS

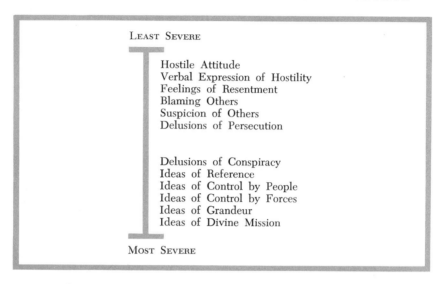

LEAST SEVERE

Hostile Attitude
Verbal Expression of Hostility
Feelings of Resentment
Blaming Others
Suspicion of Others
Delusions of Persecution

Delusions of Conspiracy
Ideas of Reference
Ideas of Control by People
Ideas of Control by Forces
Ideas of Grandeur
Ideas of Divine Mission

MOST SEVERE

Based on M. Lorr. A simplex of paranoid projection. *J. Consult. Psychol.,* 1964, **28**, 378–80.

The Paranoid State

It is difficult to distinguish the paranoid state from the vehicle that carries it through life—the paranoid personality. For paranoid personalities, suspiciousness, mistrust, and hostility—traits each of us possesses in small measure—are excessive, invariable, and permanent and may become characteristic of the total person. In that he does not blithely accept everything he encounters as true, good, and trustworthy, the paranoid personality is like all of us. The difference is that we discuss our suspicions and compare our experiences with those of others; we take positive, constructive action aimed at ameliorating our situation; we test reality.

Our ability to make a reasonable appraisal of life, our desire to see ourselves as others see us, and our attempts to comprehend the point of view of others are prime assets. They give perspective to our suspicions and doubts. In our ability to view ourselves critically we have some protection from disorder. It is the absence of this capacity that traps the paranoid personality in his own web of suspicion.

The frightened and hostile paranoid personality "reads" his environment incorrectly and interprets innocent actions as incontrovertible confirmation of dangers always secretly feared—"always secretly feared" because the inability to trust others isolates him from meaningful human connection that would enable him to exchange confidences, ask advice, and check the nature of reality. Fear feeds on itself, and the absence of access to others abandons the paranoid personality to the tortures of his distorted perceptions.

Isolation from others is caused by fear and distrust, and the isolation produces even greater fear and distrust. Suspecting that others cannot be relied on, the paranoid person must provoke, irritate, and test those about him to gain reassurance that they are no threat to him. This continued testing and provocation makes it extremely difficult to maintain compatible relationships with paranoid persons because the constant probing and testing provokes in others exactly the behavior and attitudes most dreaded by the paranoid. Paranoia thus becomes a self-confirming disorder in that its symptoms may cause a deepening of the disturbance.

The paranoid state can produce a litigious person who, feeling constantly outraged, put upon, and treated unfairly, seeks remedy in the courts and legal system by launching lawsuit after lawsuit as he acquires the reputation of a crotchety, difficult human being. In this paranoid state he can establish a standoff with society in which there is an unspoken agreement regarding mutual avoidance, "You leave me alone and I won't trouble you."

Paranoia and Delusion

The range of paranoid delusions encompasses almost every important human relationship. The delusional system may reflect anxiety about marriage, money, career, or any other aspect of existence in which plots by others could work to one's disadvantage. Delusions of persecution ("There are people plotting to destroy or debilitate me.") are coupled dynamically to delusions of grandeur ("After all, if so many are 'in' on the plot I must be someone special."). The existence of the plot shores up the shaky self-esteem of the one plotted against providing confirmation of his private self-appraisal. The egocentrism and narcissism reflected in this self-elevation tell us something of the inner needs of the patient.

The paranoid's *unconscious* self picture is not a very flattering one. It suggests unconscious inner weakness desperately covered by a conscious facade that distorts reality in an attempt to disguise a truth too terrible to be faced. Denying the essential truth of his inner state and ascribing his weaknesses and unacceptable emotions to others (projection) free the paranoid of anxiety but at an exorbitant cost to his interpersonal relations. The defensive steps taken within the psychic economy are quite sophisticated and complicated. But, in a simplified form, the following kinds of events must occur.

The paranoid must first discover that what he sees within himself is repugnant and intolerable. Unable to live with an accurate portrayal of himself and his feelings toward others he, at first, insists it cannot be so and represses this ugly and painful encounter with reality. When denial and repression fail and he becomes anxious again, drastic psychic surgery is required. He externalizes these unacceptable emotions and characteristics by ascribing them to others; he is not hostile, they are. He is loving but to no avail since others are jealous and revenge-seeking. Being "out there" makes these feelings and impulses manageable and he can, deluded about reality, defend himself against an apparently hostile, angry, threatening world. This requires an exorbitant expenditure of energy, but the paranoid pays the price to be free of the pain and anguish of the relentless anxiety that would otherwise disrupt every working hour.

The therapist's approach to the paranoiac must be a tentative one indeed. The symptoms are such that it is impossible for the patient to trust or accept the means to possible psychological redemption. Paranoia is woven into a way of life; it cannot easily reweave itself or comfortably tolerate repair.

THE SCHIZO-AFFECTIVE DISORDERS

Early conceptions of the psychoses assumed that each form of disorder was regularly associated with a particular personality or specific body type. Thus, it was natural to assume that the manic-depressive psychoses and the schizophrenias could not exist at the same moment in the same person. As is so often the case, observations in modern clinical practice made this assumption untenable. A mixture of schizophrenic and affective symptoms could and often did exist simultaneously in a patient.

The patient with a schizo-affective disorder may experience a series of bizarre hallucinations accompanied by a set of vague, ill-defined, and poorly organized delusions. The emotional state may be one of excessive elation or depression. Prognosis for such cases is somewhat better than for the classic schizophrenic reactions, but it has been observed that if these mixed symptoms appear again and again over time the likelihood is great that the schizophrenic aspects of the disorder will finally predominate.

If you accept the theoretical position of Leopold Bellak (1958), this schizo-affective pattern is best viewed as a temporary combination of symptoms reflecting the movement of an affective disorder as it shifts into a full-blown schizophrenia. At any single point in time about 10 per cent of those diagnosed schizophrenic might temporarily be labeled schizo-affective. This way-station enroute to a more serious set of symptoms of emotional disturbance is on the road to schizophrenia rather than mood disorder.

Stanley Cobb (1943) was the author and defender of this schizo-affective subdivision of the categories originally established by Kraepelin. His justification for this label is that it is descriptive of a great many cases diagnosed as affective psychosis at first, only to be rediagnosed as schizophrenia after a few years of hospitalization. The records of such patients reveal an interim stage during which signs of both symptom patterns are present.

Thus, if the defensive pattern called manic depression fails to solve the patient's problems, the next level of response to pressure may be a total schizophrenic break with reality. In the same way, depression and self-flagellation may relieve anxiety for a while but, if they fail, schizophrenic disorder may be the next response. The invention and use of the term schizo-affective serves two prime purposes: It is an accurate description of a phase of transition that sometimes comes between the affective psychoses and the schizophrenias, and it serves as a theoretical bridge between the two forms of disorder, representing an attempt to evolve a system of description of psychotic disorder a little less fixed and rigid than the original Kraepelinian conception of mental illness in man.

SUMMARY

Our somewhat ancient, classic descriptions of the schizophrenic reactions were rooted in an era in which emotional disorder was considered a physical illness capable of being described and treated like all other illnesses. The shift of modern theory to a dynamic, interpersonal conception of the causes of schizophrenia has stressed the common denominators of inadequate early development that produce severe disturbance in the cognitive, emotional, intellectual, and perceptual experience of the world.

Depending on the individual's personal history, this disturbance may take the form of schizophrenic reactions of various kinds. The simple schizophrenic is apathetic, seclusive, and withdrawn from human contact. To lead a life of minimal attachment to society, the hebephrenic breaks completely with our conception of reality and becomes delusional, hallucinatory, and incapable of communicating with others. The catatonic deals with his intense anxieties by rendering himself immobile. He dramatically turns off normal human response, and he "freezes" in panic, unable to decide which move will solve his conflicts and which will deepen them. The paranoid distorts reality but he stays tightly involved with events in the real world. He continues to respond but it is the suspicious, hostile, resentful, and irrational quality of this response that disturbs his fellow citizens.

We have had an overview of the classic forms of schizophrenic disorder, but in practice these categories of emotional distress are seldom seen in pure form. With the discovery of psychochemicals, psychotic patterns may be arrested in their early stages and never appear in their classic form. The next decade will see an increased erosion of this ancient and much patched system of nosology. Hopefully, there will develop a diagnostic approach more firmly based theoretically and a better match to the nature of patients occupying our mental hospitals.

The Disorders of
Mood and Emotion

6

Manic depressive disorders were first recorded early in man's history, and ancient descriptions of the behavior of those so afflicted resemble almost exactly their modern day equivalents. Tales of mania and melancholia reach back to the days of Homer and Hippocrates, but it was centuries before clinicians discovered that the two conditions were dynamically related facets of the same disorder. Kraepelin made official the connection between these seemingly opposite symptom patterns, but for seventeen centuries mania and depression were treated as separate, unrelated disorders of emotion. In some patients recurring and alternating depressions and manias were observed. When this oscillation was predictable it became evident that the absence of one might be occasioned by the presence of the other and that the disorder was constant while the symptoms varied in form (Cohen, 1967).

MANIA AND DEPRESSION TODAY

About one half of the manic depressive patients currently admitted to mental hospitals have a single encounter with the disorder; the other half experience successive attacks spaced over a period of time (Grinker *et al.*, 1961). First encounters most often occur between the ages of 20 and 30, with manic attacks becoming strikingly less frequent as the patient ages. Women display manic depressive disorders with substantially greater frequency than men—about 70 per cent of such hospitalized patients are female.

109

The classic, cyclical form of this disorder has decreased in modern times. Where once it was a common concern of therapists, it has now been relegated to a position of almost casual interest and a clinical curiosity. Fewer than 15 to 25 per cent of patients diagnosed manic depressive display this unmistakable alternation between the two aspects of the disorder (Rennie, 1942). Distinct cycles of improvement, deterioration, and alternation of patterns of symptoms are not the sole province of the manic depressive disorders; they simply are most visible there. Today a full fledged depression does not often move directly to its manic opposite nor does the reverse frequently occur. For that matter, many of the cases of "cyclothymia" (alternating mania and depression) reported in the historical past actually referred to manic and depressive symptom pictures separated by several years. Even then the clinical picture of cyclothymia was more theoretical than clinical. Mania and depression—and their alternation—were, in those days, ascribed to an unknown internal organic reaction, and little credence was given to the possibility that life circumstances could influence the timing of the appearance of the symptoms (Huston, 1967).

If manic reactions are indeed a defensive attempt to ward off depression, then this frantic search for a way out of conflicts and frustrations may, when it fails, trigger the very emotional state it seeks most to avoid. Whether the attempt to solve problems is manic or depressive in form, either may seem to the patient a superior alternative to the total break with reality that characterizes schizophrenia. The manic depressive has serious disturbances of mood, but he does not always experience the massive ego-fragmentation of other forms of psychosis.

Typically, 20 per cent of the first admissions to mental hospitals each year include patients diagnosed schizophrenic, while 14 per cent will bear the label of the depressive or manic. In mania and melancholia, joy and sorrow are exaggerated and become oppressive and disturbing accompaniments to living. Since emotion is so much a part of human nature, it is not surprising that disorders of mood were among the earliest psychic problems recognized by man.

The disorders of mood evident in mania and melancholia constitute the primary form of the disorder; the companion thought disturbances of schizophrenia or psychosis are ancillary aspects of the disorder.

MANIC REACTIONS

For diagnostic purposes, three degrees of manic activity are described: hypomania, acute mania, and delirious or hyperacute mania. These dimensions refer primarily to the intensity of excited behavior displayed by the patient. It is predictable that with an individual's increasing agitation and excitement, his capacity for making accurate judgments about the real world will disintegrate and his relationship to it will deteriorate rapidly (Noyes and Kolb, 1958). Roughly 30 per cent of those admitted to hospitals with affective disorders will display manic symptoms in varying degrees.

Hypomania

In the hypomanic, or subacute, stage this disorder is almost indistinguishable from "normal" excitement and freedom from inhibition. In a society where the "go-getter," the smooth talker, the supersalesman, and the charmer are admired, the energy, drive, and activity of the hypomanic will certainly be approved and rewarded. Such social reward and enthusiastic approval will prod the manic into even greater displays of overactive behavior.

A steady state of hypomania can easily and profitably be maintained in our society. Everyone knows persons capable of the successful and simultaneous juggling of an incredible number of interests, projects, and hobbies, persons whose energy supply seems inexhaustible in their various roles contributing to problem solving, innovation, and change. These are the people eagerly accepted and widely admired, even though it has been suggested that some of their effectiveness can be traced to the stimulus value they provide to others rather than the organized effort they actually deliver. A great many enthusiastic followers are needed to tend to the mundane details of implementing the brilliant ideas cast off in rapid-fire fashion by a highly active, slightly manic innovator. Sometimes an ideas-first-details-later form of brainstorming is exactly the push needed to produce change, and the stabilized hypomanic may thus become a cultural hero in a bustling, active society.

DAVE B.

As Dave liked to say, "Sleeping is a bad habit; Thomas Edison never slept more than 42 minutes a night." Dave could never quite accomplish this, but he frequently worked through the night without tiring and a cat nap seemed to revitalize him completely. Dave's reputation for having a finger in 10 full scale projects at the same time was accurate. His secret was speed and organization wedded to a high energy level and an insatiable interest in whatever was new. Dave seldom finished what he began since the mundane details of execution bored him once he had generated the original idea. Dave had tried, briefly, all the usual hobbies and interests but abandoned each in turn once he had mastered its intricacies. He did everything so well and so vigorously that few of his friends were aware of how restless and depressed he became at those odd times when he found himself "between" projects.

If one's usual level of output is less than manic, the beginning stage of hypomania will be acutely obvious to others (Cameron, 1942). As a previously steady mood shifts into a higher gear, the level of activity rises, behavior becomes more spontaneous and outgoing, and the patient experiences an increased alertness in sensory perception and thought processes. The rate of speech is altered and a "pressured" or "driven" quality is added to it. The rapid coursing of speech ricochets from topic to topic, never pausing, rarely tolerating interruption, and welcoming each new idea with unbounded enthusiasm. Speech becomes a dodging, darting reflection of thoughts racing at a desperate pace.

As the victim moves deeper into hypomanic behavior, he becomes increasingly distractable and excessively responsive to a tumult of ideas, each jostling the other to command his attention. The hypomanic begins to resemble a man after his third martini—gay, witty, and laughing a little too loudly in response to every new twist and turn of the conversation.

This hyperactivity and increased alertness is matched by an expanded sense of well-being and self-confidence. All things seem within the hypomanic's grasp if only he can apply enough energy and inventiveness. Risks become challenges, and by sheer daring the hypomanic sometimes succeeds where others might fail. He sketches large on a broad canvas suited to the reach of his thought. The internal psychic experience of the hypomanic must resemble a movie run at an increasingly rapid speed and unable to be slowed down.

When the outer limits of hypomania are reached, the qualities that initially evoked great approbation disintegrate into a less appealing form. Blithe confidence crosses the line into intolerable arrogance. When his ideas are questioned and followers fail to respond anymore to the now rough blandishments of his charm, the victim is liable to level accusations of little faith and limited vision at those who would abandon him. Enthusiasm becomes anger and resentment, and the more sober judgment of others seems to be gross disloyalty.

The broad efficiency of his judgment suffers in direct relation to the hypomanic's compulsive need for activity. As plans fail or fall short of the mark and his ability to deal with and recover from failure diminishes, he desperately throws good effort after bad and, doubling his wager in an unreasoning attempt to recoup his losses, spirals more rapidly into regions of heavy loss. At this juncture, his symptoms have escalated beyond a permanent hypomanic style of life. As the chaos spreads, the patient rushes frenetically into the acute stage of mania.

Acute Mania

In the acute stage the victim is belligerently incapable of accepting criticism, restraint, or domination by others. As the live wire, life of the party who has rid himself of the inhibitions that enmesh most of us, he experiences an irresistible sense of freedom from inner conflict. In the acute stage he becomes a gross caricature of his hypomanic self and an increasing nuisance to his friends and the general public. Convinced of the absolute correctness of his judgment, and suspicious of the plotting, jealousy, and interference that seems to surround him at every turn, he reaffirms his own importance with an expansive delusional system that drives him further from a rational examination of his emotional difficulties (Schwartz, 1961).

Having cast off his inhibitions, he is likely to violate the mores of proper behavior and good taste by becoming aggressive, vulgar, and insensitive to how others view him. There will be a corresponding decay in personal habits and grooming since he is unconcerned about what others think of him. Reality and proper comportment will be twisted and bent out of shape by a frantic urge to activity. The case of Joe A. is illustrative of this stage.

TOMORROW THE WORLD

JOE A.

The police had delivered Joe to the emergency entrance of the hospital in an agitated, disheveled, and wild-eyed state. The police were gentle with him and kept nodding, smiling, and trying to soothe him. Joe wasn't really violent just then since he was busily engaged in presenting a rapid-fire commentary on his life to the police in the squad car. Joe was going to do this and Joe was going to do that. Joe had connections. Joe knew people in high places. And Joe was going to make both officers full partners in a new enterprise that would make millions. I caught the tail end of the conversation as they urged him into the hospital and it sounded—at a speed of delivery barely intelligible—approximately like this:

"You look like a couple of bright, alert, hard working, clean-cut, energetic, go-getters and I could use you in my organization! I need guys that are loyal and enthusiastic about the great opportunities life offers on this planet! It's yours for the taking! Too many people pass opportunity by without hearing it knock because they don't know how to grasp the moment and strike while the iron is hot! You've got to grab it when it comes up for air; pick up the ball and run! You've got to be decisive! decisive! decisive! No shilly-shallying! Sweat! Yeah, sweat with a goal! Push, push, push, and you can push over a mountain! Two mountains, maybe. It's not luck! Hell, if it wasn't for bad luck I wouldn't have any luck at all! Be there firstest with the mostest! My guts and your blood! That's the system! I know, you know, he, she, or it knows it's the only way to travel! Get 'em off balance, baby, and the rest is leverage! Use your head and save your heels! What's this deal? Who are these guys? Have you got a telephone and a secretary I can have instanter if not sooner? What I need is office space and the old LDO [long-distance operator]. . . ." *

Hyperacute Mania

The inevitable toll of hyperactive behavior is about to be collected, however. The human vehicle can operate at top speed only for a limited period of time without breakdown. Hyperacute, or delirious, mania is the final stage of a desperate attempt to resolve one's problems, but it is a state rarely witnessed in this age of tranquilizers. The classic madman of the cinema is a close approximation to this condition. The patient is close to delirium, he is confused, wildly excited, impervious to outside influence, violent when crossed, severely disoriented, and incoherent. By this time he may be hallucinatory with savage visual and auditory experiences that have little correspondence to reality. His disordered behavior continues (unless quelled by drugs) until the state of total exhaustion is reached.

Drugs administered early in the course of an expanding manic attack are now startlingly effective. In the era prior to this age of chemistry, manic patients were removed to surroundings that were quiet and unstimulating. This measure was effective primarily because there seemed to be a circular, self-stimulating sequence in manic behavior which subsided when the environment was structured to soothe and calm.

The terminal or hyperacute phase of mania is not easily distinguishable from a full-blown violent catatonic excitement—incomprehensible disorganization marks both states. In many respects manic actions are an attempt to manipulate, push, and shove life into a shape more rewarding to the victim. Mania is a redoubling of effort to make the world yield what the individual needs desperately.

DEPRESSIVE REACTIONS

The agitation of mania is linked dynamically to the onset of depression, even though the surface behaviors seem polar opposites. In theory, the rapidly mounting spiral of frenetic activity of the manic reflects an attempt on his part to deny that he senses the massive depression that is

* From E. B. McNeil. *The Quiet Furies.* Englewood Cliffs, N.J.: Prentice-Hall, Inc., © 1967, p. 147. Reprinted by permission of the publishers.

about to engulf him. The manic runs away from depression by plunging into activity so all-consuming that it drowns out the "quiet voice" of depression. In mania he denies that he is sensitive to a loss in self esteem or threatened loss of a love object on which he is dependent (Gibson, 1958; Gibson, Cohen, and Cohen, 1959).

Depression is most often described in terms of its severity: simple, acute, and hyperacute (delirious or stuporous). A special category is reserved for agitated depressions in which the patient is hyperactive and upset about the delusional content of his thinking, e.g. the fear that the end of the world is imminent (Kraines, 1957).

Simple Depression

The simple phase of depression resembles the behavior of most of us when we are feeling less than joyous about life. Dejected and discouraged, the simple depressive exudes an air of sadness as he sits slumped in a chair without the energy or motivation to do much of anything. His usual level of physical activity slows down as does his thinking (Bellak, 1952).

The patient may think mostly about his feelings of worthlessness. He sees himself as a failure, unliked, unloved, sinful, and due shortly to receive the punishment he so richly deserves. Attempts to reason with him or to demonstrate that the world is not nearly so forlorn or without hope as he reports it to be are useless, of course. He accepts full blame for his sad state of affairs and resists attempts to dissuade him from this conviction.

His sense of hopelessness increases as his rate of activity decreases. He becomes preoccupied with internal miseries, severs communication with the outside world, and suffers disruptions in his usual patterns of eating and sleeping. He is convinced that things couldn't be worse than they are and that the future promises only compounded catastrophe and further pain. He may think of ending it all both as a well-deserved punishment and as the only rational solution to woes without number (Campbell, 1953).

Acute Depression

As the depression moves into an acute stage, thinking may become increasingly delusional. The punishment the victim feels he deserves is now certain to take place and promises to be even more severe than he imagined when his depression was simpler in degree. His self-accusations expand and deepen, and their logical justification becomes even less clearly connected to reality. Contact with others is eliminated, and the world may appear distorted and alien. Before long, a variety of delusional as well as real somatic symptoms may occupy the patient's attention since he has estranged himself from the outside world and is focused almost exclusively on his internal experience.

Soon, somatic changes appear with greater variety and severity, e.g. constipation, loss of sexual impulse, or cessation of menstrual periods. With his attention focused to an unusual degree on his bodily discomfort, the victim is certain that this is the beginning of the end, and in 75 per cent of such patients ideas of death and suicide appear (Arieti and Meth, 1959). The possibility of suicide is a very real one for an acutely depressed patient since he views his world through eyes that perceive only gloom and doom. There is danger that the depressive may decide to take loved ones with him to a fantasy heaven where they all will be free of the burden of living. The newspapers regularly carry accounts of depressed mothers who kill themselves and their children to spare them the miserable life they envision lies ahead.

In the case of Ralph R., the first appearance of simple depression went unnoticed. When depression became acute he was hospitalized but this state soon gave way to a hyperacute, stuporous condition in which he resembled a mumbling vegetable more than a human being.

EVERYTHING STINKS. INCLUDING ME.
RALPH R.

Ralph had begun to sink deeper and deeper into a massive depression and was now unable to think clearly or communicate coherently . . . . He was delusional about his worthlessness and sinfulness and was convinced that the whole world knew him for what he was—an abomination in the sight of God. He was certain that he was undergoing God's personal punishment for his many misdeeds and began to hallucinate the voice of Jesus and the Virgin Mary. He heard the voices asking him to kill himself and join them in the other world. . . .

Ralph plunged even deeper into depression and became a vegetable. When spoken to, he seemed to pay no attention since his energies were devoted to excluding extraneous noise in order to hear more clearly the voices that now spoke to him incessantly. His regression to childish behavior, including wetting and soiling himself, boded ill for his recovery.

It has been nearly eight months since Ralph has spoken coherently to anyone. Even when suffering discomfort or unhappiness, he will not complain. He seems to feel that he deserves anything that happens to him since he is such a failure as a human being.*

* From E. B. McNeil. *The Quiet Furies*. Englewood Cliffs, N.J.: Prentice-Hall, Inc., © 1967, p. 160. Reprinted by permission of the publishers.

Hyperacute Depression

A patient may be free of hallucinations yet fail to respond when in the throes of a stuporous depression. When severely regressed and childlike he must be fed, washed, diapered, and tucked into bed and he becomes unresponsive, inert, mute, hallucinatory and absorbed with concerns about sin and death.

How is it possible to account for the existence of psychic forces so powerful that they can reduce a fullgrown adult to a helpless, vegetative state? The most popular explanation is one referring to the early training the child experiences (Cohen, Baker, Cohen, Fromm-Reichmann, and Weigert, 1954). The conclusion of Cohen *et al.*, following an intensive study of twelve cases of manic-depressive psychosis, is that the adult depressive was excessively indulged early in life (always accepted, loved uncritically, and excused for wrong doing). As the child got older, he learned that parental approval was forthcoming only if he rigidly conformed to specific demands for obedience and achievement. This history of early acceptance and later severe demands for performance culminates in the formation of an adult who cannot possibly achieve at a level adequate to satisfy his fantasy of what he should have accomplished.

If this theoretical interpretation is accurate, we have determined a part of the formula for rearing an adult depressive: teach the child he is accepted first for himself; teach him later that love is contingent on performance; then set the standards of performance so high that a sense of guilt and failure are inevitable.

Agitated Depression

An agitated depression is, dynamically, similar to every other form of depression. The mood of sadness and melancholia are the same, but retardation of action and thought are missing in agitated depression. Obsessed with ideas of suicide, imminent destruction, and catastrophe, agitated depressives pace restlessly and are unable to sleep or eat since they are so aware of dangers to which others seem oblivious. Speech is pressured, as it is in manic attacks, and its content is worried and anxious matching the harried, pained, concerned thoughts of the victims. They cry doom and may sit by themselves issuing repetitive warnings to everyone, bewailing the condition of the world, and crying over their terrible fate.

In many respects, agitated depression is an exaggerated version of excessive and irremedial grief over loss of a loved one. In a milder form, this phenomenon is apparent in any adult under severe pressure and unable to find a reasonable solution to life's problems. In normal life these periods of agitation are brief and specific to the situation of the moment; for the full-blown, agitated depressive this agitation becomes a prolonged part of existence. In the depressive personality, internal anxiety is projected on the outside world—a world that then appears fragile and ready for destruction. This world view is a reflection of the patient's internal experience.

THE INVOLUTIONAL PSYCHOTIC
REACTIONS

The designation "involutional psychotic reaction" is frequently a diagnostic "extra" in modern nosological systems. These psychotic reactions differ little from any other, but they are given a special title because they appear in middle or late middle life and because they occur during a period of metabolic and endocrinal change. The implied causative links of age, altered endocrine functioning, and psychotic reaction are too loose for clinical comfort, but the diagnosis has a long history (Ford, 1967).

The human involutional period covers roughly the ages of 40 to 55 in women and 50 to 65 in men. As Cameron (1963) has noted, the involutional age is also the age at which depressive and paranoid reactions are most common. Since so few demonstrably direct links exist between metabolism and abnormal behavior, the designation "involutional" tells us little about the patient, the etiology of the observed reaction, or profitable approaches to therapy. Even the clue that this reaction appears two to three times more frequently in women than in men is not particularly helpful since its meaning is not yet clear.

The psychological response of women to the primary sign of involution—menopause—is considered crucial to the appearance of psychotic reactions. When menstruation becomes irregular and then stops—gradually or abruptly—the female genitalia begin to display signs of atrophy, and a series of vasomotor (circulatory) symptoms of varying degrees of distressfulness may appear. Menopause signals an end to reproductive functions, and the fear of being less than a whole, productive woman can find its reflection in the psychological state of the female and induce extreme mood swings, irritability, depression, and other emotional disturbances. If the woman is convinced that she is a useless appendage to society and if she grows envious of her younger, still fertile counterparts, she can react to menopause as a traumatic experience (White, 1964).

The male equivalent of menopause is called the andropause, or male climacteric. This is only an approximate equivalent to menopause since there is little convincing clinical evidence that similar physiological events are occurring (Noyes and Kolb, 1958). It is true that the aging male undergoes some form of disturbance in neurological and endrocrinological balance as his gonadal functions change, but this is likely to occur late in life for most males.

For both men and women it is a trying task to distinguish between the purely *physical* symptoms of aging and declining sexual function and the *psychological* reactions to awareness of these events. In a culture so desperately devoted to the joys of youth and to the discrediting of age, the involutional period can pose a particularly excruciating threat.

In classic form, this period was described as producing involutional melancholia—a delusional, anxious, agitated depression. This reaction often had visible precursors in the form of neurotic-like symptoms that are transient and mild in form. Attempted suicide was not uncommon for these patients, since they may develop a severe and profound depression underscored by their conviction of total worthlessness and uselessness to society (Barnett, Lefford, Pushman, 1953).

JUDITH B.

Judith's two children were grown and gone and, try as he would, her husband Ed seemed unable to fill the void they left. Judith always treated her children as her "light and life" during their growing years and this left little energy for her husband. Her overprotectiveness of the children had been suffocating to them and each had broken free of her meddling at an early age. Now they seldom visted her and the significance of their flimsy excuses was not lost on her. Judith was convinced that her children hated her because she had been an evil mother who had destroyed their chance for happiness. When both the son and daughter got divorced, Judith shouldered all the blame. She became irritable and depressed and this mood alternated with a hysterical agitation. After two dramatic but ineffectual attempts at suicide, Judith was hospitalized. She has a drugged calmness about her now, but she continues to have a worried and pained facial expression and is easily upset by even the most commonplace events.

There is reason to believe that the severity of the symptom pattern is, in part, due to the social role designed for older persons in our culture. If age brought increased rank, greater reverence, and an honored position as it does in some societies (Japan, China, etc.) we might witness less distress in aging people. Without this social rank, chaotic fantasies of personal guilt and worthlessness coupled with deranged physiological functioning are not unusual in persons going through the crisis of aging (Wittenborn and Bailey, 1952).

Age and Involution

Age is a vital factor in this diagnosis but it is used in a highly circular fashion. Failing all else, a patient displaying depressive or paranoid symptoms is tossed into the involutional pigeonhole if he or she is middle-aged. If a younger person displays a similar set of symptoms he or she is sometimes, startlingly, classified as involutional in anticipation of the actual event. Since age is too elastic a measuring device to be employed effectively in making a diagnosis of involutional psychotic reaction, the category is used less and less in modern clinical practice.

There are psychological problems peculiar to middle age, and these certainly warrant consideration as a part of the total spectrum of psychotic reactions. Biologically we do decline with age. We learn less rapidly, react with less speed, have a diminished sensory apparatus, and display clear bodily evidence of waning strength and vigor. Any or all of these events are capable of wounding our vanity and of whispering in our ear a tale of declining ability. Yet, these varied changes are responded to with greater or lesser grace depending upon the personal history of the individual. We can only comprehend involutional psychotic reactions if we have a full understanding of the psychological context into which they must be fitted (Szalita, 1966).

If psychosis is a behavioral reaction to stress, and if stress is defined in terms of threatening elements within the self and the environment, then we can only deal with involutional psychotic reactions successfully if we know the individual intimately and can make a proper appraisal of stress and threat as *he* sees it. One man's success may well be another man's failure, and it is in the personal interpretation of events that the key to involutional psychosis may be found.

What is most difficult to comprehend about this syndrome is the reported "normality" of the patient prior to the appearance of the symptoms. To the layman it may seem that this patient population is drawn from the ranks of the ordinary and untroubled, while, in reality, victims of this disorder are produced by a life devoid of preparation for the critical test of aging.

Middle and older age is an inevitable time of balancing-the-accounts and a time of measuring the discrepancy between what one aspired to and what one achieved. The specter of death always lurks in the background, and this can provoke serious distress and a deep sense of longing for the chance to do it all over again (Gilbert, 1952). Even the depths of despair and self-accusation are not totally free of secondary gain, since these behaviors usually evoke increased care and consideration from others. The hospitalization of the involutional may be a poor solution to a problem of living.

SUMMARY

The disorders of mood and emotion are differentiated from the schizophrenias described in the last chapter mainly in terms of the kind and quality of emotional, cognitive, and intellectual disorientation each experiences. The disorientation and disorganization of the manic and the depressive are produced by the behavioral disorder rather than in reaction to it. In this sense both kinds of emotional disorders are active responses to the world and to the people in it, and internal appraisals of how one is doing in accomplishing ambitions and goals in life. Depression is an unrealistic confession of failure just as manic behavior is a feverish denial of it.

Alternating mania and depression are less frequently seen in modern practice than in times past and a different view of manic depression exists today since we look to a psychogenic rather than organic basis for the problem.

The exaggeration of mood and loss of control over it in mania is divided, for convenience, into three degrees of severity: hypomania, acute mania, and hyperacute mania. Normal mood swings of joy and exultation over happy events are attached to reality and are self-limiting, i.e. calm returns following the celebration. When moods reach unusual heights, level off briefly, and then escalate further, we are faced with serious emotional disorder.

The depths of hyperacute depression and the active heights of mania both reflect reactions to a life circumstance in which the contrast between what one is and what one feels he ought to be is intolerably anxiety provoking. These aspirations and ambitions deeply ingrained in childhood have become the adult measure of personal worth, and when the gap between "is" and "ought to be" forces itself into consciousness, disordered behavior may result. The manic redoubles his efforts to close the gap, but the depressive accepts this discrepancy and blames himself for its existence. When the manic's attempts at last minute remedy fail (as they must), he too gives up and joins the depressive.

The involutional psychotic reactions occupy a special, and puzzling, niche among the mood disorders. They clearly are dysfunctions of the emotions, but their appearance in middle age (at the time of physiological alterations in reproductive capacity) has long led us a merry chase by suggesting that these mood disorders have a physiological rather than psychogenic basis. At best, causation seems to be an interaction of the two and modern hospitals treat it accordingly.

The disorders of mood and emotion, being free of the bizarre distortions of schizophrenia, have always seemed to have a more hopeful prognosis. Perhaps this optimism exists because the disorders seem to "overtake" otherwise reasonably normal persons who have managed to survive most of the other perils of human existence. As we will see when we discuss methods of therapeutic treatment, the disorders of mood and emotion *are* more responsive to our ministrations.

The Organic
Disorders

7

One of the penalties of growing old is the increased risk of senile psychotic disorder. The psychoses of senility are the most frequent but not the sole form of severe psychological disturbance based on organic changes that come with advanced age. Aging is a particular problem for those in Western industrialized society since the advances of medical technology have allowed a stretching of the *average* life span (Burgess, 1960). We live longer because medical advances equip us to fight the ravages of age and more of us are alive today because more of us survive death in infancy. Surviving the perils of infancy does not, of course, assure us of a longer life span. Only one person in twenty-five lived to be over sixty-five at the turn of the century, but by 1960 we had cut this ratio in half. In the next two decades we will probably increase by half again the number of persons destined to exceed the three score measure of age.

With age comes physical and psychological disorder (Arnhoff, 1961; Himwich, 1962). Disturbances of a psychological sort are shaped by the configuration of one's previous years and reflect the role and status of the elderly in our society. Emotional disturbance cannot be disentangled from the issues of diminished self-esteem and an eroded sense of usefulness resulting from forced retirement and the loss of a productive role in our culture. As a man's income, prestige, family position, and relevance to society diminish, his ego dissolves, and this loss is reflected in his management of the later years. Old age is also a time of fear—fear of change and fear of death (Straker, 1963).

The life of a senior citizen with acute or chronic brain disorder could

123

hardly be described as his "golden years." Aging is complicated by acute and chronic symptoms of brain disorder and cerebral incompetence. In such cases, the older person may become the victim of disorganization in memory, learning, judgment, comprehension, emotional control, and sensory and motor response.

ACUTE BRAIN DISORDER

Acute brain syndromes are biochemical changes in brain functions that produce temporary disorganization of behavior. When cerebral incompetence is acute there is a sudden onset of delirium, stupor, or coma. Behavioral disorders that accompany those states have, at one time or another, been labeled acute toxic confusional states, symptomatic psychoses, or delirious syndromes. The patient in this stuporous condition is brought to full, normal consciousness only with great difficulty, and he can be maintained in an alert state for very short periods. In contrast, the patient in a coma is suffering a more severe brain disorder and seems both to be awake and unconscious at the same moment. The comatose patient is unresponsive to the outside world. But, these are changes in brain function that can be reversed with proper treatment.

Delirium presents a special case, since it can be produced by toxic states induced by drugs or an elevated temperature attendant on infection or disease. In delirium the normal integration and continuity of behavior decays, and psychological chaos takes its place. The patient at first tries to adjust by making a series of motor responses to his physiological condition (restlessness, irritability, and distortion of thought, feeling, and reaction). As the physiological distress deepens he becomes more confused in the attempt to order the jumble of his thoughts and perceptions, and he may become incoherent and disoriented. Preoccupied with an internal physiological crisis, he can no longer assimilate the burden of additional psychological stimulation from the outside world. The consequent cognitive instability may produce delusions and hallucinations— the victim becomes unable to control the mixture of conscious and unconscious thoughts that now flood his awareness, and what is real and unreal become confused. Past, present, and future are merged into a misshapen mass of current experiences.

The severity of the symptoms an individual displays correlates roughly to the amount of damage his central nervous system has sustained. If the disorder is acute, the prognosis is good because the usual healing mechanisms of the body will, before long, remedy or compensate for this breakdown of its functions. When drug intoxication is relieved, a high fever reduced, or nutritional deficiency remedied, the nervous system and the brain may again become dependable organs for rational use. The patient, once the delirium has passed, can again make sense of psychological events in his life.

CHRONIC BRAIN DISORDER

Brain lesions, infection, or the normal degenerative processes that come with age all can produce brain damage that is chronic—damage that cannot be reversed by known medical techniques. The victim of a chronic brain syndrome suffers progressive deterioration of various intellectual, cognitive, and emotional functions. He may suffer the loss of concentration, of memory, of the ability to deal with life in symbolic terms, and of the ability to differentiate objects one from another. Fragmentation of thought is particularly evident, since the patient suffers constant interference by extraneous thoughts coupled with the loss of ability to focus attention on the matter being discussed. Behavior ceases to be rational, and the irrationality is produced by a badly functioning nervous system that fails to integrate internal and external stimuli and response systems.

On the nonintellectual side, the chronic brain disordered patient will be less able to select proper patterns of behavior or to regulate them once chosen. The control and inhibition of certain parts of behavior will malfunction in such a way that material long repressed or suppressed may make its appearance without the usual signs of guilt, embarrassment, or shame. Personal habits of order and neatness may deteriorate severely, speech may be slurred, emotional instability is frequent, and the damaged person may weep or laugh inappropriately. Delusional beliefs long suppressed by a rational view of the world may make their appearance, and these may be coupled with moderate or severe hallucinations. Awareness of the inappropriateness of his actions is usually absent since he loses the capacity to stand back from the self and make judgments about his behavior.

With aged patients (in their 70's) a mixture of cerebral arteriosclerosis and senile brain disease of a diffuse sort can account for as high as 30 per cent of first admissions to mental hospitals (Fishbein, 1962). The advances made by medicine in keeping us alive have thus steadily altered the form and kind of psychotic problem that is admitted to our hospitals. Let us now look briefly at the prime sources of such disturbance.

SENILE BRAIN DISORDER

Senile dementia can develop early or late in life and may take place suddenly or develop over an extended period of time. And, for some patients, senile brain disorder will produce simple deterioration without marked overtones of manic, depressed, or paranoid patterns of behavior. But, its advanced state is one of extensive incapacitation and helplessness. As the patient begins to forget essential facts, he also suffers a loss in good judgment and becomes incapable of dealing with symbols and abstractions as he once could. While he may be unable to tell you what he had for lunch, he can have excellent recall for events in the remote past. Memory lapses are troublesome, of course, and the senile patient may, in desperation, make up details (confabulate) to fill the ever increasing number of gaps in his memory (Ferraro, 1959). In very severe cases, the behavior of the senile patient may appear similar to that of the arteriosclerotic. In the early stages the disorders can usually be distinguished from one another.

As brain and central nervous system cells die and are not replaced by the growth of new cells, deterioration becomes more marked. With continued deterioration there will be a peeling off of layers of civilization with those things learned last being lost first. Controls the patient once ably exercized over his emotions become ineffectual, giving free rein to depression, paranoid thoughts, and aggressive reactions (temper tantrums, violent response)

"The return of the repressed" is one way of describing the release of unconscious content once carefully monitored by its victim. These release symptoms produce behavior that is usually shocking to the young relatives of these older persons since the aged have always had many virtues and few sins attributed to them. Long suppressed sexual, aggressive, greedy, or inconsiderate thoughts may appear, and if the patient is mobile this turn of events may involve him in distasteful encounters with the law. The two most common brain syndromes of the aged are senile brain disease (atrophy and/or degeneration of parts of the central nervous system) and cerebral arteriosclerosis (the thickening of arteries in the brain), accounting for nearly 80 per cent of their brain disorders (Marks, 1961).

With judgment and memory impaired, confused in orientation to time, place, or person, delusional and perhaps hallucinating, the typical hospitalized patient would be a female (they live longer than men) about 75 years old. There is only a low correlation between the amount of physical or central nervous system damage and the severity of psychosis, however.

TABLE 7.1 SYMPTOM PATTERNS IN THE EARLY * STAGES OF SENILE PSYCHOSES COMPARED WITH CEREBRAL ARTERIOSCLEROSIS

SYMPTOM	SENILE PSYCHOSIS	CEREBRAL ARTERIOSCLEROSIS
Appearance of pattern of symptoms.	Gradual, progressive, long lasting.	A brain "accident," dramatic, short duration, end in death.
Intellectual impairment and paranoia.	Common	Uncommon
Headaches, dizziness, convulsions, depression, emotional outbursts.	Uncommon	Common
Fluctuations in symptom pattern.	Uncommon	Common

* At later stages, progressive intellectual impairment marks all such damaged patients.

After J. C. Coleman. *Abnormal Psychology and Modern Life.* Scott, Foresman & Co., 1964.

This is to say, simply, that a postmortem of the senile brain tells us little of the behavior of the afflicted individual. All old, senile persons don't become psychotic but this physiological stress may trigger a psychosis in persons needing full command of all their capacities to make an adequate adjustment to the demands of life.

The case of John and Nancy B. illustrates some of the characteristics of senile psychosis and some of the difficulties that arise in caring for senile persons in the home.

OLD FOLKS AT HOME

JOHN AND NANCY B.

They were up at strange hours of the night calling for help or attention and drifted off into brief naps all during the day. Sometimes they even slipped into a light sleep while you were talking to them.

In the middle of a conversation, either or both of them might suddenly burst into tears over the least trifle. Sometimes John would get weepy and insist he was being mistreated and Nancy would join in the unhappy demonstration without the slightest justification. As rapidly as they cried, they could also express bitterness and recrimination. Often it was about the behavior of people at the moment, but just as often the resentment was directed at persons long dead and involved incidents that had taken place as long as 50 years ago.

. . .

Nancy seemed better preserved than John, but she was beginning to talk loosely of plots to get her money, and she became coarse if not vulgar. Her food seemed poisoned to her and her eyes would flash with suspicion at every meal. She would taste the food tentatively, watch to see if anyone looked guilty or was watching her, and in a loud, stagey voice announce, "I'm not very hungry today. I think I won't eat." *

It is difficult to measure the amount of senile psychotic deterioration among the approximately 20 million persons over 65 years of age in our country since many senile sufferers are cared for at home and not recorded among the total number. The degree of senile deterioration is rarely measured exactly, and borderline symptoms of psychosis may be masked by the failing health of the victim.

Fate does not always hold deterioration in store for aging persons, even though the population of mentally ill at advanced ages has been estimated to be as high as 50 per cent. With increasing age many persons just begin to reach the height of their spiritual, material, or artistic contribution. We can admire the golden years, but we must be realistic about the truth that the body's ability to resist disease and to recover decreases to match the loss in all the other senses, energies, and capacities. Senility will be the ultimate fate of many of us.

DISORDER AND INFECTION

One of the most dramatic instances of damage to brain and nervous tissue occurs as a consequence of cerebral syphilis. Syphilis, untreated, kills or maims human beings and an interpretative history of the rampage of the syphilis spirochete would cover centuries of the congress of man with his fellow human beings. Its origin is obscure, and the time of the first appearance of syphilis on earth has yet to be agreed upon. Syphilis seems to have existed for centuries, and its spread across the planet could well have been a part of the great voyages of discovery of Columbus and Vasco De Gama. This infection certainly was the camp follower of every army in history. The mixture of sex, war, and exploration brought syphilis to the four corners of the earth.

The syphilis spirochete is extremely virulent and can penetrate the

* From E. B. McNeil. *The Quiet Furies.* Englewood Cliffs, N.J.: Prentice-Hall, Inc., © 1967, pp. 203–04. Reprinted by permission of the publishers.

defenses of the body with startling ease. The modern miracle of penicillin and antibiotic drugs should long ago have banished this infestation, but the stubborn resistance of man to education has produced a rising rate of disease and the formation of newer, more resistant strains of greater virulence (Bruetsch, 1959).

TABLE 7.2   THE STAGES OF SYPHILIS—INFECTION TO CEREBRAL DAMAGE

TIME	SYMPTOMS
10–40 days after infection	A sore (hard chancre) at point of infection. Vanishes in 4–6 weeks.
3–6 weeks later	Skin rash (brown colored) resembling measles or smallpox. May be accompanied by indigestion, fever, headaches.
. . . . . .	Latent period—no symptoms but spirochete attacking tissues, cells, organs, or blood vessels.
10–30 years later	Vision failure, heart attack, mental disturbance, motor-coordination difficulties.

Within 10 to 30 years after infection, the syphilis spirochete can begin to take its toll of the brain and central nervous system. If the blood vessels and heart are its target, death is sudden. If the nervous system is the focus, we have paresis (a paralytic disorder of the central nervous system). Only a small percentage of those with untreated syphilis suffer paresis, but an untreated case is regularly fatal.

When general paresis strikes, the patient responds in terms congruent with his life history and may experience manic expansiveness and euphoria or severe depression. Either emotional extreme of this disorder may be marked by disorientation, motor incapacity, delusions, hallucinations, and destruction of intellectual and cognitive capacities. In its simple or demented form we can witness the reduction of a previously integrated personality to its lowest common demoninator of disorganization.

With treatment, about 50 per cent of syphilitic patients show improvement or recovery, a small percentage die during treatment, and a slightly greater number show little improvement. The key issues are, of course, prevention, early detection, and treatment. Our society, unfortunately, is not yet ready to accept this disease as a social equivalent to all others.

The organic consequences of this "social" disease—translated into psychotic disorder—are severe. The case of Jack O. demonstrates the paretic destruction of a capable human being.

THE SWINGER—TWENTY YEARS LATER
JACK O.

Jack had devoted a great deal of his time to being a fastidious dresser who was always close to the newest fashion trends. He knew style, had excellent taste, and would fuss over some tiny detail of his attire until it was just right and suited him exactly. But, Jack started to get sloppy. He did only an approximate job of shaving and sometimes he forgot to do it at all. His shirts were worn more than once, his shoes lost their unfailing luster, his tie knot became lumpy, and he went too long between haircuts. His eating habits became gross and his apparel was stained with a variety of foods. This was so out of character for Jack that it evoked comment by all who knew him.

My contact with Jack was on a referral basis from the company physician who wanted psychological tests done on him. Jack was quite willing to be tested but he was a difficult subject since he ran off at the mouth at great length about past accomplishments and future grandiose plans. The degree of intellectual and cognitive deterioration revealed by the tests was severe. The loss in his capacity to reason, to solve problems, and to perform visual-motor tasks was astonishing in such a young man, and much of the content of the projective tests was distorted, bizarre, and disconnected. Tests designed to reveal organic impairment suggested diffuse damage to the central nervous system and these findings fit closely the results obtained by a complete neurological examination.*

DISORDER AND DAMAGE
TO THE BRAIN

Damage to the brain or central nervous system can occur insidiously as a consequence of some abnormality of tissue growth that gradually compresses the brain cells within the skull. Or, the sudden death of brain tissue can, as in the following case, occur as the result of a violent accident.

GASOLINE AND ALCOHOL—IN EQUAL PARTS
NORM R.

Norm R. survived the crash but he ceased to exist just as surely as if he had died in the wreckage. He was alive—if you could call it living.

---

* From E. B. McNeil. *The Quiet Furies.* Englewood Cliffs, N. J.: Prentice-Hall, Inc., © 1967, pp. 197–98. Reprinted by permission of the publishers.

When Norm's head hit the windshield, a part of his skull was depressed by the impact. A large blood vessel in the brain was ruptured by small fragments of the skull, and there was widespread cerebral laceration. Following remedial surgery, Norm was comatose for two days and survival in any form remained an unanswered question. Once past this first crisis, he was watched closely for behavioral signs that would indicate the rate at which the body was repairing itself. Progress was slow and painful, and Norm posed an unusually vexatious home care problem when he finally was well enough to leave the hospital.

. . .

The worst part for Norm and those caring for him, especially the children, was the impairment of his memory. So many details of Norm's past life were gone that he had to invent new ones to fill in the vacant space. Where parts were missing, new and plausible substitutes were invented to take their place. Whenever Norm made an effort to reconstruct the world as it had once been, he became acutely aware of his inability to concentrate for even a brief period of time, and he would get a headache and become totally fatigued by the vain effort.*

Injury to the brain in which the patient survives but his behavior is seriously altered has always existed in man, since the skull offers a re-

TABLE 7.3   SYMPTOMS OF CEREBRAL DAMAGE

BRAIN DAMAGE	SOURCE	SYMPTOMS
Cerebral Concussion	Mild injury (accident, blow)	Brief confusion, disorientation, memory loss, headache, clouding of consciousness, some amnesia, rapid recovery.
Cerebral Contusion	Brain bruised by sudden compression against skull.	Concussion symptoms on a more severe scale. Delirium, impairment of intellectual functions. Slower recovery and persistence of symptoms past time of damage.
Cerebral Laceration	Cutting or tearing of brain tissue, often object penetration of brain, internal bleeding.	Like extremely severe contusion, may be comatose, all bodily systems may function erratically. Delirium following coma may be marked by delusions, hallucinations, anxiety, confusion, memory loss, excitement, agitation, etc.

* From E. B. McNeil. *The Quiet Furies.* Englewood Cliffs, N. J.: Prentice-Hall, Inc., © 1967, pp. 186–87. Reprinted by permission of the publishers.

markable but imperfect protection for the brain. Automobile accidents have vastly increased the rate of serious brain damage and produced a grisly but rich source of increased variety of kinds of possible damage.

Brain injuries may make drastic changes in usual patterns of behavior, but these changes do not always mean confinement to a mental institution. This fate is reserved for a small minority of all those so injured. Even the fabled Private Eyes of popular fiction need not anticipate residence in in a mental hospital though they are bludgeoned unconscious with remarkable frequency.

Most head injuries produce an acute phase of altered behavior followed by recovery. For these cases there may be nothing more than a disruption of normal brain function following a mild concussion and brief loss of consciousness. Some disorientation or moderate confusion may exist for a short span of time but within hours or, at most, days, these symptoms are relieved. In addition, a retrograde amnesia may exist in which the patient can recall events remote in time but has lost memory of the events just preceding loss of consciousness.

If the brain is severly bruised or compressed within the skull, the symptoms of disorder increase in intensity and duration. A boxer, for example, may be hospitalized in a comatose state for hours, days, or weeks. When the trauma involves a shattered skull and laceration of the brain, the extent and variety of the behavioral defects that occur will vary accordingly. There is a general rule of thumb that, in combination, the amount of damage to the brain and the stability of the personality before injury summate to produce the final pattern of behavior that will be visible to the onlooker (Brosin, 1959).

The patient's reaction to the injury is a vital contributor to the final outcome, and it is difficult to disentangle the consequences of the injury itself from the patient's reaction to knowing his brain has been damaged. A stable, mature, well-adjusted person weathers brain damage much better than his unstable, inadequate counterpart. How a person's behavior changes, then, will depend on his psychic condition before the event, the extent of the damage, and the strategic location of the insult to his nervous system.

With tumorous growth in the brain a succession of shifting symptom patterns will be evident since the internal pressure and tissue destruction will be progressive and subtle (Mulder, 1959). The rate at which a tumor grows and the behavioral changes that will accompany it are unpredictable since they vary with the individual's physiological and psychological state. By the same token, the point at which the patient will have insight into the nature and irreversability of this condition will be unique to each case.

With non-benign tumors, little except surgery will prove effective since the malignant growths must be removed to ease pressure on the brain. And, surgery itself may contribute additional complications to the already strained behavior of the patient. The remedial destruction of tumorous and adjoining tissue to relieve pressure produces additional damage.

When damage is produced by toxic phenomena (severe infection, high temperature, carbon monoxide, poisoning, drugs, glandular dysfunction, etc.) a cardinal sign is the confusion and personality disintegration typical of delirium. Delirious reactions can be produced by a number of toxic substances and by a variety of conditions, but the clinical picture does not differ essentially from other kinds of acute or chronic brain disorder once the damage is done.

SUMMARY

The marvelously complicated organ called the brain allows us to have the unique characteristics that make us human. And, when the brain and related parts of our central nervous systems lose their capacity to sense, perceive, learn, remember, and control response—when the brain can no longer integrate and regulate the massive details of living—then we assume a dehumanized level of adjustment and interaction with the world. When an intact brain could just barely maintain an acceptable psychological life for an individual, then the damaged organ may prove insufficient to the task and psychosis will make its appearance.

Acute brain disorder and chronic brain disorder differ primarily in terms of the extent of cerebral damage sustained by the patient, the length of time it takes to recover normal balance, and the seriousness of the psychological disorganization produced. Whether the brain disorder is insidious in onset (senile brain disorder) or the sudden consequence of the death of brain cells (accident, trauma, virulent infection), the extreme forms of damage effect disorganization of most systems of human behavior.

When the physical incapacity is compounded by a breakthrough of psychotic processes, the picture is even more grim and unappealing. Psychosis following brain damage may display inappropriate extremes of emotional response (mania or depression), cognitive or perceptual deviation (hallucinations and delusions), suspicion and hostility (paranoia), or withdrawal from reality and retreat into a life of fantasy (the schizophrenias). In such cases, the damage to the brain does not "cause" the psychosis. It simply makes a nonpsychotic adjustment less possible for those whose lives had been reasonably free of distress in the past.

ORDER FROM DISORDER: THE THERAPIES *IV*

The Somatic
Therapies

8

American society—as no other in history—has taken the position that everyone should be mentally healthy and believes that human psychic suffering can be relieved through some mixture of individual psychotherapeutic, psychosocial, and organic therapies. Ours is a treatment-oriented society, and the management of emotional disorders has included a wide range of usual and unusual means of producing change in man's psychic apparatus and behavior. It is obvious that an astute therapist will use a variety of methods to achieve the greatest purchase on the patient's problem, but, for the sake of clarity, the organic, physical, or somatic techniques will be considered here, and psychotherapeutic techniques will be discussed in the next chapter.

The somatic therapies can be as basic as prescribing prolonged, drugged sleep or as severe as psychosurgery in which brain damage or other insult to the nervous system is employed for curative purposes. Sleep therapy is an ancient approach that had a brief resurgence when the Russians reported new success with electronarcosis, a process that involves rendering the patient unconscious by applying an electric current to the brain. An instrument called an electrosone is used in this procedure. Low voltage electric current to the "sleep centers" of the brain induce a brief but deep sleep from which the patient is reported to emerge refreshed and revitalized. Related treatment in America has been focused on a prolonged drug narcosis which seems to produce approximately the same effects. These methods have not been widely adopted by American psychotherapists who have been deeply involved in other basic somatic treatments of disorder.

THE SHOCK THERAPIES

Chemical Shock

In 1932 the Polish psychiatrist Manfred Sakel (1900–1957) developed insulin coma therapy in Vienna. When enough insulin is introduced into the blood stream, a condition of lowered blood sugar (hypoglycemia) results, and the patient slips into a coma-like state. The accidental discovery of this condition stimulated a flurry of experimentation with insulin. Physicians and psychiatrists were hard-pressed to explain why certain psychotic symptoms decrease following this event, but the desperate desire for some sort of effective therapy produced two related swirls of activity: the application of chemically induced shocks for patients bearing all kinds of symptoms; and, experimentation with a variety of chemical compounds producing approximately the same effect. The induction of the hypoglycemic state is not an event witnessed comfortably by the squeamish, but its beneficial effects are well-documented for certain of the chronic psychoses.

Although individuals vary in their tolerance for insulin, a daily increasing dose of it can produce a comatose state. Once aroused from shock (by means of raising the blood sugar level via tube feeding of orange juice) the schizophrenic patient will most often experience a temporary amnesia for recent events but will be able to communicate in a clearer and more rational manner. For some patients this improvement fades rapidly after the initial shock treatments. For others there is an increase in the period of lucidity, and psychotherapeutic treatment can be applied with some success.

The Hungarian psychiatrist Ladislaus von Meduna (1896–1964) became convinced that epilepsy and schizophrenia were incompatible diseases and reasoned that schizophrenia, then, could be cured by the administration of convulsive agents that would induce its incompatible opposite. The use of Metrazol (a synthetic preparation of camphor) to produce brief epileptic-like convulsions was a short-lived chapter in the history of treatment. Metrazol proved to be too erratic and unreliable, proper dosages were difficult to determine, and the convulsions were too violent.

Indoklon inhalation therapy is used in some modern hospitals (Kalinowsky, 1967a) for the treatment of schizophrenia. Indoklon (an ether compound) turned out to be the only pharmacological convulsive agent that was not more dangerous or less reliable than Metrazol, and it is used in treatment of schizophrenics when other methods fail.

Somatic shock treatment has had a checkered career in the management of schizophrenia (Kalinowsky and Hoch, 1961; Sargant and Slater,

1964). Lehmann (1967) reports a case of hebephrenia, for example, in which 200 electroconvulsive treatments and 50 subcoma insulin treatments were administered to a patient during the course of one year. Kalinowsky (1967a) reports that few therapists now use insulin coma with schizophrenics. He admits improvement in schizophrenics is slow and advises a minimum administration of 40 to 60 comas.

Conflicting claims have been made for the degree of success of chemical shock treatment for schizophrenics. Malzberg (1938) tells of improvement of 54 per cent and recovery of 13 per cent of patients so treated (compared with 19 per cent improvement and 3.5 per cent recovery in untreated cases), and Kalinowsky and Hoch (1952) describe a remission rate of 40 to 50 per cent in insulin treatment of schizophrenia. They conclude that catatonics and paranoids respond better to insulin treatment than do hebephrenic or simple schizophrenics. Even in those instances in which coma induction has provided symptomatic relief, the rate of readmission to mental hospitals within 5 years following discharge remains discouragingly high and differs little from that of untreated patients (Hinko and Lipschutz, 1947).

Sakel's original claims of successful treatment with insulin ranged as high as 75 per cent, but his work was not accepted everywhere because this treatment was not easy to manage and the theoretical rationale for its effectiveness was vague and difficult to believe. The hazards of treatment (irreversible coma, circulatory or respiratory collapse) and the need for extensive medical and nursing care during the 30 to 50 hours of coma made it a particularly difficult form of therapy.

The results of artificially induced deep coma are not fully explainable either on a physiological or psychological basis, but the empirical effect they produce—relief from severe symptoms—has been sufficient to encourage their use. These methods are still used in cases of schizophrenia that fail to respond to less drastic forms of therapy. In its heyday, chemical shock was used on every imaginable category of emotional disorder and proved most effective with depressive cases.

Electroconvulsive Therapy

In about 47 A.D., Scribonius Largus used an electric eel to administer nonconvulsive shock to relieve the headaches of a Roman emperor. Although the first convulsive use of electric shock was probably accomplished by the French physician J. B. LeRoy in 1755, its modern history dates from the work of Cerletti and Bini in Rome in 1938. Interestingly, determination of a safe dosage for human beings was accomplished by studying the dosage given to stupefy hogs for execution in a Roman slaughter house. This less dangerous and less complicated means of inducing convulsions, and the positive results it produced, made it a frequently used treatment for schizophrenics.

The procedure for the artificial production of convulsive seizures in mental patients involves, first, the injection of a curare-like muscle relaxant to soften the severity of the seizure and to prevent fractures during the convulsion. This is followed by the application, via electrodes placed at both temples, of from 70 to 130 volts for a period of about 0.5 seconds to induce a seizure lasting slightly less than one minute. The seizure resembles the grand mal attack experienced by epileptics. Treatments are administered 2 or 3 times a week and may range from 5 to 30 or more in number. After shock there is an impairment of memory and ability to learn, but this and confusional states clear up after a short time. Persisting brain damage is rare. Research explorations of variations and modifications in electroshock have focused on the spacing of treatments (Sargant, 1961) and on combining treatment with varied tranquilizing and antidepressant drugs (Cannicott, 1963; Wittenborn, Plante, Burgess, and Livermore, 1961).

Theories of exactly how an electroconvulsive shock works in treatment to alter human cognition, perception, emotion, and behavior are many, contradictory, and confusing. This is to say we are unclear about why it works but are willing to accept the simple fact that it does. Philosophical, psychological, and physiological explanations of all sorts have been tendered. It has been suggested, for example, that the increased attention of preparation for treatment is the most helpful aspect of the process. It has also been suggested that electroshock is viewed by the patient as a symbolic and well-deserved death for imaginary sins committed in the past. Is it a barbarous, sadistic assault on helpless patients or is it an alteration of brain function that allows the patient to regroup his psychic forces? Most physiological explanations are speculative in the extreme (shock acts as a biological stressor that forces the brain to mobilize its resources to face an emergency), and there is almost no experimental substantiation of them. It has also been suggested that shock unlocks a powerful chemical in the brain and that this chemical restores order to a disordered mind.

The effectiveness of electroshock has been greatest for the depressions. Improvement is dramatic and rapid in retarded or agitated depressive patients, and results are almost equally as good for manic patients. Improvement is not cure and it does not indicate a complete remission of symptoms; it does mean that better contact can be established with the patient during the time for intensive treatment.

In a number of studies, reports of recovery from depression have varied from 40 to 50 per cent recovered (Noyes and Kolb, 1958). The rate of spontaneous recovery from manic-depressive disorders has always been high, but comparisons of recovery rates for patients in the years before and after the discovery of electroshock (Bond, 1954) revealed an improved rate and a greatly shortened stay in the hospital after electroshock. While patients treated with electroshock experienced a more frequent recurrence of the disorder, they have had to remain hospitalized only one half the time of patients in the years before its discovery.

Catatonics have responded well to electroconvulsive therapy and simple and hebephrenic patients less well but, now, psychoactive drugs have replaced convulsive shock as a preferred treatment. For paranoid patients, since their symptom patterns seem to reflect a life-long pattern of difficult relationships with others, the results of electroshock are disappointing. Electroshock alleviates symptoms briefly, but relapse to the previous state of disorder occurs before long.

As with all other forms of treatment of schizophrenics, electroconvulsive therapy is most likely to have a favorable outcome if the disorder had an acute onset and has existed for only a brief period before treatment is begun.

Table 8.1 lists indicators of favorable and unfavorable prognosis following electroconvulsive therapy, but it is important to keep in mind that those conditions that indicate a greater or lesser chance of recovery following shock are the same ones that would weigh favorably or less favorably in the balance of recovery without therapy.

TABLE 8.1   PROGNOSIS FOLLOWING ELECTROCONVULSIVE THERAPY *

GREATER	LESS
Recent onset of disorder	Disorder has existed for some time
Rapid onset of disorder	Slower onset of disorder
Stable personality before disorder becomes apparent	Unstable personality before breakdown becomes apparent
High anxiety about the disorder	Low anxiety about the disorder
External stress more important than internal factors in causing the disorder	Internal factors outweight external stresses in causing the disorder

° From I. Rosen and E. Gregory. *Abnormal Psychology.* Philadelphia: W. B. Saunders Co., 1965.

PSYCHOSURGERY

At about the time of widespread interest in the "shock" therapies, Egas Moniz (1874–1955), a Spanish neurologist, came to believe that recurrent morbid ideas circulated in a cyclic fashion in the diseased brain of some patients and produced mental disorder. To temper and short-circuit this reaction, Moniz began surgically to disconnect the frontal lobes from the rest of the human brain in patients with "intractable" phychoses.

This procedure calmed some agitated patients, but it made vegetables of others—they walked and talked, and looked like human beings but they were without ambition, tact, imagination, or consciousness of the self (Greenblatt, 1967). Anxiety disappeared but it carried with it many of the features that made a person human. A part of the brain tissue, once destroyed, will not regenerate or replace itself. The person that once was is destroyed with surgical disconnection of the fibers of the frontal lobes from the rest of the brain.

This was a sad chapter in the history of somatic therapy, a chapter written by those who decided psychosurgery was necessary to "cure" mental illness. Opening the skull to let the evil spirits out had been practiced since the beginning of civilized history; unfortunately it produced a sophisticated modern counterpart. Surgeons disconnected parts of the brain from others to produce emotional and cognitive alteration in their patients but brain damage, once accomplished, ruled out alternative forms of therapy and treatment. Specialists literally "cut themselves off" from the possibility that therapy of other kinds may have succeeded.

In the brief period in which psychosurgery flourished (approximately 15 years), thousands upon thousands of patients were reduced to a state of damaged passivity that solved a cultural problem at the expense of the individual patient. We were awakened from the nightmare of psychosurgery by psychopharmacological advances that reduced the need for such drastic treatment nearly to zero. It is a chapter in treatment history that should not be forgotten by future generations of therapists. It was a savage surrender of therapy to surgery that spread rapidly across the world leaving in its wake an untold number of damaged human beings.

PSYCHOPHARMACOLOGY

The discovery of psychoactive chemicals offered a way out for therapists caught in the bear-trap of unresponsive cases that were excessively demanding of time and effort with little to justify this expenditure. If you were of an age to witness the magical transformation of hospital wards as the psychochemical era was ushered in, you might better comprehend the importance of the event. Patients once uncontrollable and intractable became docile, almost rational, and manageable, if not curable. The first application of the stimulants, depressants, and tranquilizers in mental hospitals was shockingly random and indiscriminate considering that so little was known of their effect on various patterns of disorder. Treatment today is much more sophisticated: the unwanted and unexpected side-effects are fewer, interaction effect of various drugs is better understood, and the results achieved in the drugged state are better controlled.

Drugs gave the harried ward physician time to pause and make a new evaluation of the complex problem of caring for an increasing number of severely disturbed human beings pumped into the mental hospitals by an expanding population. Drugs were as old as man foraging among the shrubs, plants, and roots of antiquity seeking relief from painful difficulties, and modern physicians have re-examined the old-wives' tales of leaf, root, and fermented juice cures of the ancients in the search for new compounds for remedy of emotional disorder.

The history of drug use in therapy is one of a sudden and explosive proliferation of a multitude of psychoactive agents, most of which were over-promoted by the drug companies. As Peterson (1966) indicated, "In common with virtually all new medical treatments, the considerable real worth of these drugs in the treatment of mental disorders was at first exaggerated through the use of inadequately designed research. Only 10 of the roughly 1,000 studies concerned with chlorpromazine therapy that were published between 1952 and 1956, for example, could be described as controlled" (p. 19). Research with drugs has hardly been a model of scientific excellence.

Placebos and their effects make the task of evaluation of drug therapy particularly difficult. Almost the entire catalogue of possible symptoms a human being can experience seems to be capable of relief by the harmless "sugar pill" doctors have employed for hundreds of years to achieve peace of mind for their patients. The magic of the placebo is amazing. Placebos even produce "side effects" of a kind that would be reasonable if the patient had been administered an actual medicine. In a study of thousands of patients, over 60 per cent reported relief from headaches after getting placebos, and similar percentages of relief have been reported for neuroses, colds, coughs, gastro-intestinal disorders, and a variety of other illnesses.

When drugs are evaluated scientifically, attention must be paid to this psychic component of scientific findings. All too often the enthusiasm of the researcher bent on proving his point interferes with an objective appraisal of the effects of the drug. Another peril is the conduct of research "in house" by drug companies with a vested interest in the compound. The general practitioner, harried by a multitude of responsibilities, may take at face value the questionable scientific findings presented in glowing terms in the drug company's brochure.

Peterson (1966) observes that despite these problems of evaluation there are several advantages to the use of drugs in therapy. Both clinically and scientifically, drugs have the advantage of control of the intensity and duration of treatment, and they cost less in time, effort, and money. Drugs can be an adjunct to other forms of therapy and produce effects (unlike psychosurgery where the act once done cannot be reconsidered) which can often be reversed.

The Tranquilizers

It is conceptually convenient to cast complex drugs into simple categories in which a single effect is ascribed to a single drug, but this seldom matches the fact of drug use. The first antidepressants, for example, increased the motor activity of patients but, at the same time, left them with depressive thoughts. Drugs, it was suggested, make the patient more "reactive" to stimuli but do little to change the content of his thoughts and perceptions.

There is no drug that acts on behavior alone; all drugs alter body chemistry and change the internal physical balance. The action of the drug differs from the drug's effect. Thus, tranquilizers (ataractics) are designed to have an effect on the patient's level of anxiety; but they may also have a sedative side effect. The patient may not, subjectively, be able to tell if he is tranquil or merely sleepy. The effect of either action may be a desired one, however.

The sedatives (barbiturates) produce an effect that resembles the tranquility of other drugs. They were first used medically in 1903 as a means of chemical restraint to replace the unpopular physical restraints (strait-jackets, etc.) long in use in asylums (Sharoff, 1967). The use of barbiturates was soon extended to include the treatment of schizophrenias of all kinds by continuous sedation for long periods of time. Today, sedatives (Nembutal, Amytal, Phenobarbital, etc.) are used to take the sting out of the psychic pains of rage, anxiety, guilt, and other unpleasant emotions. Restlessness and instability decrease when the depressant effect of these drugs occurs, but there is seldom a freeing of the patient from his psychotic symptoms. Sedatives are used primarily to deal with crisis situations in which unusual emotional stress is being experienced or is anticipated.

TRANQUILIZERS

THE PHENOTHIAZINES		RAUWOLFIA ALKALOIDS
Sparine		Serpasil
Vesperin		Harmonyl
Mellaril		Moderil
Compazine		Raudixin
Dartac		
Stelazine		
Permitil		
Thorazine		

MINOR TRANQUILIZERS

Librium	Softran	Listica
Valium	Soavitil	Levetran
Serax	Trancopal	Quiactin
Miltown, Equanil	Levanil	Ultran
Solacen	Striatran	Sycotrol

Tranquilizers are usually subdivided into major and minor, or strong and weak, categories. It is estimated that tranquilizers constitute about 10 per cent of the nearly 65 million prescriptions dispensed each year by pharmacists and that, for the general practitioner of medicine, tranquilizing agents make up the third most common drug prescribed. The bulk of this mass of "tranquility pills" being taken to calm our society is made up of minor tranquilizers. Surprisingly, there is no reliable evidence that these minor tranquilizers are any better than the harmless sugar coated placebos.

The tranquilizers are about a decade and a half old, dating from about 1953, and they are probably improperly named (Denber, 1967). It is true they appear to make agitated patients more "tranquil" but it is the progressive disappearance of symptoms in acute and chronic psychoses that makes the "tranquilizers" so valuable. Thus, the drugs are anti-anxiety and anti-psychotic in action. A detailed account of which drug is proper for which particular set of psychotic symptoms is not possible. Each drug does not have nearly so specific an action and, as we have seen, diagnosis and symptom description is far from an exact science.

Denber (1967) suggests that the following are among the many conditions appropriate for tranquilizer therapy: acute schizophrenia; manic, involutional, and senile psychoses; agitated depression; acute alcoholic and epileptic psychoses; psychoses due to mental deficiency or organic brain disorder. This prescription of tranquilizers applies equally to those displaying borderline psychotic symptoms. In short, tranquilizers are used with almost all kinds of disorder. Denber's list of symptoms so treatable (regardless of diagnosis) include tension, anxiety, hyperactivity, agitation, impulsiveness, aggressiveness, and auditory or visual hallucinations.

It is apparent that a great deal of art and trial and error characterize the use of psychoactive chemicals. As Fink and Itil (1967) observed, "The ways in which the organic therapies of schizophrenia are associated with alterations in behavior are unclear . . . [and] duration of illness, length of hospitalization, type of onset, previous treatment, age, social class, and educational level influence the selection of treatment" (p. 661–62). Some tranquilizers are known to have antidepressant effects as well, and this further scrambles the hoped for treatment utopia of one patient —one pill.

The tranquilizers once in most frequent use with psychotic patients were reserpine and chlorpromazine. Reserpine comes from the snakeroot plant (rauwolfia) and has been used in India for thousands of years. This drug was used initially to treat high blood pressure (hypertension) and to calm anxious and agitated patients. Its effectiveness was questioned by researchers (Segal and Shapiro, 1959), since placebos properly administered seemed to produce much the same benefit for patients.

Chlorpromazine was described as the drug that produces "indifference." It was used to limit anxiety and agitation in patients. Recently, it has been administered in combination with other drugs and has produced better results than a simple placebo (Fink, Klein, and Kramer, 1963). A number of controlled, long-term studies report an adequate level of effectiveness of chlorpromazine (Caffey, Diamond, Frank, Grasberger, Herman, Klett, and Rothstein, 1964; Casey, Bennett, Lindley, Hollister, Gordon, and Springer, 1960).

The rauwolfia derivatives have fallen into some disfavor in recent recent years, and the use of phenothiazines has increased accordingly. This has occured primarily because the phenothiazines have produced fewer side effects and more immediate results in the patient.

As we noted earlier, a simple schema of one drug-one patient is unworkable. Thus, no simple chart of psychosis and appropriate drug dosage level can be presented. In general, however, the major tranquilizers are administered to those with acute or chronic psychoses, agitated depressions, and organic brain disorders of many kinds. The rauwolfia compounds are used for both acute and chronic schizophrenia and for agitated states apparent in the manic psychoses or senile conditions. The minor tranquilizers are most often administered to neurotic rather than psychotic patients, but they have been used adjunctively with major tranquilizers.

Scientific assessment of the effect of tranquilizers on psychotics has most often failed to indicate that one drug is markedly better than the next for a specific disorder. All seem, in varying degrees, to produce the necessary sedative, tranquilizing, and anti-psychotic effects.

The Antidepressants

In the late 1950's the antidepressant drugs were discovered as an enlightened accident in the search for new and better tranquilizers. These new drugs acted as antidepressants, stimulants, or euphoria-producers in distressed patients but had no significant effect when administered to "normals." Since depression ranks close to schizophrenia as a serious mental health problem, these discoveries marked an important therapeutic stride forward.

Depression can exist as a separate symptom of psychological difficulty, of course, but it is often an important component of syndromes such as psychosis, organic brain disease, and the like. Some remedy for this condition was available before the discovery of the antidepressants in the form of amphetamine substitutes (Ritalin, Meratran). These mood-elevators, however, often had fairly severe side-reactions (jumpiness, insomnia, loss of appetite, jitters, etc.); the euphoria lasted only a few hours and was followed by an even deeper depression. Increased tolerance was usual and the escalation of dosage needed to produce an effect was excessive. Substitutes for the amphetamines proved to be little better than the originals.

The common antidepressants in use today are:

Marsilid	Niamid
Nardil	Parnate
Marplan	Tofranil
Elavil	Norpramin
Auentyl	Ritalin
Deaner	Dexedrine
Benzedrine	

The antidepressants are particularly useful in depressions marked by anxiety. These drugs trigger a chemical state of alertness in the brain that is reflected in the patient's behavior and rouses him from his inattention to the outside world. Yet, we must be aware that nearly 30 per cent of depressed patients report improvement in response to the administration of simple placebos (Cole and Davis, 1967), and this fact makes it difficult to appraise the true effect of antidepressant drugs.

The most promising effects of antidepressants are to be found in the affective disorders. Paranoid patients and classic schizophrenics of all kinds respond less well and sometimes suffer adverse effects (Hordern, Burt, and Holt, 1965; Marks and Pare, 1965). Electroconvulsive treatment for acute depressions seems still to hold a therapeutic edge over drug application since, if possible suicide is an important consideration, electroconvulsion seems to lift the depression with greater speed and certainty. Energizers, such as imipramine, phenelzine, and ipronizaid, have been compared favorably with placebo administration and electric shock (Wechsler, Grosser, and Greenblatt, 1965).

Any attempt to evaluate the many studies of antidepressants fails to be convincing at this moment, however, since one type of antidepressant may be completely ineffective with a particular patient while another very similar drug will produce dramatic effects in him. Antidepressants have been combined experimentally with tranquilizers (one for the anxiety and one for the depression), but no trustworthy and controlled studies of the outcome have yet appeared. In something of the same fashion, electroshock therapy and antidepressants have been used in combination. A burst of enthusiastic studies followed the combined application of these remedies, but conflicting and contradictory results with these combinations suggest that the hope that drugs could replace electroshock therapy or at least decrease the number of treatments necessary has yet to be realized.

The discovery of psychoactive drugs has made an astounding difference in our capacity to treat seriously disordered mental patients. Drug therapy still has the quality of an experimental art about it, and it will be some time before we sort out the ever-increasing mass of newly synthesized compounds in terms of which drug, or combination of drugs, best fits which diagnostic categories. The integration of drugs and psychotherapy has yet to be completely explored and remains a vital next step in our understanding of the treatment of severe mental disorder (Lesse, 1966).

Drugs and Child Therapy

Drugs have become an integral part of the treatment of disturbed children despite the fact that the child, as a growing organism, presents quite special problems in evaluating the effect of the drug (Fish, 1967; Fisher, 1959). When children display excessive activity and excitement or are chronically anxious, impulsive, or irritable (over-reactive), drugs are increasingly prescribed. The theoretical basis for this hasty application of drug therapy rests on the assumption that the child needs to be returned to a "normal" state as quickly as possible in order not to warp the course of his development.

The goal of drug therapy is to reduce or modify symptoms in order to facilitate the execution of a comprehensive plan of therapy that may include psychotherapy and/or manipulation or alteration of the child's environment. Therapists agree chemicals alone cannot undo attitudes and patterns of learned behavior that are a part of the child's disturbance.

The phenothiazine compounds (tranquilizers) are recommended for children with schizophrenia or organic brain disease. If the schizophrenic child patient fails to respond, the rauwolfia alkaloids are suggested despite the fact they have a less reliable action (Fish, 1967). For older children (adolescents) stimulants, antidepressants, and tranquilizers are used very much in the same fashion as for adults. This delicate therapeutic task of drugging children should not be viewed lightly by the therapist. In the words of Barbara Fish (1967):

> Drugs would destroy therapy if the doctor used them as a quick expedient to avoid responsibility for the child's complex problems in living or if he saw drugs as the ultimate weapon of authority to enforce compliance on a problem child or if he felt drugs were a measure of desperation to be used only after all other measures had failed. Children differ from adults only in that they are frequently more acutely aware of the doctor's unconscious intent and are less tolerant of his rationalizations (p. 1471).

An interesting sidelight to this observation is that again and again results obtained by drugs are inexplicably opposite from those intended by the chemical therapy. Some violently hyperactive children can receive a mixture of powerful sedatives and tranquilizers only to display even more frantic and frenetic behavior. Then, for reasons that remain unknown, they are calmed and "slowed down" when their medication is shifted to an energizing drug such as benzedrine. There is an appalling shortage of adequate information about drug action in both adults and children, but it seems somehow less ethical to drug uncomprehending children in our present state of scientific ignorance.

THERAPY AND PROGNOSIS

Whether the method is exclusively psychotherapeutic or a mixture of somatic treatment and psychotherapy, there exists a broad general hypothesis (based on clinical experience) regarding prognosis for the various psychoses and prediction of length of stay in a psychiatric hospital.

Being hospitalized is, in itself, a unique social and group experience for each patient. Hospitalization provides a sudden and drastic separation from the problems, pressures, and difficulties that make life on the outside impossible at the same moment that it thrusts the patient into strange surroundings, reduces his freedom of action, and severs him from the support of family and loved ones (Jersild, 1967; Ackerman and Kempster, 1967). The hospitalized person must learn how to act the role of a patient. This task must be faced in a new and strange setting.

In many respects the mental hospital is a setting designed with little regard for the environment from which the patient was removed and to which he must one day return. The social stigma of being hospitalized for serious emotional disorder remains so great that hospitals, as they are presently arranged, may be a necessary but socially and psychologically costly event in the patient's life. We must one day come to view hospitals as institutions that help people to live rather than as isolated, locked buildings that house persons dangerous to themselves or to the community.

The variables that seem significant in predicting length of stay in the hospital are contained in Table 8.2.

TABLE 8.2 VARIABLES SIGNIFICANT IN CLINICAL PREDICTIONS OF LENGTH OF STAY IN PSYCHIATRIC HOSPITALS *

SHORT HOSPITAL STAY	LONG HOSPITAL STAY
Good clinical impression (in general)	Poor home situation; family not interested in his return
A good previous work record or employment available on release	Patient not motivated to leave
Family interest in patient	Diagnosed "organic disorder" on admission
Alcoholism a major symptom	Long psychiatric history, i.e. chronic case
Patient motivated to leave hospital	Passive, withdrawn
Previous stays in hospital have been brief	
First hospitalization; first psychotic attack	

* Based on R. Johnston and B. F. McNeal. Statistical versus clinical prediction: Length of neuropsychiatric hospital stay. *J. Abnorm. Psychol.*, 1967, 72, 335–40.

It is obvious that the diagnosis itself is not a trustworthy index, alone, of the hospital experience of the patient.

Prognosis includes more than length of hospitalization as an indicator; it includes some estimate of the relative freedom from symptoms for the patient in the years following hospitalization. Table 8.3 indicates that young depressives fare much better than young schizophrenics. The rate of readmission for those diagnosed schizophrenic is the vexing problem all therapists face when they undertake treatment.

TABLE 8.3   PROGNOSIS FOR YOUNG SCHIZOPHRENICS AND DEPRESSIVES—THREE
YEARS AFTER DISCHARGE FROM A MENTAL HOSPITAL *

	READMITTED TO HOSPITAL	FREE OF SYMPTOMS
Depressive	20%	34%
Schizophrenic	72%	11%

* Adapted from J. A. Clark and B. L. Mallett. A follow-up study of schizophrenia and depression in young adults. *Brit. J. Psychiat.*, 1965, **109**, 491–99.

Prognosis among the various psychotic disorders would suggest that hebephrenic and simple schizophrenics do least well, paranoiacs occupy an intermediate position, and acute catatonics bear the best prognosis. Chronic catatonics are, judged by the continued recurrence of the disorder, not very hopeful cases (Lehmann, 1967). If the disorder occurs in childhood or before puberty, the prognosis is poor whatever the diagnosis. In recent years, the ability of the patient to cooperate with drug therapy has become an added indicator of prognosis.

The average schizophrenic has from four to five times better chance for a favorable therapeutic outcome today than he might have had fifty years ago. Nearly one half of those suffering acute breakdowns are released from the hospital within six months to one year, and an even higher percentage may eventually expect to return home. Today, fewer schizophrenics vegetate in the back wards of hospitals deprived of all treatment; some end up as stablized chronic cases that don't get worse but simply don't improve, and many more experience a remission of symptoms that will allow a restricted but modestly normal life back in the community. Even the once dim prospect of full and permanent recovery exists for more of our psychotic population than has ever existed before. Exact percentages in each of the above categories are difficult to obtain and of questionable reliability, but there is little question of the broad accuracy of this appraisal of the efficacy of various kinds of treatment of psychosis today.

Hospitals are, of course, staffed by doctors, and some researchers (Uhlenhuth and Park, 1964) worked with depressed psychoneurotic out-patients and compared imipramine with placebo administration to ex-amine the possibility that patients got more relief from some doctors rather than others, i.e., their subjective response to either the drug or a placebo depended on their perception of, and response to, the doctor giving the drug. No significant evidence was obtained that the doctor, rather than the drug, was the source of relief.

It is an interesting commentary on the nature of psychochemical treatment that in our modern hospitals who prescribes what medicine for which disorder is closely linked to the experience and availability of the therapist (Mendel, 1967). Inexperienced therapists prescribed tran-quilizers more often than their experienced colleagues, and if the patient happens to see the doctor at a time when few therapists are available (weekends, for example) there is a greater likelihood that medicine will be prescribed for his condition. The psychoactive chemicals have proved to be a handy solution to many therapeutic challenges.

The relationship of therapy to prognosis, then, proves to be a com-plicated affair requiring substantial sophistication on the part of an in-vestigator bent on determining the source and reasons for remission of symptoms in psychotics. If somatic treatment is not the answer, then perhaps psychotherapy is what is needed. We will turn our attention to that subject in the next chapter.

SUMMARY

The historical persuasion that mental disturbance was a kind of physical illness led therapists naturally to manipulate the body chemistry and brain functioning of patients in the search for symptom relief and cure. The discovery in the 1930's that patients improved following the artificial induction of convulsive seizures led to the widespread use of insulin and metrazol as almost the sole form of treatment for psychotic patients. When the means of inducing convulsions electrically was perfected, this method soon eclipsed all others and became a standard treatment in mental institutions. Contemporary with the induction of chemical and electrical convulsions was the more radical solution of surgically produc-ing brain damage to control the symptoms of chronic patients.

Organic treatment today is almost exclusively of a psychopharmacological nature. Psychic tranquilizers, energizers, stimulants, and antidepressants are chosen to treat every conceivable kind of mental disorder, and the refinement of new psychoactive drugs is occurring at an incredible rate. A great deal of trial and error (empirical medicine) still characterizes this recent approach to organic treatment, and only a primitive beginning has been made on the development of refined techniques of drug therapy. This conclusion is most evident in drug therapy in which psychological factors such as the doctor-patient relationship play a prominent part.

Whatever the choice of therapy, evaluation of the effects of medication must take into account the condition of the patient (and his history) at the time of hospitalization. The exact relationship of therapy to prognosis in psychosis is yet an indeterminate one.

The Psychotherapies

On its surface, psychotherapy is disarmingly simple since it is essentially a process of one person talking to another until the emotional, cognitive, or behavioral disorder disappears. The usual forms of psychotherapy, according to White (1964), involve a number of related processes. Psychotherapy includes the therapeutic relationship of a client and a trained professional; it focuses on the expression of the patient's feelings and attitudes and on recognition or interpretation of these by the therapist. The desired end product of this relationship is some alteration in the feelings, attitudes, beliefs, and behavior of the patient to achieve a pattern of living less painful and unrewarding to the patient and less disruptive of his relationships with others. The varieties of psychotherapy are great; Ford and Urban (1963), for example, compare ten distinct views and approaches, but the list could be extended to much greater length. Despite the variety of forms of psychotherapy that have evolved in American psychotherapeutic practice, the most common approaches are dynamic in nature and owe an enormous debt to the influence of Sigmund Freud and psychoanalytic theory.

DYNAMIC PSYCHOTHERAPY

Psychoanalysis

Sigmund Freud (1856–1939) was the author of the theoretical principles on which psychoanalytic treatment was based, and the form of this approach to disorder in man has, among its orthodox followers, under-

154

gone startlingly little change since its exposition in the early 1900's (Freud, 1938; Freud, 1924–1953; Freud, 1953–1964). Few other forms of treatment have remained intact over so long a period of time and the critics of psychoanalysis have used this fact to level charges of "cultism," "conservatism," and "dogmatism" at its practitioners. Freud's works have been revised, modified, altered, and expanded by Neo-Freudian theorists, but these changes have found little acceptance with the orthodox psychoanalysts of this era.

The emphasis of orthodox psychoanalytic treatment has been on the analysis of unconscious material (dreams, fantasies, slips of the tongue, etc.), and the analysis of the transference relationship of patient to therapist. The psychoanalytic technique assumes that during the course of treatment repressed (unconscious) material will surface, be examined, analyzed, and interpreted until the patient is able, without conflict, to have insight about it and to assimilate it into the realm of conscious psychic processes. Once unconscious motives and forces become conscious, these theorists say, they can be dealt with and managed in voluntary ways and need no longer influence the patient from outside the reaches of his awareness.

The content of the unconscious may become visible to the therapist as the patient expresses himself in analytic sessions, but the patient is thought to resist becoming aware of the meaning of this material since it is anxiety-laden and consciously distressing. One important means of detecting the disordered perceptions, feelings, and cognitions of the patient, then, is provided in the development of what has been labeled the "transference neurosis." The psychic difficulties of the patient get expressed toward the therapist in the "transference neurosis" in a manner typical both of the patient's usual relations with others and of the unresolved feelings and conflicts he retains from his childhood experiences with significant other persons.

As the patient and therapist work to understand and resolve this inappropriate (but typical) patient reaction to the therapist, insight is gained into the unresolved childhood feelings and conflicts that are thought now to dominate the adult's relatedness to life and to the world. This stress on cognitive insight about the emotional experiences that have produced disturbed patterns of behavior is characteristic of psychoanalytic treatment methods. Using verbal means, a form of cognitive and emotional relearning (based on insight) takes place as the patient comes to realize how inaccurate and inappropriate is his style of life. The childish motives that impelled him to action in the past can now be controlled and modified by the patient.

This is a bare outline of psychoanalytic methods of treatment, and it does a disservice to the richness and complexity of the method and the theoretical principles on which psychoanalysis is based. But, classic psychoanalytic methods have not often been applied to the many varieties of psychotic and schizophrenic disorders in man which are our prime concern. The results of the application of psychoanalysis has been less than spectacular. Standard psychoanalytic procedures did not evolve from the study of psychosis, and they have not proved particularly successful in their treatment.

For traditional psychoanalysts, the approach to treatment of the psychoses is related to their conception of the difference between neurotic and psychotic adaptations to life (Mack and Semrad, 1967). Psychosis reflects a conflict between the individual and his environment while neurotic conflicts are principally within the personality, as in the conflict between necessary adult behavior and unconscious infantile urges and impulses. The psychoses are thought to be produced by defects in the ego's capacity to integrate the diverse features of life and to meet the demands for the establishment of effective interpersonal relations with people, for contact with the commonly accepted definition of reality, and for the control impulses.

The psychotic not only fails to meet these demands but he uses the quite primitive, childlike defenses of flight, inhibition, and social withdrawal to avoid the challenges of society. These simple, unsophisticated, disorganized defenses then characterize the behavior that labels him psychotic. The conflicts of the psychotic are judged to be extremely basic in nature, revolving about primary narcissism (fixation on one's self and inability to form deep relationships with others), and about disruptive experiences during early training of bodily functions (eating, waste elimination). Disordered behavior, thus, is difficult to remedy since it represents an ego hardly able to accomplish what is needed for civilized living.

Classic psychoanalytic treatment of the psychoses is unsuitable since the resources a patient needs for its success are simply not available to him; it is a method that requires a coherent degree of psychological organization the psychotic is unable to produce. Even in ideal circumstances, the psychoanalytic patient undergoes a difficult emotional ordeal; the psychotic patient cannot manage this additional burden.

Psychoanalytic practices have been modified in some respects but a more important event has been the development of the psychoanalytically oriented, or based, psychotherapy called dynamic psychotherapy. The trappings of psychoanalysis were abandoned, its principles were modified and mixed with those of other disciplines (learning theory, for example), and rigid procedures were replaced with a more flexible approach to treatment (Alexander and Selesnick, 1966).

Psychotherapy

Redlich and Freedman (1966) describe, for example, common-ground analytic psychotherapy. This form of therapy, an offshoot of classic psychoanalytic techniques, is now the method most often taught practitioners in training centers. In concert with chemotherapy, this is what most neurotic or psychotic patients will be given in the way of individual treatment.

In this conception, the "doctor who wants to help you" is an integral part of any psychotherapy, not only because the role of doctor is highly sanctioned and prestigious in our society but because he brings to the relationship an objective interest in the patient's problems and a positive regard for the patient as a person. The confidence and security of the patient-therapist relationship does not mean uncritical support or acceptance of the way the person is, but it promises help where help is most needed.

In this setting and with this relationship, discussion between patient and therapist focuses on the patient's perceptions of his problems, his emotions, and his behavior. The therapist attempts to clarify aspects of the patient's difficulties in order both to increase the patient's awareness about how such situations arise and to have the patient take a closer look at himself and others and the nature of his relationship to the world. In this sense the therapist offers a set of trained eyes with which to examine the patient's life. The new perceptions, new cognitions, and new patterns of response the patient must acquire are learned with the help of the teacher-therapist.

Following an initial appraisal of the nature of the patient's problem and determination of the capacity to profit from a "talking therapy," a variety of supportive, directive, or persuasive techniques may be applied to the principal complaints and problems. As therapeutic progress is made, it is hoped that the patient will be able to understand the nature of his problems, to change the nature of his response to others, and to lead a life in which he can, on his own, continue to change and mature. Dynamic psychotherapy is designed to mark the initiation of a lifetime of continued self-appraisal and the beginning of a more comfortable adjustment.

We referred to psychotherapy as a talking cure, and this technique has obvious limitations for psychotic patients. The symbolic abstraction that is language and the world of ideas, concepts, and thoughts are most comfortable and useful for the undisturbed members of our middle socioeconomic classes and may be alien to the disturbed members of the more heavily populated lower socioeconomic classes. The capacity of many members of our society to respond profitably to a talking relationship with a therapist may be quite limited by the nature of their early experience and training.

This limitation of direct verbal psychotherapy with seriously disturbed persons is best illustrated in a clinical observation by Joseph Church (1961), "Many schizophrenics . . . not only express bizarre ideas but express them bizarrely" (p. 159). There can be no better example of the bizarre interaction of language and thinking than that of the patient who became fascinated with the name CHURCH and studied it until he became aware that it "both begins and ends with CH, which are the third and eighth letters of the alphabet; and so the word can be written 38UR38" (p. 159). This observation was then mixed with knowledge of the Korean War, the then important 38th parallel, and the symbol for uranium. The patient was convinced that Professor Church was "imbued with atomic energy" since the two H's in his name indicated H^2 or heavy hydrogen. In such an instance language becomes the vehicle for expression of a reality "shot through with baffling or malevolent forces." If the language and the meaning of language are disturbed for a patient, it becomes quite a complicated matter to use verbal therapy to alter his psychotic state.

The goals of dynamic psychotherapy, as Coleman (1964) views them, include insight into and resolution of handicapping or disabling conflicts, an improved sense of self and delineation of one's identity, alteration of undesirable patterns and habits of reaction, improved competency in interpersonal relationships, and the modification of inaccurate assumptions about the self and the world to make it possible to have a more meaningful and fulfilling way of life.

The goals of psychotherapy and the methods of achieving these goals have varied widely in the past and will continue to vary in days to come. Difficulties in achieving the basic step—reaching the psychotic patient— have most often required the use of adjunctive means such as drugs to pave the way for the verbal psychotherapeutic transaction.

Will (1967) notes that despite the limitations on psychotherapeutic intervention in schizophrenia there exists a core set of principles that apply to such therapy when attempted:

1. The behavior of the schizophrenic is viewed as dynamically purposeful and capable of being understood.
2. Current behavior is related to past experience but the present—in the form of the therapist-patient relationship—is emphasized.
3. Symbolic and nonverbal activity are treated with as much importance as words.
4. The patient-therapist relationship is used as a tool to reduce anxiety

and to provide opportunities for the patient to learn about himself and grow.

5. The therapist refuses to accept patient behavior at face-value when it is directed at destroying the therapeutic relationship, e.g. hostility, withdrawal, etc.

Psychotherapy becomes, then, a special social process instituted to help the schizophrenic find his way back from the depths of his disturbance. The task is to get the schizophrenic to abandon past patterns of living and learn new ones. The therapist becomes a person capable of dealing with destructive psychotic patterns of living in a more benign and understanding way than have others in the past life of the schizophrenic.

There are obvious complications in this therapeutic transaction. Chronically disordered patients (hebephrenics or paranoid schizophrenics, for example) may have settled into a way of life that is unsatisfactory but is judged by them to be safer than taking a chance on the possibility of a better life. In addition, hospitalization can become a comfortable way of life that fosters a dependency that vitiates the desire to change.

The psychotic patient—whether acute or chronic—is being asked by the therapist to undertake what he both needs and fears most, a human relationship. Trapped in a web of disordered emotional, cognitive, intellectual, and perceptual disortions of the world, the demands of therapy may be far more than he can manage. Psychotherapy with psychotics is an unusually demanding task that can only succeed if conducted by a mature therapist in full command of his own personal and psychological life.

It would take us too far afield to draw an extended series of comparisons between classic psychoanalytic and modified psychodynamic theory and practice but some common features of modern theories and practices might help us understand the form this evolution has taken. Sundberg and Tyler (1962) indicate that despite the differing emphasis contained in the varieties of current psychodynamic views, these views share many similarities.

Most current methods of psychotherapy concentrate on "bringing about *a sufficient lowering of the patient's level of anxiety so that he will be able to permit himself to explore the painful areas of his experience*" (p. 293). Thus, the privacy, confidentiality, and freedom from interruption characteristic of the therapeutic interview is valued in common by all forms of therapy.

All therapists must be capable of learning to deal with anxious human beings. In this respect, a therapist must be a person emotionally stronger than the patient and must be able to share this emotional strength with him. Modern psychotherapists must also be able to create a secure patient-therapist relationship that can become a vehicle for productive change in the patient. As Sundberg and Tyler (1962) note, Freud and the classic position insisted, at first, that insight be achieved in therapy. Later, the relationship of therapist and patient—marked by the transference phenomenon—assumed greater importance. Countertransference —how the therapist reacts and relates to the patient—for example, became an issue of prime importance to traditional therapists.

There are other common factors worth mentioning. Whatever the theoretical disposition of the therapist, for example, he must deal with the problem of establishing a connection between the patient's inner and outer worlds. A patient's internal reaction to the forces of the real world is not always predictable and may not match the "normal" experience. In a sense every therapist must learn to see the world through his patient's eyes and must find the means of making the internal and external worlds compatible, or at least capable of being dealt with. It is evident that this goal is most difficult to achieve among severely disturbed patients whose contact with the real world is weakest.

Finally, some action must take place. The patient must do more than ruminate philosophically about the nature of his plight. He must commit himself to action, he must try to alter his style of life, and he must make decisions about how he will meet present and future challenges. This suggests that every therapist must find the means of shifting the patient from a passive pattern of response to an active attempt to make life different for himself.

The methods by which these goals are accomplished differ between therapists subscribing to different treatment philosophies, but the goals seem to be held in common. The methods of most modern therapies are modifications of classic psychoanalysis in which there has been a shift in emphasis, a modification of basic doctrine, and a revision of technique to suit current problems of this era.

Two additional modern issues need discussion at this point: the use of drugs in therapy and the effectiveness of psychotherapy. The discovery of psychoactive drugs promises to modify the form of dynamic psychotherapy even more radically than in the past, but justification for this necessary change becomes apparent when the scientific evidence for the effectiveness of psychotherapy is examined.

1. Drugs and Psychotherapy

Mortimer Ostow (1962) has tackled the difficult issue of the use of pharmaceutic agents as an integral part of psychotherapy. To illustrate the use of drugs with paranoid schizophrenia and paranoia, Ostow recounts a case in which he reports, with staggering and refreshing honesty, that the "conduct of the drug therapy was rather clumsy" (p. 222). Overdosage—one of the most frequent pitfalls of drug therapy—is described, but the greatest value in this case study is the sensitive and detailed account of the treatment.

Ostow considers the possible complications of mixing a "talking cure" with chemical agents but concludes, "a drug can. . . undo the ego distortion and disruption which are responsible for the florid symptoms of an acute neurotic or psychotic crisis" (p. 4). Ostow is fully cognizant of the palliative nature of drug use and notes that, "the pathogenic process will sooner or later reassert itself, and unless it is countered by one of these pharmaceutic agents, it will once more bring about the clinical picture of neurosis or psychosis" (p. 4).

Drugs can reassemble a fragmented ego, protect the patient from times of acute stress, relieve painful symptoms, and establish a basic security from which psychotherapy can then proceed. Drugs, however, are also a tempting substitute for therapeutic acumen and can sometimes be used when the therapist becomes uncertain of the course he ought to pursue or anxious about the rising distress of the patient. A drug cannot give insight into the dynamic interrelation of parent and child (LaVietes, 1967) nor can it substitute for taking a more realistic view of one's self and how one relates to one's fellow man (Frank, 1967). The patient freed of the oppression of his symptoms may, in fact, resist the painful encounter with himself that is an integral part of psychotherapy.

As Ostow (1962) suggests, the behavioral consequences of drug-ingestion do not always match the glowing descriptions promulgated by drug manufacturers. Psychiatry has certainly been revolutionized by the refinement of drug therapies, but their use needs to be regulated by practical clinical experience and modified by the individual variations that inevitably occur and always defy the generalizations drug sellers make.

Drugs, according to Ostow, have their effect primarily on the level of psychic energy and the form of psychic functioning. The idea of psychic "energy" has a prolonged history as an early and vital aspect of Freud's view of man. But, times have changed since Freud and the pure vision of psychoanalysis and psychotherapy has for some years been corrupted by new drug discoveries. Interestingly, by all modern accounts, Freud would have been the first theorist to have accepted drugs as an adjunct to the therapeutic process.

There, of course, is no rational basis on which psychotherapists reject drugs as helpful agents. If drugs are dispensed with sufficient regard to their effect and the consequence this effect has in the therapeutic process, they can make an enormous contribution to the welfare of the patient. The difficulty is that drugs can easily dominate the relationship of therapist and patient to the detriment of both. Drugs clearly are the wave of the future and therapists *must* learn to use them and to adapt their therapeutic approach accordingly. The patient—the primary source of our concern—should be granted the advantage of whatever modern therapeutic science can offer him. But, drugs should be used as therapy rather than as a means for subduing psychotic patients.

2. Is Psychotherapy Effective?

Most professionals believe psychotherapy works—makes a significant difference in the lives of their patients—but this belief is an article of clinical faith that has yet to be subjected to a valid scientific test and this faith is least tested with psychotics. There have been a number of attempts to capture the elusive truth of the matter.

Research in the last decade and a half was stimulated by the work, in England, of H. J. Eysenck (1952). Eysenck and his coworkers divided neurotic patients into three groups: those treated psychoanalytically, those treated with nonpsychoanalytic psychotherapy, and those who received no psychotherapy at all or were treated by physicians without psychiatric training. Eysenck reviewed a number of studies of results obtained for these three groups of patients and concluded that psychotherapy of any variety is of little value for neurotic patients.

There were, of course, a great many outcries against this conclusion. Without incontrovertible evidence to contradict Eysenck's claims, these outcries were necessarily limited to criticism of Eysenck's interpretation of the statistical data published by others. Some theorists concluded that Eysenck had done no more than compound a number of errors by treating the reported outcomes of therapy as if they were equivalent from study to study, i.e., he assumed that the patients in the various reports were equally disturbed to begin with, were of approximately the same age, sex, socioeconomic and intellectual status, and had received equally good therapy.

Conclusions about the helpfulness of the patient-therapist relationship, when compared with other forms of assistance to patients, can only be made when an adequately designed and controlled experiment is accomplished. This will be a massive undertaking that cannot reasonably be begun until it is possible to reach agreement about the meaning of such words as "cured," "improved," and "symptom-free." In addition, we must agree about the instruments of measurement used to assess the condition of the patient prior to treatment, the nature of the therapeutic experience, and the condition of the patient following treatment. Follow-up of psychotic patients returned to the community has been so sparse that little more than statistical (head-counting) evidence has been accumulated to date. The effectiveness of psychotherapy with psychotics must, truthfully, be reported as essentially unknown at this time.

The question of effectiveness of psychotherapy will probably, one day, be answered on a conditional basis, i.e., effectiveness depends upon the nature of the patient, his circumstances and life history, his therapist, and the social environment in which the transaction takes place.

VARIATIONS IN PSYCHOTHERAPY

American psychotherapists have been a restless breed when it comes to innovation and experimentation with treatment techniques and devices. We will take time to explore the principles of new approaches primarily because they seem increasingly to be useful in solving the problem of too few therapists and too many patients.

Experimentation continues, and the reader should have some sense of the variety of techniques and approach employed. For example, fellow patients have been pressed into therapeutic service when they can be useful as "intermediate therapists," capable of reaching patients who don't trust the ward physician (Pfeiffer, 1967). In Boston, beer and tender loving care have been applied in a hospital setting. Patients have an afternoon "beer and social hour," are expected to behave in a mature fashion, and respond extremely well (Volpe and Kastenbaum, 1967).

Rubins (1967) has used multiple therapists in an assault on the patient's problems; Rosen (1953) has employed a direct and forceful approach in which he becomes a magical and powerful person to the patient, fearlessly entering the patient's fantasy world and interpreting its meaning to him. Frieda Fromm-Reichman (1959), with an infinite patience peculiar to her, has used her unusual sense of empathy, sympathy, and understanding to pentrate the psychotic world, while Searles (1965) has used his own emotional response to patients as a therapeutic clue to the patients' impulses, feelings, and behavior.

The variations and possibilities are incalculable. Let us first examine a long-lasting variation (group psychotherapy), and then appraise one of the most recent innovations (behavior therapy), to gain an understanding of the current therapeutic scene.

Group Psychotherapy

Since problems of human adjustment inevitably involve relationships with other people, planned group interaction guided by trained persons could be effective in altering the cognitive, perceptual, emotional, and behavioral patterns of patients. The patient can learn, in group sessions, that he does not stand alone and troubled in the world. Awareness that others feel the same impulses, make the same mistakes, and suffer the same social rebuffs can be a valuable insight.

Sharing problems with others has an age-old curative effect, just as investing a part of one's self in helping others seems to benefit disturbed persons. A patient in group therapy can avoid the painful direct confrontation that might characterize his interaction with a personal therapist until the moment he feels ready to manage it comfortably. The approaches to the conduct of group sessions vary widely and are subject to constant experimentation (Dreikurs, 1956; Mullan, 1957). Although group therapy has most often been applied to neurotic disorders, Peyman (1956) reports its application to schizophrenics with some success.

Gruen (1966) has recently suggested that in those who remain in group therapy (from one quarter to one third drop out) certain personality characteristics are evident. Thus, the flexible perception of authority, the ability to express rather than suppress or repress anger, and the willingness to establish emotional relationships with others seem to contribute to a successful experience with this form of therapy. These characteristics are not usual in psychotic patients.

There is less than adequate evidence regarding the degree and extent of effectiveness of these group efforts at psychotherapy. Forms of group therapy have been experimented with in at least as great variety as individual methods, but adequate systematic appraisal of the outcome of group therapy has been lacking. Clinical impressions of success have been abundant, but a fully controlled matched study (with follow-up over time) is rare.

What is intriguing about group therapy is the quality of social naturalness it suggests. Somehow, there seems hope for disturbed man if, working with his fellow human beings, he can come to understand more of himself and learn to deal more effectively with others.

Most often, when groups of patients are a heterogeneous collection (rather than all of one diagnostic kind), therapists tend to exclude paranoid patients (for fear they will incorporate other group members in their delusional system), hypermanic patients, and hallucinating psychotics (Wolf, 1967). Ambulatory psychotics in fair contact with others can be included in the group. Combined individual and group psychotherapy for the same patient has become an increasingly favored method (Sager, 1967), but this combination too is limited primarily to psychotic patients in fairly good contact with others and free of massive distortions of the real world (Whitaker and Lieberman, 1964).

Group psychotherapy is a step forward in our treatment methods, but it remains talk therapy and interpersonal therapy restricted to a limited segment of the psychotic population. Simple schizophrenics, hebephrenics, paranoids, and catatonics are all possible candidates for the method if they are in remission from the most destructive of their symptoms and have begun to re-establish contact with others. This is too limited a reach for any therapeutic technique designed to service the large population of hospitalized psychotic patients.

Behavior Therapy

A recent approach to producing change in human behavior patterns is reported by Bandura (1967). Behavioral psychotherapy proceeds on the premise that much of what has been designated as pathology (disease) might better be viewed as a distorted way of coping with the environment the individual has learned while growing up. Psychotherapeutic treatment should consist, then, of a process of social relearning using the basic principles of learning theory. This new and vigorous theoretical offshoot has stimulated a great deal of experimentation designed to elaborate the details both of method and theory (Bandura and Walters, 1963; Eysenck, 1964; Urban and Ford, 1967).

Behavioral therapy deals frequently with the "models" that pattern behavior and serve as examples for the younger members of our society. Modeling, reinforcement, and extinction procedures, they believe, can be used to shape behavior initially or to reorganize or eliminate abnormal behavior when applied appropriately, consistently, and with the proper timing. These methods of reinforcing certain patterns of behavior while extinguishing other less desirable ones can be applied without the complex and detailed training required for traditional psychotherapists.

Behavior learning methods demand discipline and control on the part of the behavioral "therapist." The use of operant techniques, i.e., punishment and reward following responses to modify behavior. Operant learning techniques can be used to increase certain behaviors while decreasing the appearance of others and, thus, will help to shape human beings into an acceptable form.

Reese (1966) outlines a series of steps for operant conditioning of behavior. To begin with, it is important to specify what pattern of behavior the socializer wishes to establish. Is it the elimination of passivity, aggressiveness, bizarre actions, fears, or delusional thoughts? The question that must be asked is, what *exactly* do you wish the person to do when you have successfully completed training, and what measure will you use to decide whether the learning has been accomplished? The difference between how the person acts now and how you wish him to perform in the future, then, measures the size of the task at hand.

The next step is to set up a favorable situation in which the behavioral modification can occur—where there is minimal distraction, where there is time available, where the behavior that is the target is not contaminated by other behaviors, etc. In this setting some basic motivation must be established, i.e., what will reward or reinforce the desired behavior? The reward may range from adult attention and approval to candy, privilege, or escape from unpleasantness. These rewards, or reinforcers, are then withheld from the subject or granted him according to a schedule designed to extinguish unwanted behaviors and reinforce desired ones. Extraneous and unintended rewards are eliminated in order not to confuse the process of modifying the person's behavior (a favorite food can absorb his attention while learning is supposed to be taking place).

The shaping of behavior can now proceed with reward or reinforcement until the final desired behavior is achieved. In great part, success in this venture is dependent on a planned and organized program of reinforcement of behavior in the beginning and a fading-out or intermittent reinforcement as the desired behavior begins to appear in a regular and predictable fashion.

These behavioral modification methods can produce learning and desirable behavior only if properly applied. The plan of behavior reinforcement cannot demand more than the person is capable of delivering, and it must be timed with an eye to his basic ability and his emotional response to training. It need not be an unkind or heartless method. It is, rather, systematic. But, the objection traditional theorists and practitioners have had to operant conditioning is its suggestion of inhumanity, its treatment of the human being as an organism, an animal, an object to be manipulated. The method works but the arguments about applying it to human beings will rage for many years to come.

Behavior therapy has become the most visible expression of the theoretical move away from a medical or disease model of psychopathology. To demonstrate the direction this movement has taken, we can describe the control of the behavior of schizophrenic patients in an institutional setting. Ayllon and Haughton (1962) decided that schizophrenics who would not eat their meals could have this behavior extinguished if only positive reinforcement (by ward personnel) for its continuance could be curtailed. In a hospital setting the researchers asked the staff to stop coaxing patients to eat. All rewards or reinforcements (extra attention, for example) for refusing to eat were withdrawn, and the patients simply went without food if they resisted attending meals at the proper time. Before long, patients went willingly and on time when meals were announced. It was further reported that patients who had refused on past occasions now ate heartily (Allyon and Michael, 1959).

In this and related ways, behavior therapists have demonstrated the ability of their methods to modify the deviant and distorted actions of severely disturbed persons. They insist, then, that much of what we have traditionally called "illness" might better be considered imperfect social learning that is remediable when the principles of learning are applied to its correction (Lindsley, 1960).

Behavioral therapists agree that the patient's behavior, broadly defined to include not only his motor expression but his concepts and his emotions, is what any therapist must deal with and must modify if treatment is to succeed. It is in the conceptualization of disorder and in the means of treatment that the greatest theoretic difference with traditional therapy occurs. Behavioral theorists feel that, unwittingly, many traditional psychotherapists employ behavioral means for inducing change in their patients and that these methods should be acknowledged and made explicit rather than implicit.

The therapist-patient relationship, for example, has long been cherished as a pivot point of therapeutic interaction in classic theory and practice (Goldstein, Heller, and Sechrest, 1966), yet even this, behavior theorists insist, must be scrutinized in a clear scientific light. This vaguely defined and shadowy concept, say behavioral therapists, can, if properly treated scientifically, be made to lose its mystery without altering the positive, behavior-changing function it has always served (Wilson, Hannon, and Evans, 1968). If the therapist is viewed as a "social reinforcer" (Krasner and Ullmann, 1965; Posner, 1967), then the nature of his verbal behavior must be analyzed in learning-theory terms to understand the specific means by which it facilitates change in patients.

In some forms of behavioral therapy—"intervention" therapy, for example (Ayllon, Haughton, and Hughes, 1965)—the classic patient-therapist relationship has only minor importance as the therapist, like an engineer, manipulates the patient's environment. The complaint behavioral therapists have is that the unanalyzed, barely understood patient-therapist relationship may as often reinforce deleterious patient behaviors as it does positive constructive ones (Allyon and Michael, 1959). What behavioral therapists call for, then, is a scientifically delineated means of controlling the relationship of therapist and patient in order to maximize the behavior modification they see as the goal of therapy (Wolpe and Lazarus, 1966).

This approach to psychotherapy has not gone unchallenged by theorists of other persuasions. Therapists oriented to more traditional methods have asked not only how permanent change can occur without a close,

intimate therapist-patient relationship but how the seemingly very complicated psychic process of man can be reorganized by simple learning
procedures. Some of the principal charges leveled against behavior
therapy have been that it is superficial, i.e., it avoids consideration of the
basic causes of symptoms, and that, consequently, its "cures" can only be
temporary. Psychotherapists of traditional bent insist that, at best, behavior therapy may force the psychic apparatus of the individual to substitute another (and perhaps more damaging) symptom for the one
undergoing treatment. It is, they argue, like reducing a fever through
the liberal use of aspirin. The fever is gone but the disease remains. This
may work with the simple neuroses displaying focal symptoms (specific
fears, phobias, or precise behavior patterns), but the complex psycho-
neuroses and the psychoses would resist so mechanical an approach.

With regard to the issue of symptom substitution, Cahoon (1968) reap-
praised the available information, reformulated the question, and concluded that it is probable that dynamic forms of psychotherapy as well
as behavior therapy are equally guilty of eliminating one set of symptoms
only to find them replaced by their manifestation in a different form. He
discovered that the statement that "removing symptoms without dealing
with underlying causes" is a gross oversimplification of the facts and has
only added to the argument between dynamic and behavior therapists.

Behaviorists insist patients become symptom-free and no new symptoms develop following application of their treatment methods; dynamic
theorists insist this cannot possibly be true and is an apparent rather than
real outcome of the reinforcement, punishment, desensitization, and
reconditioning approaches behavior therapists use. The evidence support-
ing each point of view is too lengthy to reproduce here. It is sufficient to
indicate at this juncture that most of the dialogue between the adherents
of these different points of view has not been fruitful. It has been very
much like a dialogue in which neither listener understands the language
of the other.

In both clinical practice and research, behavior therapy has made inroads into the problems of severe psychological disorder in children. Most
of the work accomplished to date has had neurosis or behavior disorder
as its target, but autism and childhood schizophrenia have also been explored (Davison, 1964; 1965). Schizophrenic children who inflicted injury
on themselves were treated by Lovaas, his coworkers, and others (Lovaas,
Freitag, Gold, and Kassorla, 1965; Lovaas, Schaeffer, and Simmons, 1965;
Tate and Baroff, 1966; Wolf, Risley, and Mees, 1964). Therapists oriented
more to classic psychotherapeutic methods have not, however, felt quite
comfortable with the physical punishment used as a means to a therapeutic end. This use of punishment as a negative reinforcement in

autistic children has raised the hue and cry of "childhaters" among classic psychotherapists (Marshall, 1966; Wetzel, Baker, Roney, and Martin, 1966; Zimmerman and Zimmerman, 1962).

Research evaluations of the relative success or failure of these attempts to modify the behavior of autistic and psychotic children has, most often, been uncontrolled and less than convincing, scientifically. It ranks, as a number of behavior therapists have indicated, with the unreliable early studies of the effects of classic forms of psychotherapy.

Behavior therapy has taken psychoanalytic theory as its principal protagonist by insisting on a learning rather than a talking cure of disorder. Eysenck (1959) contrasts behavior therapy with traditional psychotherapy, much to traditional psychotherapy's disadvantage. Eysenck maintains that psychotherapy is based on an inconsistent theory never properly postulated in testable scientific form and that its evidence is clinical and impressionistic—a personal experience not capable of being controlled or subject to experimental demonstration.

Behavior therapy is not only considered more scientific by its supporters but its abandonment of concepts such as repression, the unconscious, defense mechanisms, interpretation of symptoms, symbols, and dreams is regarded as a scientific breakthrough. Behavior therapy focuses on the symptom rather than its origins in early development or its underlying (unconscious) dynamics. Emotional disorder, then, is an excessive load of incorrect, undesirable, and unnecessary behavioral responses that must be unlearned by the patient.

Traditional dynamic theory has been accused of cloaking the meaning of its work in obscure and cultish terms little capable of being understood by most persons. It is equally true that behavior therapy has semantic problems of a serious sort that are yet to be resolved. As Gelfand and Hartmann (1968) indicate, "A confusing variety of terms has been used to describe essentially identical manipulations; for example, desensitization, reciprocal inhibition, counterconditioning, deconditioning, and unconditioning have all been used to describe a single technique . . ." (p. 205).

Behavior therapy has been most practiced on and achieved its greatest success with quite specific complaints—in particular, the phobias. It is in the elimination of unwanted anxieties and fears that it has made its mark, just as psychoanalytic theory has had its greatest impact on the neurosis labeled hysteria. For the first time in some years brisk winds of conflict are stirring, and the psychoanalytic theoretical viewpoint faces a challenge that may well modify it in dramatic and beneficial ways. The claims of behavior theorists are, perhaps, as excessive as those of their traditional predecessors. It is possible, of course, that some of the behavior usually attributed to internal psychic conditions might better be traced to external, environmental circumstances that can be altered by patterned learnings and shaped to a more desirable form. But, the test of any theoretical or therapeutic advance is to be found in the effectiveness it eventually displays—the test of time must still be met before we accept the claims of this approach to the cure of man's disorders.

THERAPY AND THE FUTURE

From its quite specific beginnings focused on cerebral pathology in the individual, psychological concern has been extended to man as a growing, learning, social being. As Redlich and Freedman (1966) have observed, "Large-scale migrations in our time, as the result of war, political and racial persecution, economic depression, and population explosions have uprooted and upset millions of people" (p. 824). These are the problems that confront preventative therapy directed at the psychoses.

The frontiers of therapy with psychosis must one day include consideration of the nature of marriage, the child-rearing experience, the transaction called education, and the pressures of the adult role in business, industry, and the military. Man's community life, his standards, ethics, and religious values must also be viewed as an integral part of an appraisal of man-in-society in order to design institutions beneficial to him.

If speculations about the future are made, it would be reasonable to predict that between now and the end of the twentieth century we should witness a startling transformation of traditional definitions of the practice of psychotherapy. The years ahead might see a shift of emphasis away from immersion in individual psychotherapy and toward concern with the total condition of man as a political, economic, social, and psychological creature. The medical, or illness, model of emotional disturbance is liable to be substantially altered, and mental health manpower shortages may be relieved by abandoning the concept of an elite priesthood of therapists who alone possess the secret knowledge needed to assist disordered man.

It seems inevitable that scientific progress will bring more complete understanding and control over human disorder. Man will create new problems for himself, but we are well on the way to solving some of the age-old difficulties which have long plagued us. We will, in the future, move into the community to reach the source of disordered life via community mental health centers and shift to an emphasis on a sociocultural theory of mental disorder (Caplan and Caplan, 1967). The Federal government will invest much more heavily in mental health in the years ahead (Yolles, 1967); it is calculated that 500 federally supported community mental health centers will be in operation during 1970 and this will, hopefully, be just a beginning in the battle against psychosis.

This is an optimistic conclusion, but our society is in a unique position to be the first to determine exactly what is needed, when, and in what amounts to solve one of man's most ancient problems.

SUMMARY

A summary of the impact of psychotherapeutic techniques on psychotic disorder must, unfortunately, be brief at this stage in our knowledge. Whether the method is classic psychoanalysis or its eclectic and dynamic psychotherapeutic offshoots, it seems that most forms of "talk-therapy" are best suited for a patient whose disorder has not made massive inroads into the intellectual, emotional, cognitive, and perceptual parts of his life.

Patients whose previous history would suggest a good prognosis with whatever form of treatment applied are the best candidates for psychotherapy as they are the best candidates for organic or somatic therapy. It is probably true that the dominance of somatic methods of treatment in modern times can be traced to the severe limitations that must be imposed on psychotic candidates for psychotherapy.

While many psychotherapeutic methods have been tried experimentally, no clear-cut therapeutic breakthrough has been achieved to date. Group psychotherapy has permitted therapists to reach a larger patient population, but it continues to reach a limited segment of the seriously disturbed population and its effectiveness has yet to be adequately studied. Behavior therapy is a promising new approach to treatment, but it has yet to explain fully the complexities of psychosis and schizophrenia.

Perhaps the hope for the future is to be found in the massive infusion of federal funds to support the cause of mental health. The establishment of community mental health centers may be the answer as new ways of prevention, amelioration, and social after-care are devised to make the treatment of psychosis a phenomenon that is less alien to the citizens of our culture.

References

ACKERMAN, N. W. and KEMPSTER, S. W. Family therapy. In A. M. Freedman and H. I. Kaplan (eds.), *Psychiatry*. Baltimore: The Williams & Wilkins Co., 1967. Pp. 1244–48.

ADAMS, H. "Mental illness" or interpersonal behavior? *Amer. Psychol.*, 1964, 19, 191–97.

ALEXANDER, F. C. and SELESNICK, S. T. *The History of Psychiatry*. New York: Harper & Row, Publishers, 1966.

American Psychiatric Association Diagnostic and Statistical Manual for Mental Disorders. Washington, D. C.: American Psychiatric Association, 1952.

ARIETI, S. *The Intrapsychic Self*. New York: Basic Books, Inc., Publishers, 1967.

ARIETI, S. and METH, J. M. Rare, unclassifiable, collective, and exotic psychotic syndromes. In S. Arieti (ed.) *American Handbook of Psychiatry. Vol. I.* New York: Basic Books, Inc., Publishers, 1959. Pp. 547–63.

ARNHOFF, F. N. Concepts of aging. In P. H. Hoch and J. Zubin (eds.), *Psychopathology of Aging*. New York: Grune & Stratton, Inc., 1961. Pp. 136–48.

ASH, P. The reliability of psychiatric diagnosis. *J. abnorm. soc. Psychol.*, 1949, 44, 272–77.

AUGENBRAUN, BERNICE, REID, HELEN L., and FRIEDMAN, D. B. Brief intervention as a preventive force in disorders of early childhood. *Amer. J. Orthopsychiatr.*, 1967, 37, 697–702.

AYLLON, T. and HAUGHTON, E. Control of the behavior of schizophrenic patients by food. *J. Experimental Analysis of Behavior*, 1962, 5, 343–52.

AYLLON, T., HAUGHTON, E., and HUGHES, H. B. Interpretation of Symptoms: Fact or Fiction. *Behavioral Res. and Therapy*, 1965, 3, 1–7.

172

AYLLON, T. and MICHAEL, J. The psychiatric nurse as a behavioral engineer. *J. Experimental Analysis of Behavior*, 1959, **2**, 323–34.

BALLARD, D. M., GLASER, HELEN H., HEAGARTY, MARGARET C., and PIVCHIK, ELIZABETH C. Failure to thrive in the "neglected" child. *Amer. J. Orthopsychiatr.*, 1967, **37**, 680–90.

BANDURA, A. Behavioral psychotherapy. *Sci. Amer.*, 1967, **216**, 78–86.

BANDURA, A. A social learning interpretation of psychological dysfunctions. In P. London and D. Rosenhan (eds.), *Foundations of Abnormal Psychology*. New York: Holt, Rinehart & Winston, Inc., 1968. Pp. 293–344.

BANDURA, A. and WALTERS, R. H. *Social Learning and Personality Development*. New York: Holt, Rinehart & Winston, Inc., 1963.

BARNETT, J., LEFFORD, A., and PUSHMAN, D. Involutional melancholia. *Psychiatr. Quart.*, 1953, **27**, 654–62.

BATESON, G. Minimal requirements for a theory of schizophrenia. *Arch. gen. Psychiatr.*, 1960, **2**, 477–91.

BEERS, C. *A Mind That Found Itself*. New York: Longmans, Green & Co. Ltd., 1908.

BELLAK, L. *Manic-Depressive Psychosis and Allied Conditions*. New York: Grune & Stratton, Inc., 1952.

BELLAK, L. *Schizophrenia: A Review of the Syndrome*. New York: Logos Press, 1958.

BENJAMIN, J. D. Some considerations in biological research in schizophrenia. *Psychosom. Med.*, 1958, **20**, 427–45.

BERGLER, E. Further studies of depersonalization. *Psychiatr. Quart.*, 1950, **24**, 268–77.

BIRD, B. Feelings of unreality. *Internat. J. Psychoanal.*, 1957, **38**, 256–65.

BLANK, H. R. Depression, hypomania, and depersonalization. *Psychoanaly. Quart.*, 1954, **23**, 20–37.

BOCKOVEN, V. S. *Moral Treatment in American Psychiatry*. New York: Springer, 1963.

BOISEN, A. Types of dementia praecox: A study in psychiatric classification. *Psychiatr.*, 1938, **1**, 233–36.

BOND, E. D. Results of treatment in psychoses—with the control series. *Amer. J. Psychol.*, 1954, **110**, 881–87.

BOWLBY, J. *Maternal Care and Mental Health*. Monograph series #2, World Health Organization, Geneva, 1951.

BRADLEY, C. *Schizophrenia in Childhood*. New York: The Macmillan Company, 1941.

BRADLEY, C. and BOWEN, M. Behavior characteristics of schizophrenic children. *Psychiatr. Quart.*, 1941, **15**, 296–315.

BRILL, H. Classification in psychiatry. In A. M. Freedman and H. I. Kaplan (eds.), *Psychiatry*. Baltimore: The Williams & Wilkins Co., 1967. Pp. 581–89.

BROSIN, H. W. Psychiatric conditions following head injury. In S. Arieti (ed.), *American Handbook of Psychiatry, Vol. II*. New York: Basic Books, Inc., Publishers, 1959. Pp. 1175–1202.

BRUETSCH, W. L. Neurosyphilitic conditions. In S. Arieti (ed.), *American Handbook of Psychiatry, Vol. II*. New York: Basic Books, Inc., Publishers, 1959. Pp. 1003–20.

BULLE, P. H. and KONCHEGUL, L. Action of serotonin and cerebrospinal fluid of schizophrenics on the dog-brain. *J. clin. exp. Psychopathol.*, 1957, **18**, 287–91.

BURGESS, E. W. *Aging in Western Societies*. Chicago: University of Chicago Press, 1960.

BUSS, A. H. *Psychopathology*. New York: John Wiley & Sons, Inc., 1966.

BUSS, A. H. and LANG, P. J. Psychological deficit in schizophrenia. I. Affect, reinforcement, and concept attainment. *J. abnorm. Psychol.*, 1965, **70**, 2–24.

CAFFEY, E. M., JR., DIAMOND, L. S., FRANK, T. V., GRASBERGER, J. C., HERMAN, L., KLETT, C. J., and ROTHSTEIN, C. Discontinuation or reduction of chemotherapy in chronic schizophrenics. *J. chronic Diseases*, 1964, **17**, 347–58.

CAHOON, D. D. Symptom substitution and the behavior therapies: a reappraisal. *Psych. Bull.*, 1968, **69**, 149–56.

CAMERON, N. The place of mania among the depressions from a biological standpoint. *J. of Psychol.*, 1942, **14**, 181–95.

CAMERON, N. *Personality Development and Psychopathology*. Boston: Houghton Mifflin Company, 1963.

CAMERON, N. A. Paranoid disorders. In A. M. Freedman and H. I. Kaplan (eds.), *Psychiatry*. Baltimore: The Williams & Wilkins Co., 1967. Pp. 665–75.

CAMERON, N. and MAGARET, ANN. *Behavior Pathology*. Boston: Houghton Mifflin Company, 1951.

CAMPBELL, J. D. *Manic-Depressive Disease*. Philadelphia: J. B. Lippincott Co., 1953.

CANNICOTT, S. M. Technique of unilateral electronconvulsive therapy. *Amer. J. Psychiat.*, 1963, **120**, 477–80.

CAPLAN, G. and CAPLAN, RUTH B. Development of community psychiatry concepts. In A. M. Freedman and H. L. Kaplan (eds.), *Psychiatry*. Baltimore: The Williams & Wilkins Co., 1967. Pp. 1499–1516.

CARY, ARA C. and REVEAL, MARY T. Prevention and detection of emotional disturbances in preschool children. *Amer. J. Orthopsychiatr.*, 1967, **37**, 719–24.

CASEY, J. F., BENNETT, I. F., LINDLEY, C. J., HOLLISTER, L. E., GORDON, M. H., and SPRINGER, N. N. Drug therapy in schizophrenia. *A.M.A. Arch. gen. Psychiatr.*, 1960, **2**, 210–20.

CATTELL, J. P. Depersonalization phenomena. In S. Arieti (ed.), *American Handbook of Psychiatry, Vol. III.* New York: Basic Books, Inc., Publishers, 1966. Pp. 88–102.

CHAPMAN, L. J. and CHAPMAN, JEAN. Genesis of popular but erroneous psychodiagnostic observations. *J. abnorm. Psych.*, 1967, **72**, 193–204.

CHURCH, J. *Language and the Discovery of Reality.* New York: Random House, Inc., 1961.

CLAUSEN, J. A. Family structure, socialization, and personality. In Lois Hoffman and M. Hoffman (eds.), *Review of Child Development Research.* New York: Russell Sage Foundation, 1966. Pp. 1–53.

COBB, S. *Borderlands of Psychiatry.* Cambridge: Harvard University Press, 1943.

COHEN, MABLE B., BAKER, GRACE, COHEN, R. A., FROMM-REICHMANN, FRIEDA, and WEIGERT, EDITH V. An intensive study of twelve cases of manic-depressive psychosis. *Psychiatry*, 1954, **17**, 103–37.

COHEN, R. A. Manic-depressive reactions. In A. L. Freedman and H. I. Kaplan (eds.), *Psychiatry.* Baltimore: The Williams & Wilkins Co., 1967. Pp. 676–88.

COLE, J. O. and DAVIS, J. M. Antidepressant drugs. In A. M. Freedman and H. I. Kaplan (eds.), *Psychiatry.* Baltimore: The Williams & Wilkins Co., 1967. Pp. 1203–75.

COLEMAN, J. C. *Abnormal Psychology and Modern Life.* Chicago: Scott, Foresman & Company, 1964.

COLEMAN, J. C. *Abnormal Behavior.* Dubuque, Iowa: William C. Brown Company, Publishers, 1966.

DAIN, N. *Concepts of Insanity in the United States, 1789–1866.* New Brunswick, N. J.: Rutgers University Press, 1964.

DAVIDSON, M. A., McINNES, R. G., and PARNELL, R. W. The distribution of personality traits in seven-year-old children: A combined psychological, psychiatric, and somatotype study. *Brit. J. Educ. Psych.*, 1957, **27**, 48–61.

DAVISON, G. C. A social learning theory programme with an autistic child. *Behavior Res. and Therapy*, 1964, **2**, 149–59.

DAVISON, G. C. The training of undergraduates as social reinforcers for autistic children. In L. P. Ullmann and L. Krasner (eds.), *Case Studies in Behavior Modification.* New York: Holt, Rinehart & Winston, Inc., 1965. Pp. 146–48.

DENBER, H. C. B. Tranquilizers in psychiatry. In A. M. Freedman and H. I. Kaplan (eds.), *Psychiatry.* Baltimore: The Williams & Wilkins Co., 1967. Pp. 1251–63.

DREIKURS, R. The contribution of group psychotherapy to psychiatry. *Group Psychotherapy*, 1956, 9, 115–25.

DURELL, J. and SCHILDKRAUT, J. J. Biochemical studies of the schizophrenic and affective disorders. In S. Arieti (ed.), *American Handbook of Psychiatry, Vol. III.* New York: Basic Books, Inc., Publishers, 1966. Pp. 423–57.

EATON, J. W. and WEIL, R. J. *Culture and Mental Disorders.* New York: Free Press of Glencoe, Inc., 1955.

EISENBERG, L. Psychotic disorders. I. Clinical features. In A. M. Freedman and H. I. Kaplan (eds.), *Psychiatry.* Baltimore: The Williams & Wilkins Co., 1967. Pp. 1433–38.

EKSTEIN, R., BRYANT, K., and FRIEDMAN, S. W. Childhood schizophrenia and allied conditions. In Bellak, L. (ed.), *Schizophrenia.* New York: Logos Press, 1958. Pp. 555–693.

ELKIND, H. B. and DOERING, C. G. Epidemiology of mental disease: Further studies. I. Variation in diagnosis. Reprint #5 on Schizophrenia. *Statistical Studies from the Boston Psychopathic Hospital*, 1928.

ELLIS, A. Should some people be labelled mentally ill? *J. consult. Psych.*, 1967, 31, 435–46.

EYSENCK, H. J. The effects of psychotherapy: An evaluation. *J. consult. Psychol.*, 1952, 16, 319–24.

EYSENCK, H. J. Learning theory and behavior theory. *J. ment. Sci.*, 1959, 105, 61–75.

EYSENCK, H. J. *Behavior Therapy and the Neuroses.* London: Pergamon Press, 1960.

EYSENCK, H. J. *Experiments in Behavior Therapy.* London: Pergamon Press, 1964.

FARINA, A. and HOLZBERG, J. D. Attitudes and behaviors of fathers and mothers of male schizophrenic patients. *J. abnorm. Psychol.*, 1967, 72, 381–87.

FELIX, R. *Mental Illness: Progress and Prospects.* New York: Columbia University Press, 1967.

FERRARO, A. Senile psychosis. In S. Arieti (ed.), *American Handbook of Psychiatry, Vol. II.* New York: Basic Books, Inc., Publishers, 1959. Pp. 1021–45.

FINK, M. and ITIL, T. M. Schizophrenia. VI. Organic therapy. In A. M. Freedman and H. I. Kaplan (eds.), *Psychiatry.* Baltimore: The Williams & Wilkins Co., 1967. Pp. 661–64.

FINK, M., KLEIN, D. F., and KRAMER, J. C. Clinical efficacy of chlorpromazine-procyclidene combination, imipramine and placebo in depressive disorders. *Psychopharmacologia*, 1963, 7, 27–38.

FISH, BARBARA. Organic therapies. In A. M. Freedman and H. I. Kaplan (eds.), *Psychiatry.* Baltimore: The Williams & Wilkins Co., 1967. Pp. 1468–72.

FISHBEIN, M. Statistics and the epidemiology of arteriosclerosis. *Postgrad. Med.*, 1962, 31, 311–12.

FISHER, S. *Child Research in Psychopharmacology.* Springfield, Ill.: Charles C Thomas, Publisher, 1959.

FLECK, S. The role of the family in psychiatry. In A. M. Freedman and H. I. Kaplan (eds.), *Psychiatry.* Baltimore: The Williams & Wilkins Co., 1967. Pp. 213–24.

FLECK, S., LIDZ, T., and CORNELISON, ALICE R. Comparison of parent-child relationships of male and female schizophrenic patients. *Arch. gen. Psychiatr.,* 1963, **8,** 1–7.

FORD, H. Involutional psychotic reaction. In A. M. Freedman and H. I. Kaplan (eds.), *Psychiatry.* Baltimore: The Williams & Wilkins Co., 1967. Pp. 697–703.

FORD, I. H. and URBAN, H. B. *Systems of Psychotherapy.* New York: John Wiley & Sons, Inc., 1963.

FOUCAULT, M. *Madness and Civilization: A History of Insanity in the Age of Reason.* New York: Pantheon Books, Inc., 1965.

FOULDS, G. The reliability of psychiatric, and the validity of psychological diagnosis. *J. ment. Sci.,* 1955, **101,** 851–62.

FRANK, J. D. Evaluation of psychiatric treatment. In A. M. Freedman and H. I. Kaplan (eds.), *Psychiatry.* Baltimore: The Williams & Wilkins Co., 1967. Pp. 1305–09.

FREEDMAN, A. M. and KAPLAN, H. I. *Psychiatry.* Baltimore: The Williams & Wilkins Co., 1967.

FREEMAN, H. Physiological studies. In L. Bellak (ed.), *Schizophrenia.* New York: Logos Press, 1958. Pp. 174–215.

FREEMAN, W. and WATTS, J. W. *Psychosurgery in the Treatment of Mental Disorders and Intractable Pain.* Springfield, Ill.: Charles C Thomas, Publisher, 1950.

FREUD, S. *The Basic Writings of Sigmund Freud.* (A. A. Brill, trans.), New York: Modern Library, Inc., 1938.

FREUD, S. *Collected Papers.* (Joan Riviere, trans.), London: The Hogarth Press, 1924–1953.

FREUD, S. *The Standard Edition of the Complete Psychological Works of Sigmund Freud.* (James Strackey, trans.), London: The Hogarth Press, 1953–1964.

FROMM-REICHMANN, FRIEDA. *Psychoanalysis and Psychotherapy: Selected Papers of Frieda Fromm-Reichmann.* Chicago: University of Chicago Press, 1959.

FULLER, J. L. and THOMPSON, W. R. *Behavior Genetics.* New York: John Wiley & Sons, Inc., 1960.

GARDNER, G. GAIL. The relationship between childhood neurotic symptomatology and later schizophrenia in males and females. *J. neur. Ment. Dis.,* 1967, **144,** 97–100.

GELFAND, DONNA M. and HARTMANN, D. P. Behavior therapy with children:

a review and evaluation of research methodology. *Psych. Bull.*, 1968, **69**, 204–15.

GIBSON, R. W. The family background and early life experience of the manic-depressive patient: A comparison with the schizophrenic patients. *Psychiatr.*, 1958, **21**, 71–90.

GIBSON, R. W., COHEN, MABEL R., and COHEN, R. A. On the dynamics of the manic-depressive personality. *Amer. J. Psychiatr.*, 1959, **155**, 1107–07.

GILBERT, J. *Understanding Old Age.* New York: The Ronald Press Company, 1952.

GILLINA, J. Magical fright. *Psychiatr.*, 1948, **11**, 387–400.

GLUECK, S. and GLUECK, ELEANOR. *Family Environment and Delinquency.* Boston: Houghton Mifflin Company, 1952.

GOLDFARB, W. Effects of early institutional care on adolescent personality (graphic Rorschach data). *Child Developm.*, 1943, **14**, 213–23.

GOLDFARB, W. Variations in adolescent adjustment of institutionally reared children. *Amer. J. Orthopsychiatr.*, 1947, **17**, 449–57.

GOLDSTEIN, A. P., HELLER, K., and SECHREST, L. B. *Psychotherapy and the Psychology of Behavior Change.* New York: John Wiley & Sons, Inc., 1966.

GREENBLATT, M. Psychosurgery. In A. M. Freedman and H. I. Kaplan (eds.), *Psychiatry.* Baltimore: The Williams & Wilkins Co., 1967. Pp. 1291–95.

GRINKER, R. R., MILLER, J., SABSHIN, M., NUNN, R., and NUNNALLY, J. C. *The Phenomena of Depressions.* New York: Hoeber, 1961.

GRINKER, R. R. and SPIEGEL, J. P. *Men Under Stress.* New York: McGraw-Hill Book Company, 1945.

GRUEN, W. Emotional encapsulation as a predictor of outcome in therapeutic discussion groups. *Int. J. Group Psychotherapy*, 1966, **16**, 93–97.

HARLOW, H. F. The nature of love. *Amer. Psychologist*, 1958, **13**, 673–85.

HARLOW, H. F. Love in infant monkeys. *Sci. Amer.*, 1959, **200**, 68–74.

HARLOW, H. F., and HARLOW, MARGARET K. A study of animal affection. *Nat. Hist.*, 1961, **70**, 48–55.

HARLOW, H. F., and HARLOW, MARGARET K. The effect of rearing conditions on behavior. *Bull. Menninger Clinic*, 1962, **26**, 213–24.

HARLOW, H. F., and HARLOW, MARGARET K. The effect of rearing conditions on behavior. In J. Morey (ed.), *Sex Research: New Developments.* New York: Holt, Rinehart & Winston, Inc., 1965. Pp. 161–75.

HARVEY, O. J., HUNT, D. E., and SCHRODER, H. M. *Conceptual Systems and Personality Organization.* New York: John Wiley & Sons, Inc., 1961.

HIMWICH, H. E. Research in medical aspects of aging. *Geriatrics*, 1962, **17**, 89–97.

HIMWICH, H. E. Psychopharmacology. In A. M. Freedman and H. I. Kaplan (eds.), *Psychiatry.* Baltimore: The Williams & Wilkins Co., 1967. Pp. 67–76.

HIMWICH, W. A. and HIMWICH, H. E. Neurochemistry. In A. M. Freedman and H. I. Kaplan (eds.), *Psychiatry*. Baltimore: The Williams & Wilkins Co., 1967. Pp. 49–67.

HINKO, E. and LIPSCHUTZ, L. Five years after shock therapy. *Amer. J. Psychiatr.*, 1947, **104**, 387–90.

HOCH, P. and ZUBIN, J. (eds.), *Current Problems in Psychiatric Diagnosis*. New York: Grune & Stratton, Inc., 1953.

HOLLINGSHEAD, A. B. and REDLICH, F. C. *Social Class and Mental Illness*. New York: John Wiley & Sons, Inc., 1958.

HORDERN, A., BURT, C. G., and HOLT, N. F. *Depressive States*. Springfield, Ill.: Charles C Thomas, Publisher, 1965.

HORWITT, M. K. Fact and artifact in the biology of schizophrenia. *Science*, 1956, **124**, 429–30.

HUMPHREYS, L. G. Characteristics of type concepts with special reference to Sheldon's typology. *Psych. Bull.*, 1957, **54**, 218–28.

HUNT, W., WITTSON, C., and HUNT, E. A theoretical and practical analysis of the diagnostic process. In P. Hoch and J. Zubin (eds.), *Current Problems in Psychiatric Diagnosis*. New York: Grune & Stratton, Inc., 1953. Pp. 53–65.

HUSTON, P. E., Psychotic depressive reaction. In A. M. Freedman and H. I. Kaplan (eds.), *Psychiatry*. Baltimore: The Williams & Wilkins Co., 1967. Pp. 688–97.

JACKSON, D. D. A critique of the literature of the genetics of schizophrenia. In D. D. Jackson (ed.), *The Etiology of Schizophrenia*. New York: Basic Books, Inc., Publishers, 1960.

JACKSON, D. D. Schizophrenia. *Scientific Amer.*, 1962, **207**, 65–75.

JACO, E. G. *The Social Epidemiology of Mental Disorders*. New York: Russell Sage Foundation, 1960.

JACOBSON, EDITH. Depersonalization. *J. Amer. Psychoanal.*, 1959, **7**, 581–610.

JELLINEK, E. Some principles of psychiatric classification. *Psychiatr.*, 1939, **2**, 161–65.

JERSILD, EALINE A. Group therapy for patients' spouses. *Amer. J. Nursing*, 1967, **67**, 544–49.

KALINOWSKY, L. The convulsive therapies. In A. M. Freedman and H. I. Kaplan (eds.), *Psychiatry*. Baltimore: The Williams & Wilkins Co., 1967. Pp. 1279–85.

KALINOWSKY, L. Insulin coma therapy. In A. M. Freedman and H. I. Kaplan (eds.), *Psychiatry*. Baltimore: The Williams & Wilkins Co., 1967(a). Pp. 1285–91.

KALINOWSKY, L. B. and HOCH, P. H. *Shock Treatments, Psychosurgery and Other Somatic Procedures in Psychiatry* (2nd ed.). New York: Grune & Stratton, Inc., 1952.

KALINOWSKY, L. B. and HOCH, P. H. *Somatic Treatments in Psychiatry*. New York: Grune & Stratton, Inc., 1961.

KALLMANN, F. J. *Heredity in Health and Mental Disorder.* New York: W. W. Norton & Company, Inc., 1953.

KALLMANN, F. J. The genetics of mental illness. In S. Arieti (ed.), *American Handbook of Psychiatry.* New York: Basic Books, Inc., Publishers, 1959. Pp. 175–95.

KALLMANN, F. J. (ed.). *Expanding Goals of Genetics in Psychiatry.* New York: Grune & Stratton, Inc., 1962.

KANNER, L. Early infantile autism. *Amer. J. Orthopsychiatr.,* 1949, **19,** 416–26.

KANNER, L. *Child Psychiatry* (3rd ed.). Springfield, Ill.: Charles C Thomas, Publisher, 1957.

KANNER, L. History of child psychiatry. In A. M. Freedman and H. I. Kaplan (eds.), *Psychiatry.* Baltimore: The Williams & Wilkins Co., 1967. Pp. 1313–15.

KAUFMAN, I. *et al.* Treatment implications of a new classification of parents of schizophrenic children. *Amer. J. Psychiatr.,* 1960, **116,** 920–24.

KESSLER, JANE W. *Psychopathology of Childhood.* Englewood Cliffs, N. J.: Prentice-Hall, Inc., 1966.

KETY, S. S. Biochemical theories of schizophrenia, Part II. *Science,* 1959, **129,** 1590–96.

KIEV, ARI. Prescientific psychiatry. In S. Arieti (ed.), *American Handbook of Psychiatry, Vol. III.* New York: Basic Books, Inc., Publishers, 1966. Pp. 166–79.

KLINE, N. S., and OPPENHEIM, A. N. Constitutional factors in the prognosis of schizophrenia: Further observations. *Amer. J. Psychiatr.,* 1952, **108,** 909–11.

KLINE, N. S., and TENNEY, A. M. Constitutional factors in the prognosis of schizophrenia. *Amer. J. Psychiatr.,* 1950, **107,** 434–41.

KRAEPELIN, E. *One Hundred Years of Psychiatry.* New York: Citadel Press, 1962.

KRAINES, S. H. *Mental Depressions and Their Treatment.* New York: The Macmillan Company, 1957.

KRASNER, C., and ULLMANN, L. P. *Research in Behavior Modification.* New York: Holt, Rinehart & Winston, Inc., 1965.

KRETSCHMER, E. *Physique and Character.* New York: Harcourt, Brace & World, Inc., 1925.

LANG, P. J., and BUSS, A. H. Psychological deficit in schizophrenia. II. Interference and activation. *J. abnorm. Psychol.,* 1965, **70,** 77–106.

LA VIETES, RUTH L. Psychotic disorders II: Treatment. In A. M. Freedman and H. I. Kaplan (eds.), *Psychiatry.* Baltimore: The Williams & Wilkins Co., Inc., 1967. Pp. 1438–41.

LAZARUS, R. S. *Personality and Adjustment.* Englewood Cliffs, N. J.: Prentice-Hall, Inc., 1963.

LEA, H. C. *Materials Toward a History of Witchcraft, Vol. III.* Philadelphia: University of Pennsylvania Press, 1957.

LEHMANN, H. E. Schizophrenia. IV. Clinical features. In A. M. Freedman and H. I. Kaplan (eds.), *Psychiatry.* Baltimore: The Williams & Wilkins Co., 1967. Pp. 621–48.

LEMKAU, P. V., and CROCETTI, G. M. Vital statistics of schizophrenia. In L. Bellak (ed.), *Schizophrenia.* New York: Logos Press, 1958. Pp. 64–81.

LESSE, S. Psychotherapy plus drugs in severe depressions: Technique. *Compreh. Psychiatr.*, 1966, 1, 224–31.

LEWIS, N. D. C., and PIOTROWSKI, A. A. Clinical diagnosis of manic-depressive psychosis. In P. Hoch and J. Zubin (eds.), *Depression.* New York: Grune & Stratton, Inc., 1954.

LIDZ, T. *et al.* Schizophrenia and the family. *Psychiatry,* 1958, 21, 21–27.

LIDZ, T., FLECK, S., and CORNELISON, ALICE R. *Schizophrenia and the Family.* New York: International Universities Press, 1965.

LINDSLEY, O. R. Characteristics of the behavior of chronic psychotics as revealed by free-operant conditioning methods. *Dis. Nerv. Syst.*, 1960, 21, 66–78.

LONDON, P. The major psychological disorders. In P. London and D. Rosenhan (eds.), *Foundations of Abnormal Psychology.* New York: Holt, Rinehart & Winston, Inc., 1968. Pp. 391–426.

LOVAAS, O. I., FREITAG, G., GOLD, V. J., and KASSORLA, I. C. Experimental studies in childhood schizophrenia: analysis of self-destructive behavior. *J. Exp. Child Psychol.*, 1965, 2, 67–84.

LOVAAS, O. I., SCHAEFFER, B., and SIMMONS, J. B. Building social behavior in autistic children by use of electric shock. *J. Exp. Res. in Personality*, 1965, 1, 99–109.

LUNDIN, R. W. *Principles of Psychopathology.* Columbus, Ohio: Charles E. Merrill Books, Inc., 1965.

MACK, J. E., and SEMRAD, E. V. Classical psychoanalysis. In A. M. Freedman and H. I. Kaplan (eds.), *Psychiatry.* Baltimore: The Williams & Wilkins Co., 1967. Pp. 269–319.

MAHLER, MARGARET S., FURER, M., and SETTLAGE, C. F. Severe emotional disturbances in childhood: Psychosis. In S. Arieti (ed.), *American Handbook of Psychiatry.* New York: Basic Books, Inc., Publishers, 1959. Pp. 816–39.

MALITZ, S. Drug therapy: Antidepressants. In S. Arieti (ed.), *American Handbook of Psychiatry, Vol. III.* New York: Basic Books, Inc., Publishers, 1961. Pp. 477–507.

MALITZ, S., and HOCH, P. H. Drug therapy: Neuroleptics and tranquilizers. In S. Arieti (ed.), *American Handbook of Psychiatry, Vol. III.* New York: Basic Books, Inc., Publishers, 1966. Pp. 458–76.

MALZBERG, B. Outcome of insulin treatment of one thousand patients with dementia praecox. *Psychiatr. Quart.*, 1938, **12**, 528–53.

MARKS, H. H. Characteristics and trends of cerebral vascular disease. In P. H. Hoch and J. Zubin (eds.), *Psychopathology of Aging*. New York: Grune & Stratton, Inc., 1961. Pp. 69–99.

MARKS, J., and PARE, C. M. B. *The Scientific Basis of Drug Therapy in Psychiatry*. New York: Pergamon Press, 1965.

MARSHALL, G. R. Toilet-training of an autistic eight-year-old through conditioning therapy: a case report. *Behavior Research and Therapy*, 1966, **4**, 242–45.

McNEIL, E. B. Psychology and aggression. *J. Confl. Res.*, 1959, **3**, 195–244.

McNEIL, E. B. *The Quiet Furies*. Englewood Cliffs, N. J.: Prentice-Hall, Inc., 1967.

MEHLMAN, B. The reliability of psychiatric diagnosis. *J. abnorm. soc. Psychol.*, 1952, **47**, 577–78.

MENDEL, W. M. Tranquilizer prescribing as a function of the experience and availability of the therapist. *Amer. J. Psychiatr.*, 1967, **124**, 16–22.

MENNINGER, K. Concerning our advocacy of a unitary concept of mental illness. In L. Appleby, J. Scher, and J. Cumming (eds.), *Chronic Schizophrenia*. New York: Free Press of Glencoe, Inc., 1960. Pp. 54–67.

MENNINGER, K., MAYMAN, M., and PRUYSER, P. *The Vital Balance*. New York: The Viking Press, Inc., 1963.

MORA, G. History of psychiatry. In A. M. Freedman and H. I. Kaplan (eds.), *Psychiatry*. Baltimore: The Williams & Wilkins Co., 1967. Pp. 2–34.

MOWRER, O. H. *Abnormal Reactions or Actions?* Dubuque, Iowa: William C. Brown Company, Publishers, 1966.

MULDER, D. W. Psychoses with brain tumors and other chronic neurologic disorders. In S. Arieti (ed.), *American Handbook of Psychiatry, Vol. II*. New York: Basic Books, Inc., Publishers, 1959. Pp. 1144–62.

MULLAN, H. Trends in group psychotherapy in the United States. *Int. J. soc. Psychiatr.*, 1957, **3**, 224–30.

MURPHY, LOIS B. Learning how children cope with problems. *Children*. U. S. Department of Health, Education and Welfare, Children's Bureau, July–August, 1957.

MURRAY, H. A. *Explorations in Personality*. New York: Oxford University Press, Inc., 1938.

NORRIS, V. *Mental Illness in London*. Maudsley Monograph #6, Institute of Psychiatry. London: Chapman and Hall Ltd., 1959.

NOYES, A. P., and KOLB, L. C. Psychotic disorders. In *Modern Clinical Psychiatry*. Philadelphia: W. B. Saunders Co., 1958. Pp. 353–448.

OPLER, M. K. Cultural differences in mental disorders: An Italian and Irish contrast in the schizophrenics—U.S.A. In M. K. Opler (ed.), *Culture and Mental Health.* New York: The Macmillan Company, 1954, Pp. 425–42.

OSTOW, M. The biological basic of human behavior. In S. Arieti (ed.), *American Handbook of Psychiatry.* New York: Basic Books, Inc., Publishers, 1959. Pp. 58–87.

OSTOW, M. *Drugs in Psychoanalysis and Psychotherapy.* New York: Basic Books, Inc., Publishers, 1962.

PARNELL, R. W. Physique and mental breakdown in young adults. *Brit. Med. J.*, 1957, **1**, 1485–90.

PASTORE, N. The genetics of schizophrenia: A special review. *Psych. Bull.*, 1949, **46**, 285–302.

PETERSON, E. *Psychopharmacology.* Dubuque, Iowa: William Brown Company, Publishers, 1966.

PEYMAN, D. A. R. An investigation of the effects of group psychotherapy on chronic schizophrenic patients. *Group Psychotherapy*, 1956, **9**, 35–39.

PFEIFFER, E. Patients as therapists. *Amer. J. Psychiatr.*, 1967, **123**, 1413–18.

PHILLIPS, L. A social view of psychopathology. In P. London and D. Rosenhan (eds.), *Foundations of Abnormal Psychology.* New York: Holt, Rinehart & Winston, Inc., 1968. Pp. 427–59.

PLANANSKY, K. Heredity in schizophrenia. *J. nerv. met. Dis.*, 1955, **122**, 121–42.

POSNER, E. G. Training behavior therapists. *Behavior Res. and Therapy*, 1967, **5**, 37–41.

RAINER, J. D. Genetics and psychiatry. In A. M. Freedman and H. I. Kaplan (eds.), *Psychiatry.* Baltimore: The Williams & Wilkins Co., 1967. Pp. 37–49.

REDLICH, F. C., and FREEDMAN, D. X. *The Theory and Practice of Psychiatry.* New York: Basic Books, Inc., Publishers, 1966.

REES, L. Constitutional factors and abnormal behavior. In H. J. Eysenck (ed.), *Handbook of Abnormal Psychology.* New York: Basic Books, Inc., Publishers, 1961. Pp. 344–92.

REESE, ELLEN. *The Analysis of Human Operant Behavior.* Dubuque, Iowa: William C. Brown Company, Publishers, 1966.

RENNIE, T. A. C. Prognosis in manic-depressive psychoses. *Amer. J. Psychiatr.*, 1942, **98**, 801–14.

RENNIE, T. A. C., SROLE, L., OPLER, M. K., and LANGNER, T. S. Urban life and mental health. *Amer. J. Psychiatr.*, 1957, **113**, 831–37.

RIMLAND, B. *Infantile Autism.* New York: Appleton-Century-Crofts, 1964.

ROBBINS, R. *The Encyclopedia of Witchcraft and Demonology.* New York: Crown Publishers, Inc., 1959.

ROSEN, E., and GREGORY, I. *Abnormal Psychology.* Philadelphia: W. B. Saunders Co., 1965.

Rosen, J. *Direct Analysis; Selected Papers*. New York: Grune & Stratton, Inc., 1953.

Rosenthal, D. Problems of sampling and diagnosis in the major twin studies of schizophrenia. *J. Psychiatr. Res.*, 1962, 1, 116–34.

Rubin, L. S. Patterns of adrenergic-cholinergic imbalance in the functional psychoses. *Psych. Rev.*, 1962, 69, 501–19.

Rubins, J. L. Multiple therapists. In A. M. Freedman and H. I. Kaplan (eds.), *Psychiatry*. Baltimore: The Williams & Wilkins Co., 1967. Pp. 1248–50.

Sager, C. J. Combined individual and group psychotherapy. In A. M. Freedman and H. I. Kaplan (eds.), *Psychiatry*. Baltimore: The Williams & Wilkins Co., 1967. Pp. 1241–44.

Sarbin, T. R. On the futility of the proposition that some people be labeled "mentally ill." *J. consult. Psychol.*, 1967, 31, 447–53.

Sargant, W. The physical treatment of depression: Their indicators and proper use. *J. Neuropschiatr.*, 1961, 2, 1–10.

Sargant, W. and Slater, E. *An Introduction to Physical Methods of Treatment in Psychiatry* (4th ed.). Baltimore: The Williams & Wilkins Co., 1964.

Sarlin, C. N. Depersonalization and derealization. *J. Amer. Psychoanal. Assoc.*, 1962, 10, 784–804.

Schmidt, H., and Fonda, C. The reliability of psychiatric diagnosis: A new look. *J. abnorm. soc. Psychol.*, 1956, 52, 262–67.

Schofield, W., and Belian, Lucy. A comparative study of the personal histories of schizophrenic and nonpsychiatric patients. *J. abnorm. soc. Psychol.*, 1959, 58, 59.

Schwartz, D. A unitary formulation of the manic-depressive reactions. *Psychiatr.*, 1961, 24, 238–45.

Searles, H. J. *Collected Papers on Schizophrenia*. New York: International Universities Press, 1965.

Segal, M. M., and Shapiro, K. L. A clinical comparison study of the effects of reserpine and placebo on anxiety. *A.M.A. Arch. Neurol. Psychiatr.*, 1959, 81, 392–98.

Selling, L. S. *Men Against Madness*. New York: Garden City Books, 1943.

Selye, H. *The Stress of Life*. New York: McGraw-Hill Book Company, 1956.

Shakow, D. Psychological deficit in schizophrenia. *Behav. Sci.*, 1963, 8, 275–305.

Sharoff, R. L. Sedatives. In A. M. Freedman and H. I. Kaplan (eds.), *Psychiatry*. Baltimore: The Williams & Wilkins Co., 1967. Pp. 1275–77.

Sheldon, W. H. *Varieties of Human Physique*. New York: Harper & Row, Publishers, 1940.

Sheldon, W. H. *et al. Atlas of Man: A Guide for Somatotyping the Adult Male at All Ages*. New York: Harper & Row, Publishers, 1954.

SHIELDS, J., and SLATER, E. Heredity and psychological abnormality. In H. J. Eysenck (ed.), *Handbook of Abnormal Psychology.* New York: Basic Books, Inc., Publishers, 1961.

SINGER, MARGARET T., and WYNNE, L. Differentiating characteristics of the parents of childhood schizophrenics, childhood neurotics, and young adult schizophrenics. *Amer. J. Psychiatr.,* 1963, **120,** 234–43.

SINGER, MARGARET T., and WYNNE, L. C. Thought disorder and family relations of schizophrenics: III. Methodology using projective techniques. *Arch. Gen. Psychiatr.,* 1965(a), **12,** 187–200.

SINGER, MARGARET T., and WYNNE, L. C. Thought disorder and family relations of schizophrenics: IV. Results and implications. *Arch. Gen. Psychiatr.,* 1965(b) **12,** 201–12.

SPITZ, R. A. Hospitalism. *Psychoanal. Stud. Child.,* 1945, **1,** 53–74.

SPITZ, R. A. Anaclitic depression. *Psychoanal. Stud. Child.,* 1946, **1,** 313–42.

STRAKER, M. Prognosis for psychiatric illness in the aged. *Amer. J. Psychiatr.,* 1963, **119,** 1069–75.

SUMMERS, M. *Malleus Maleficarum.* Eng. Trans. London: The Pushkin Press, 1928.

SUNDBERG, N. D., and TYLER, LEONA E. *Clinical Psychology.* New York: Appleton-Century-Crofts, 1962.

SZALITA, ALBERTA B. Psychodynamics of disorders of the involutional age. In S. Arieti (ed.), *American Handbook of Psychiatry, Vol. III.* New York: Basic Books, Inc., Publishers, 1966. Pp. 66–87.

SZASZ, T. The myth of mental illness. *Amer. Psychol.,* 1960, **15,** 113–18.

TATE, B. G., and BAROFF, G. S. Aversive control of self-injurious behavior in a psychotic boy. *Behavior Res. and Therapy,* 1966, **4,** 281–87.

THRONE, M. L., and GOWDEY, C. W. A critical review of endogenous psychotoxins as a cause of schizophrenia. *Can. Psychiatr. Assoc. J.,* 1967, **12,** 159–74.

TORRANCE, P. *Gifted Children in the Classroom.* New York: The Macmillan Company, 1965.

UHLENHUTH, E. H., and PARK, LEA C. The influence of medication [imipromine] and doctor in relieving depressed psychoneurotic outpatients. *J. Psychiatr. Res.,* 1964, **2,** 101–22.

ULLMAN, M., and GRUEN, A. Behavioral changes in patients with strokes. *Amer. J. Psychiatr.,* 1961, **117,** 1004–09.

URBAN, H. B., and FORD, D. H. Behavior therapy. In A. M. Freedman and H. I. Kaplan (eds.), *Psychiatry.* Baltimore: The Williams & Wilkins Co., 1967. Pp. 1217–24.

VOLPE, ANNE, and KASTENBAUM, R. Beer and TLC. *Amer. J. Nursing,* 1967, **67,** 100–03.

WECHSLER, H., GROSSER, G. H., and GREENBLATT, M. Research evaluating antidepressant medications on hospitalized mental patients: A survey of published reports during a five-year period. *J. nerv. ment. Dis.*, 1965, **141**, 231–39.

WEINER, H. Schizophrenia. III. Etiology. In A. M. Freedman and H. I. Kaplan (eds.), *Psychiatry*. Baltimore: The Williams & Wilkins Co., 1967. Pp. 603–21.

WETZEL, R. J., BAKER, J., RONEY, M., and MARTIN, M. Outpatient treatment of autistic behavior. *Behavior Research and Therapy*, 1966, **4**, 169–77.

WHITAKER, D. S. and LIEBERMAN, M. A. *Psychotherapy Through the Group Process*. New York: Atherton Press, 1964.

WHITE, R. W. *The Abnormal Personality*. New York: The Ronald Press Company, 1964.

WHITEHORN, J. C. Studies of the doctor as a crucial factor for the prognosis of schizophrenic patients. *Internat. J. soc. Psychiatr.*, 1960, **6**, 71–77.

WILL, O. A., JR. Schizophrenia. V: Psychological treatment. In A. M. Freedman and H. I. Kaplan (eds.), *Psychiatry*. Baltimore: The Williams & Wilkins Co., 1967. Pp. 649–61.

WILSON, G. T., HANNON, ALMA E., and EVANS, W. I. M. Behavior therapy and the therapist-patient relationship. *J. Consult. Clin. Psych.*, 1968, **32**, 103–09.

WITTENBORN, J., and BAILEY, C. The symptoms of involutional psychosis. *J. consult. Psychol.*, 1952, **16**, 13–17.

WITTENBORN, J. R., PLANTE, M., BURGESS, F., and LIVERMORE, N. The efficacy of electroconvulsive therapy, pronoizid and placebo in the treatment of young depressed women. *J. neu. mem. Dis.*, 1961, **133**, 316–32.

WITTENBORN, J., and WEISS, W. Patients diagnosed manic-depressive psychosis —manic state. *J. consult. Psychol.*, 1952, **16**, 193–98.

WOLF, A. Group psychotherapy. In A. M. Freedman and H. I. Kaplan (eds.), *Psychiatry*. Baltimore: The Williams & Wilkins Co., 1967. Pp. 1234–42.

WOLF, M. M., RISLEY, T., and MEES, H. Application of operant conditioning procedures to the behavior problems of an autistic child. *Behavior Res. and Therapy*, 1964, **1**, 305–12.

WOLPE, J., and LAZARUS, A. A. *Behavior Therapy Techniques*. New York: Pergamon Press, 1966.

WOOLLEY, D. W. *The Biochemical Bases of Psychoses*. New York: John Wiley & Sons, Inc., 1962.

WORTIS, J. Psychopharmacology and physiological treatment. *Amer. J. Psychiatr.*, 1963, **119**, 621–26.

WORTIS, J. Psychopharmacology and physiological treatment. *Amer. J. Psychiatr.*, 1964, **120**, 643–48.

WYNNE, L. C., and SINGER, MARGARET T. Thought disorder and family relations of schizophrenics: II. A classification of forms of thinking. *Arch. Gen. Psychiatr.*, 1963, **9**, 199–206.

YARROW, L. J. Separation from parents during early childhood. In M. Hoffman and L. Hoffman (eds.), *Child Development Research*. New York: Russell Sage Foundation, 1964.

YARROW, L. J. Maternal depreviation. In A. M. Freedman and H. I. Kaplan (eds.), *Psychiatry*. Baltimore: The Williams & Wilkins Co., 1967. Pp. 1489–93.

YOLLES, S. F. United States community mental health program. In A. M. Freedman and H. L. Kapan (eds.), *Psychiatry*. Baltimore: The Williams & Wilkins Co., 1967. Pp. 1533–36.

ZIGLER, E., and PHILLIPS, L. Psychiatric diagnosis and symptomology symptomatology. *J. abnorm. soc. Psychol.*, 1961, **63**, 69–75.

ZILBOORG, G. *The Medical Man and the Witch During the Renaissance*. Baltimore: The Johns Hopkins Press, 1935.

ZILBOORG, G., and HENRY, G. W. *A History of Medical Psychology*. New York: W. W. Norton & Company, Inc., 1941.

ZIMMERMAN, E. H., and ZIMMERMAN, J. The alteration of behavior in a special classroom situation. *J. Exp. Analysis of Behavior*, 1962, **5**, 59–60.

Index